# CHALLENGES AND SOLUTIONS IN ETHNOGRAPHIC RESEARCH

*Challenges and Solutions in Ethnographic Research: Ethnography with a Twist* seeks to rethink ethnography 'outside the box' of its previous tradition and to develop ethnographic methods by critically discussing process, ethics, impact and knowledge production in ethnographic research.

This interdisciplinary edited volume argues for a 'twist' that supports openness, courage, and creativity to develop and test innovative and unconventional ways of thinking and doing ethnography. 'Ethnography with a twist' means both an intentional aim to conduct ethnographic research with novel approaches and methods but also sensitivity to recognize and creativity to utilize different kinds of 'twist moments' that ethnographic research may create for the researcher.

This edited volume critically evaluates new and old methodological tools and their ability to engage with questions of power difference. It proposes new collaborative methods that allow for co-production and co-creation of research material as well as shared conceptual work and wider distribution of knowledge. The book will be of use to ethnographers in humanities and social science disciplines including sociology, anthropology and communication studies.

**Tuuli Lähdesmäki** is a Senior Researcher and an Adjunct Professor working at the Department of Music, Art and Culture Studies, University of Jyväskylä, Finland.

**Eerika Koskinen-Koivisto** is a Post-doctoral Researcher working at the Department of Social Sciences and Philosophy, University of Jyväskylä, Finland.

**Viktorija L.A. Čeginskas** is a Post-doctoral Researcher working at the Department of Music, Art and Culture Studies, University of Jyväskylä, Finland.

**Aino-Kaisa Koistinen** is a Post-doctoral Researcher working at the Department of Music, Art and Culture Studies, University of Jyväskylä, Finland.

# CHALLENGES AND SOLUTIONS IN ETHNOGRAPHIC RESEARCH

Ethnography with a Twist

Edited by Tuuli Lähdesmäki,
Eerika Koskinen-Koivisto, Viktorija L.A. Čeginskas
and Aino-Kaisa Koistinen

LONDON AND NEW YORK

First published 2020
by Routledge
2 Park Square, Milton Park, Abingdon, Oxon OX14 4RN

and by Routledge
52 Vanderbilt Avenue, New York, NY 10017

*Routledge is an imprint of the Taylor & Francis Group, an informa business*

© 2021 selection and editorial matter, Tuuli Lähdesmäki, Eerika Koskinen-Koivisto, Viktorija L.A. Čeginskas and Aino-Kaisa Koistinen; individual chapters, the contributors

The right of Tuuli Lähdesmäki, Eerika Koskinen-Koivisto, Viktorija L.A. Čeginskas and Aino-Kaisa Koistinen to be identified as the authors of the editorial material, and of the authors for their individual chapters, has been asserted in accordance with sections 77 and 78 of the Copyright, Designs and Patents Act 1988.

All rights reserved. No part of this book may be reprinted or reproduced or utilised in any form or by any electronic, mechanical, or other means, now known or hereafter invented, including photocopying and recording, or in any information storage or retrieval system, without permission in writing from the publishers.

*Trademark notice*: Product or corporate names may be trademarks or registered trademarks, and are used only for identification and explanation without intent to infringe.

*British Library Cataloguing-in-Publication Data*
A catalogue record for this book is available from the British Library

*Library of Congress Cataloging-in-Publication Data*
A catalog record has been requested for this book

ISBN: 978-0-367-37688-8 (hbk)
ISBN: 978-0-367-37685-7 (pbk)
ISBN: 978-0-429-35560-8 (ebk)

Typeset in Bembo
by Taylor & Francis Books

# CONTENTS

List of illustrations                                                                 viii
List of contributors                                                                     x
Preface                                                                             xviii
Tuuli Lähdesmäki, Eerika Koskinen-Koivisto, Viktorija L.A.
Čeginskas and Aino-Kaisa Koistinen

Introduction: Ethnography with a twist                                                  xx
Eerika Koskinen-Koivisto, Tuuli Lähdesmäki and Viktorija L. A.
Čeginskas

**PART I**
**New collaborative practices in ethnography**                                           1

1 Poly-space: Creating new concepts through reflexive team
  ethnography                                                                           3
  *Johanna Turunen, Viktorija L. A. Čeginskas, Sigrid Kaasik-
  Krogerus, Tuuli Lähdesmäki and Katja Mäkinen*

2 Embodied adventures: An experiment on doing and writing
  multisensory ethnography                                                             21
  *Eerika Koskinen-Koivisto and Tytti Lehtovaara*

3  Ramblings: A walk in progress (or the minutes of the
   International Society of the Imaginary Perambulator)　　36
   *Matthew Cheeseman, Gautam Chakrabarti, Susanne Österlund-
   Pötzsch, Simon Poole, Dani Schrire, Daniella Seltzer and
   Matti Tainio*

## PART II
## Visuality and multi-modality in ethnography　　53

4  Participant-induced elicitation in digital environments　　55
   *Riitta Hänninen*

5  Ethical challenges of using video for qualitative research and
   ethnography: State of the art and guidelines　　68
   *Marina Everri, Maxi Heitmayer, Paulius Yamin-Slotkus and
   Saadi Lahlou*

6  Drawing and storycrafting with Estonian children: Sharing
   experiences of mobility　　84
   *Pihla Maria Siim*

7  Sharpening the pencil: A visual journey towards the outlines of
   drawing as an autoethnographical method　　100
   *Marika Tervahartiala*

## PART III
## Ethnography of power dynamics in challenging contexts　　115

8  Retrospective ethnographies: Twisting moments of researching
   commemorative practices among volunteers after the refugee
   arrivals to Europe 2015　　117
   *Marie Sandberg*

9  Ethnographic challenges to studying the poor in and from the
   global South　　131
   *Laura Stark*

10 Elite interviewing: The effects of power in interactions. The
   experiences of a northern woman　　146
   *Lotta Lounasmeri*

## PART IV
## Embodied and affective ethnography 159

11  Memory narrations as a source for historical ethnography and
    the sensorial-affective experience of migration 161
    *Marija Dalbello and Catherine McGowan*

12  The involuntary ethnographer and an eagerness to know 185
    *Sofie Strandén-Backa*

13  Ethnography, arts production and performance: Meaning
    making in and for the street 197
    *Jessica Bradley*

Ethnographic twists and turns: An alternative epilogue 213
*Tom Boellstorff*

*Index* *221*

# ILLUSTRATIONS

**Figures**

1.1 Part of the forest around the former campground in Camp Westerbork has been cleared for a field of radio telescopes. These telescopes, placed next to the memorial to the camp's victims, are visible from the site of the former camp, contributing to the bizarre experience of different worlds meeting. Photo: EUROHERIT 10
1.2 The view from the living room in the Franz Liszt Memorial Museum in Budapest. Photo: EUROHERIT. 14
1.3 Johanna at the *Voice from the Sea* sound installation in Sagres Promontory. Photo: EUROHERIT. 15
2.1 Conference venue. Photo: Tytti Lehtovaara. 26
3.1 Simon's walk. Photo: Simon Poole. 44
6.1 Drawing by a 9-year-old boy, 2018. Copyright: Inequalities in Motion. Transnational Families in Estonia and Finland Project. 91
6.2 Drawing by an 8-year-old boy, 2018. Copyright: Inequalities in Motion. Transnational Families in Estonia and Finland Project. 93
6.3 Drawing by a 6-year-old girl, 2018. Copyright: Inequalities in Motion. Transnational Families in Estonia and Finland Project. 95
7.1 Drawing by Marika Tervahartiala, 2019. Copyright: Marika Tervahartiala. 100

7.2  Drawing by Marika Tervahartiala, 2019. Copyright: Marika
     Tervahartiala. 104
7.3  Drawing by Marika Tervahartiala, 2019. Copyright: Marika
     Tervahartiala. 116
7.4  Drawings by Marika Tervahartiala, 2019, layout by Maria
     Manner. Copyright: Marika Tervahartiala. 110
7.5  Drawings by Marika Tervahartiala, 2019, layout by Maria
     Manner. Copyright: Marika Tervahartiala. 111

## Tables

5.1   Problems and proposed solutions for video research ethics 79
11.1  Summary of the record completeness and file inventory for the
      corpus 162
11.2  Dates of immigration (N=198) 164
11.3  Age at time of immigration as reported in the interviews 165
11.4  Modalities with codes and descriptions 167
13.1  Data collection across the stages 206
13.2  Data excerpt, conversation in taxi, May 2015 207

# CONTRIBUTORS

**Tom Boellstorff** is a Professor of Anthropology at the University of California, Irvine, USA. His research focuses on digital culture, disability, globalization, the history of technology, nationalism, and sexuality. A Fellow of the American Association for the Advancement of Science, his research has been supported by a range of sources including the National Science Foundation. He is author of *The Gay Archipelago: Sexuality and Nation in Indonesia*, *A Coincidence of Desires: Anthropology, Queer Studies, Indonesia*, and *Coming of Age in Second Life: An Anthropologist Explores the Virtually Human*. He is coauthor of *Ethnography and Virtual Worlds: A Handbook of Method* and coeditor of *Data, Now Bigger and Better!* His articles have appeared in *American Anthropologist*, *American Ethnologist*, *Cultural Anthropology*, *Current Anthropology*, *Annual Review of Anthropology*, *Games and Culture*, *International Journal of Communication*, *Journal of Asian Studies*, *Journal of Linguistic Anthropology*, *Journal of Virtual Worlds Research*, *Ethnos*, *GLQ*, and *Media, Culture, and Society*.

**Jessica Bradley** is an ethnographer interested in the intersection of language, education and creative practice. Her doctoral research was part of the UK-based Arts and Humanities Research Council-funded project 'Translation and Translanguaging: Investigating Linguistic and Cultural Transformation in Superdiverse Wards in Four UK Cities'. Her PhD 'Translation and Translanguaging in Production and Performance in Community Arts' considered translation and text trajectories in street arts production and performance. She is Lecturer in Literacies in the School of Education at the University of Sheffield and co-convenes the AILA Research Network in Creative Inquiry and Applied Linguistics. She has undertaken research, which explores young people's understandings of multilingualism through creative practice. With Emilee Moore and James Simpson, she is co-editor of *Translanguaging as transformation: The collaborative construction of new linguistic realities* (Multilingual Matters 2020).

**Viktorija L.A. Čeginskas**, PhD, works as a Postdoctoral Researcher in the project 'Legitimation of European Cultural Heritage and the Dynamics of Identity Politics in the EU' (EUROHERIT, ERC St.G. 2015–2020), at the University of Jyväskylä, Finland. Čeginskas has a PhD in Cultural Heritage Studies (University of Turku, Finland), and an MA in contemporary history, East-European history, and European Ethnology (Christian-Albrechts-Universität, Kiel, Germany). She has published in peer-reviewed journals, including *Santander Art and Culture Law Review*, *International Journal of Heritage Studies* and *International Journal of Multilingualism*. Čeginskas is editor of the open access journal *Ethnologia Fennica*. She recently co-edited with Sigrid Kaasik-Krogerus and Nina Sääskilahti a special issue in *European Politics and Society* (2019) and is co-author of the forthcoming monographs *Creating and Governing Cultural Heritage in the European Union: The European Heritage Label* (Routledge 2020) and *Europe from Below. Notions of Europe and the European among Participants of EU Cultural Initiatives* (Brill 2020).

**Gautam Chakrabarti** is an Assistant Lecturer in "Berlin and German Studies" at the Freie Universität Berlin (FUB), Germany; he has been a Postdoctoral Researcher in the Centre for Global Theatre History, Ludwig-Maximilians-Universität München (2016–2019), Germany. He has previously had postdoc research fellowships in The Hebrew University of Jerusalem, Israel, and the FUB. He has also taught South Asian Studies at the Humboldt-Universität zu Berlin and English and Comparative Literature at the FUB, where he did his PhD. He has earlier taught in Russian, Finnish and Indian universities. His current research, rooted in literary-cultural historiography, engages with the 'Cultural Cold War' and Eurasian cosmopolitanism/s.

**Matthew Cheeseman**, PhD, is a researcher, teacher and writer who works across fiction and non-fiction. He draws on critical theory and cultural studies, often in collaboration with artists and designers in the creation and publication of books, pamphlets and other things. At the University of Derby, UK, he is an Associate Professor of Creative Writing and Programme Leader for MA Creative Writing.

**Marija Dalbello** is a Professor of Information Studies in the School of Information and Communication at Rutgers University, New Brunswick, NJ, USA. Her teaching and publications focus on historical ethnography and migration, visuality, epistemologies of the senses, history of the book, and information history. She has published numerous essays and articles on digital mediation, visual epistemology and immigrant literacies. Her recent edited volumes include *Visible Writings: Cultures, Forms, Readings*, co-edited with Mary Shaw (2011); *A History of Modern Librarianship: Constructing the Heritage of Western Cultures*, co-edited with Wayne Wiegand and Pamela Spence Richards (2015); and a special issue of *Information Research*, "Archaeology and Information Research," co-edited with Isto Huvila, Ixchel Faniel, Costis Dallas, and Michael Olsson (2019). She is currently editing *Reading Home Cultures Through Books* with Kirsti Salmi-Niklander (forthcoming). She is writing a book, *Ellis Island as a Sensorium and an Information Machine*.

**Marina Everri**, PhD, University College Dublin, Ireland, is a Researcher in Social Psychology and systemic psychotherapist interested in understanding how current societal challenges, such as technological development and stigma and discrimination towards minority families, are transforming family relations and communication and child development. She was awarded a Marie Curie Fellowship to investigate the role of digital media in adolescents' development and parent-child communication testing and developing further the Subjective Evidence Based Ethnography protocol. Her research has contributed to theoretical advancements in adolescent and family studies through the development of innovative concepts (e.g., micro-transition and oscillations) and ethnographic/qualitative methods (e.g., stance-taking process). She is visiting fellow at the Department of Media and Communications, London School of Economics, UK, and collaborates on research projects on minority families' discrimination at the University of Parma, Italy. She is currently based in Dublin where she works as a lecturer.

**Maxi Heitmayer** is a PhD Candidate in the Department of Psychological and Behavioural Science at the London School of Economics and Political Science, UK. His dissertation project investigates smart device and social media use among adolescents and young adults using the Subjective Evidence-Based Ethnography (SEBE) protocol. The main focus of his research lies on understanding the disruptiveness of smartphones, their influence on the daily routines and habits of users, and the decisions concerning time management and attention allocation users make. His research further seeks to address challenges that data privacy regulations raise for ethnographic research involving social media, and for social media research in general.

**Riitta Hänninen**, PhD, works as a University Researcher at the Centre of Excellence in Research on Ageing and Care, Department of Social Sciences and Philosophy, University of Jyväskylä, Finland. Her research interests include the effects of new technology on the everyday lives of senior people and the relationship between technology and care. Dr. Hänninen has also studied social media influencers, the commercialization of social media, digital ethnography, and qualitative research methods in online environments. She has acted as a visiting researcher at the Department of Urban and Regional Sociology, Humboldt University, Germany, and at the Department of Social Anthropology, University of Stockholm, Sweden. Dr. Hänninen's work has been published in several peer-reviewed journals, including *Journal of Family Studies, Ethnologia Scandinavica*, and *New Media & Society*.

**Sigrid Kaasik-Krogerus**, DSocSc, is a University Lecturer at the Faculty of Arts, University of Helsinki, Finland. She has previously worked as a Postdoctoral Researcher on the research project 'Legitimation of European Cultural Heritage and the Dynamics of Identity Politics in the EU' (EUROHERIT), funded by the European Research Council. Kaasik-Krogerus specializes in media, identity, heritage, and European studies in the context of the EU and especially Central and East European countries.

**Aino-Kaisa Koistinen**, PhD in Contemporary Culture Studies, is a Postdoctoral Researcher at the University of Jyväskylä, Finland. Koistinen's expertise lies in cultural studies, media studies and feminist theory. She has worked in projects such as 'Dialogue and Argumentation for Cultural Literacy Learning in Schools' (DIALLS) funded from the EU's H2020 Program, 'Legitimation of European Cultural Heritage and the Dynamics of Identity Politics in the EU' (EUROHERIT), funded by the European Research Council, 'TRANSMEDIA LITERACY: Exploiting transmedia skills and informal learning strategies to improve formal education', funded from H2020, and 'Abusive Sexuality and Sexual Violence in Contemporary Culture' funded by Kone Foundation. She has published in journals such as *NORA – Nordic Journal of Feminist and Gender Research* and *Science Fiction Film and Television* and co-edited journal issues, such as *Somatechnics* (1/18). She is the co-editor of *Reconfiguring Human, Nonhuman and Posthuman in Literature and Culture* (Routledge 2020).

**Eerika Koskinen-Koivisto**, PhD, title of Docent, is a Postdoctoral Researcher at the Department of Social Sciences and Philosophy at the University of Jyväskylä, Finland. Her current research addresses the sense of place and community in small townships of Central Finland. Her other research interests include childhood memories, sensory ethnography, transnational family history, difficult heritage, and nostalgia. Koskinen-Koivisto is the co-Editor-in-Chief of *Ethnologia Fennica* journal. Her main publications include monograph *Her Own Worth – Negotiations of Subjectivity in the Life Narrative of a Female Labourer* (2014), theme issue *Bittersweet: Everyday life and Nostalgia for the 1950* (Journal of Finnish Studies 1/2016), and co-edited volumes *Transnational Death* (2019) and *The Routledge Handbook of Memory and Place* (2019).

**Saadi Lahlou** is a Professor in Social Psychology in the Department of Psychological and Behavioural Science at the London School of Economics and Political Science, UK, and Director of the Paris Institute for Advanced Study, France. He has directed five research units, written 200+ papers and 5 books, and built at EDF R&D the largest industry user-lab, where behaviour of volunteer workers was digitally recorded 24/7 for 10 years. His recent monograph, *Installation Theory* (Cambridge University Press, 2017) proposes a pragmatic model for the analysis of behaviour, based on 20 years of use of video ethnography in very diverse fields, from family dinners or shopping to policing, Intensive Care Units and nuclear plants.

**Tytti Lehtovaara** is a PhD Student of Ethnology at the Department of History and Ethnology, the University of Jyväskylä, Finland. In her PhD research, she studies sensory practices and memories related to female dressing. In her research, she uses dress biographical interviews and a method of experiencing together. The focus of her research is on how women speak, do, and comprise their own dress choices. She is interested in understanding the motives and meanings related to dressing, and the importance of senses in clothing consumption. Lehtovaara also has experience in using applied ethnographic methods in business and public sector development processes.

**Tuuli Lähdesmäki**, PhD, DSocSc, title of Docent, is a Senior Researcher of Art History at the Department of Music, Art and Culture Studies, University of Jyväskylä, Finland. Her research interests focus on cultural identities and identity politics, belonging, cultural heritage, strategies of interpreting the past, governance of diversities and populism. Lähdesmäki has recently led the research project 'Legitimation of European Cultural Heritage and the Dynamics of Identity Politics in the EU' (EUROHERIT), funded by the European Research Council. She is also leading JYU's consortium partnership in a project 'Dialogue and Argumentation for Cultural Literacy Learning in Schools' (DIALLS), funded from the EU's H2020 Program. She is one of the three leaders in JYU's research profiling area 'Crises Redefined: Historical Continuity and Societal Change' (CRISES) and a co-editor of *Politics of Scale. New Directions in Critical Heritage Studies* (Berghahn Books, 2019) and *Dissonant Heritages and Memories in Contemporary Europe* (Palgrave Macmillan, 2019).

**Lotta Lounasmeri** is a University Lecturer at the Centre for European Studies, University of Helsinki, Finland. She has a background in media and communication studies (PhD in 2010 from the Department of Communication, University of Helsinki). Her thesis discussed the role of journalism in the Finnish consensual political culture. A central issue was also to understand the role of elites in influencing public debate in Finland. Her research areas include political culture, political communication, journalism, and media history. Her projects have involved historical analysis of the relations of Finnish media and politics in a Nordic and European context, in an effort to understand the roots and later developments of the Finnish political culture in a comparative perspective. In her latest Academy of Finland project she studied the decision making culture in the Finnish energy sector. She has conducted numerous research projects using elite interviews as data and method.

**Catherine McGowan** is a first-year Doctoral Student in Communication, Information, and Media program in the School of Communication and Information (iSchool) at Rutgers University, New Brunswick, NJ, USA. She received her Master of Information degree from Rutgers University in January 2019 and her B.A. in philosophy from William Paterson University in 2005. She co-presented a graduate student poster, Adaptive Outreach: Transforming Archival Participation at the Society of American Archivists 2019 annual meeting. Her research interests include algorithmic aspects of society: critical analysis of data and systems that create power structures and the implications of misuse and harm, particularly within labour systems; social identity construction and expression within digital worlds; understanding the relationship between digital information and the construction of social identity and cultural knowledge; the parallels of social and computational algorithms and how they shape the development of artificial intelligence and express posthuman ideals.

**Katja Mäkinen**, MAs in Political Science and Art Education; PhD in Political Science, is a Senior Researcher in the Department of Music, Art and Culture Studies at the University of Jyväskylä, Finland. She works in the project 'Legitimation of European

Cultural Heritage and the Dynamics of Identity Politics in the EU' (EUROHERIT), funded by the European Research Council. Previously she has worked as a junior lecturer in political science and a lecturer in cultural policy at the University of Jyväskylä. Mäkinen specializes in citizenship and participation; identities; cultural heritage; spatiality and territoriality, EU's participatory governance; EU programmes on citizenship and culture; policy documents; conceptual research and ethnography. Mäkinen was the convenor of the Standing Group on Citizenship in the European Consortium for Political Research (2016–2017) and a Visiting Fellow at the European University Institute in Florence, Italy (2018). She is a co-editor of *Shaping Citizenship. A Political Concept in Theory, Debate and Practice* (Routledge 2018).

**Simon Poole** is the Senior Lead in Cultural Education and Research at Storyhouse, Chester's award-winning theatre; Programme Leader for the Masters in Creative Practice in Education at the University of Chester; Researcher at the Centre for Research into Education, Creativity and Arts through Practice (RECAP); and Researcher with the International Thriving at Work Research Group, UK. He holds positions outside of the university too, such as the Director of Research for 'Lapidus International' and Vice Chair of the Local Cultural Education Partnership. He is also Managing Director of Soil Records; Singer with 'the loose kites' and is a published poet and author.

**Marie Sandberg** is an Associate Professor, PhD in European Ethnology with a research focus on everyday life Europeanisation, European borders and migration practices. She is PI of the research network 'Helping Hands: Research Network on the Everyday Border Work of European Citizens' funded by the Danish Research Council for Independent Research, and Co-PI of the core-group project 'Diginauts: Migrants' digital practices in/of the European border regime' funded by the Velux Foundations 2018–2020. Sandberg is the Director of the Centre for Advanced Migration Studies (AMIS) at University of Copenhagen. She has published a number of peer-reviewed articles in high-ranked journals such as *Identities* and *Journal of European Studies*, as well as edited volumes. She is joint editor-in-chief (with Monique Scheer) of the international, A-ranked *Ethnologia Europaea – Journal of European Ethnology*. Sandberg is vividly engaged in discussions within international as well as Nordic fields of migration and border studies.

**Dani Schrire** is a Lecturer at the Hebrew University of Jerusalem, Israel, with a joint appointment in two graduate programs: Folklore and Folk-Culture studies and Cultural Studies. Previously, he was a postdoctoral researcher at the Institute for KAEE Göttingen, Germany, and the Katz Center for Advanced Judaic Studies at the University of Pennsylvania, USA. His research engages Jewish folkloristics, folklore and avant-garde, the development of folklore taxonomies globally, as well as collecting practices, particularly the collection of postcards. Recently he started developing a new kind of walk.

**Daniella Seltzer** is a Master's Student in the Cultural Department at the Hebrew University of Jerusalem, Israel. Her thesis focused on ultra-Orthodox women's walking, exploring their reflexivity and how they speak about their walking. She works around food justice issues, looking at urban foodways and grassroots mobilization around food waste. Daniella enjoys walking on the beach at sunset.

**Pihla Maria Siim**, MA in folklore, is a Junior Research Fellow at the Department of Estonian and Comparative Folklore (University of Tartu, Estonia), finishing her PhD thesis. Siim's research interests are related to narrative research, migration, children and mobility, multilocality and family relations. Her thesis is based on multi-sited fieldwork and concentrates on questions of identity and belonging among transnational families living in the area of Estonia, Finland and north-western Russia. Since 2013, Siim has studied transnational families in the Estonian–Finnish context in three projects led by professor Laura Assmuth (UEF). In 2018, Siim began studying trans-border commuters and returning migrants as part of the Estonian Research Council's Performative Negotiations of Belonging in Contemporary Estonia project (2018–2021), led by Dr Elo-Hanna Seljamaa. Her recent publications have touched folkloristic fieldwork practices, 'doing families' through practices of silence, and belonging and family mobilities in the Estonian–Finnish transnational space.

**Laura Stark** is a Professor of Ethnology at the University of Jyväskylä, Finland. Her research focuses on gender, urban poverty, early marriage, transactional intimacy and mobile telephony in the global South. Recent scientific articles have been published in *Ethnologia Europaea; Ethnos: Journal of Anthropology; Culture, Health and Sexuality; and Marriage and Family Review*. She is the author of *The Limits of Patriarchy: How Female Networks of Pilfering and Gossip Sparked the First Debates on Rural Gender Rights in the 19th-Century Finnish-Language Press* (Finnish Literature Society, 2011). Between 2007 and 2017 she led three major research projects on gender funded by the Academy of Finland and the Finnish Ministry of Foreign Affairs, including *'Mobile Technology, Gender and Development in Africa and India'* (2010–2013); and *'Urban Renewal and Income-Generating Spaces for Youth and Women in Addis Ababa, Ethiopia and Dar es Salaam, Tanzania'* (2013–2017).

**Sofie Strandén-Backa** is a Postdoctoral Researcher of Nordic Folklore at the Åbo Akademi University, Finland. Her field of interest covers uncomfortable matters: male and female narration about participating in the Second World War in Finland, expressions of contesting ideas about the origin of the Finland-Swedish ethnic group, and, most recently, debates about the presence of wolves in populated areas in Finland. She is particularly interested in research ethics and reflexivity, and the dialogue between the deep roots of different ways of thinking, cultural history and contemporary patterns of thought.

**Matti Tainio**, DA, is a visual artist and researcher, currently working as a Postdoctoral Researcher at Aalto University's Pori Urban Platform PUPA, Finland. His research balances between aesthetics and artistic research. His work has focused lately on the aesthetic experiences in contemporary physical activities and the experiences of darkness. His work as an artist takes place in an interdisciplinary setting where the themes of the work often intertwine with his research practice.

**Marika Tervahartiala**, MA, is a Doctoral Candidate of Art Education at the Aalto University, Finland, a drawer, a practicing visual art educator and a society engaged artwork specialist. She has been working in Kiasma, Contemporary Art Museum, Finland (various museum pedagogy positions and with Helsinki Festival Week), Aalto University, Finland (e.g. Assistant of Art Education, Substitute Art Education Lecturer) as well as a researcher in the Finnish Youth Research Network. She has conducted postgraduate studies in Crossfields Institute (Certificate Philosophy and Practice of Integrative Education) and in Arts University Helsinki (Society Engaged Art Work, will be accomplished in May 2020).

**Johanna Turunen**, MA, MSSc, is a Doctoral Candidate of Contemporary Culture Studies at the Department of Music, Art and Culture Studies, University of Jyväskylä, Finland. As part of the project 'Legitimation of European Cultural Heritage and the Dynamics of Identity Politics in the EU' (EUROHERIT, funded by the European Research Council), she analyses EU's cultural heritage policies and initiatives through insights from postcolonial/decolonial theory. In her research, Turunen focuses especially on the narrative and visual practices of defining 'Europeanness' in the European Heritage Label, the heritagization of colonial histories, decolonization of museums and theories of critical heritage studies. She is the co-editor of a themed section 'Using our pasts, defining our futures – debating heritage and culture in Europe' (2019) in the *International Journal of Heritage Studies*.

**Paulius Yamin-Slotkus** is a PhD Candidate in the Department of Psychological and Behavioural Science at the London School of Economics and Political Science, UK, and a Research Fellow and MJJ Scholar at Vilnius Gediminas Technical University, Lithuania. He has several years of experience designing, managing and researching behavioural change interventions for private and policy challenges, including posts as managing partner of the Behavioural Lab LT, consultant for the International Labour Organization and as Head of the Cultural and Behavioural Change Team at the agency of the Colombian Government in charge of civil service. His current research project makes use of first-person perspective video recordings and the Subjective Evidence-Based Ethnography (SEBE) protocol to explore how behavioural change interventions based on social norms can be used to tackle real world problems.

**Susanne Österlund-Pötzsch**, PhD, has the Title of Docent in Nordic Folkloristics, at the Faculty of Arts, Psychology and Theology, at Åbo Akademi University in Turku, Finland. She works as an archivist specialized in folklore and tradition material. Her research has focused on issues such as migration, the Swedish-speaking Finn minority in Finland, food culture and island studies. She has researched and published extensively on various aspects of walking and walking practices.

# PREFACE

Ethnography is a research method applied today by scholars not only in humanities and social sciences, but also in disciplines beyond, ranging, for example, from business to sports studies. As a method based on engagement and interaction with people in specific environments, the transformation of social, cultural, and societal relations and conditions ineluctably impact the method itself. This volume stems from scholarly interest in ethnography as a method and the potential that this method entails in transforming societies and scholarship. This interest was concretized in a conference that the editors of this book and their colleagues organized on 12–14 February 2019 at the University of Jyväskylä, Finland. The conference was titled thought-provokingly 'Ethnography with a Twist'. For the call for papers, we formulated three questions of which we wished to have a deeper discussion in the conference: 1) How does ethnographic research create substantive knowledge of current processes, phenomena, implications, and meanings of social life and culture across diverse rapidly changing, technological, natural, and/or everyday settings? 2) How can new roles and relations of researchers and their 'fields' in ethnographic research be perceived? 3) What kinds of new twists are emerging and could be explored in ethnographic research?

To our pleasant surprise, our call for papers raised a lot of interest and we received more abstracts than we expected in the preparation phase of the conference. Besides conventional paper, panel, and poster abstracts, we were delighted to receive 12 proposals for 'experimental workshops' in which their chairs were welcomed to implement joint experimental exercises or experiments, or to debate about different modes of applying or developing ethnography. In these workshops, the chairs and the participants explored ethnography regarding themes and topics, such as artistic practices, queering art, exhibition as a method, somatic tools, sensory research, motion, listening, and creative writing. Altogether more than 170 scholars from 17 countries participated in the conference to discuss methods in ethnographic research 'outside the box' and to jointly explore novel approaches to it. The broad interest for the conference indicated that there was a clear need for it: a great number of scholars perceive that they are practicing ethnography with a twist!

This edited volume is based on selected conference papers as well as elaborations of experiments implemented in or instigated by the workshops in the conference. We are also happy to include in the volume contributions from our two keynote speakers, Associate Professor Marie Sandberg and Professor Tom Boellstorff. We want to thank all the contributors to this volume for their thorough work in developing their conference papers and workshop activities into volume chapters. We are also grateful to all other participants in the Ethnography with a Twist Conference for the fruitful, critical, and interdisciplinary discussions and exchange of ideas and experiences both during and after the conference. Moreover, we want to thank all our colleagues from the University of Jyväskylä who participated in organizing the conference. We also wish to thank Senior Commissioning Editor Hannah Shakespeare and Editorial Assistant Matthew Bickerton for the smooth cooperation in the publishing process, as well as Routledge's anonymous reviewers for their fruitful comments, which helped us develop the book and sharpen our argumentation.

Finally, we want to thank the conference's core financers: the European Research Council, the Academy of Finland, and Kone Foundation. The conference, as well as this volume, was initiated by the project EUROHERIT (Legitimation of European cultural heritage and the dynamics of identity politics in the EU), led by Senior Researcher Tuuli Lähdesmäki. EUROHERIT is financed by the ERC Starting Grant under the EU's Horizon 2020 Research and Innovation Programme under grant number 636177. The projects Crossing Borders, led by Professor Sari Pöyhänen and funded by the Academy of Finland, and Intersecting Mobilities, led by Senior Researcher Tuija Sarema and funded by Kone Foundation covered a part of the conference costs. The University of Jyväskylä's current research profiling area CRISES, Crises Redefined: Historical Continuity and Societal Change, funded by the Academy of Finland, contributed to the conference budget through the salary costs of a conference secretary Urho Tulonen. Lastly, we want to thank our host departments, the Department of Music, Art and Culture Studies and the Department of History and Ethnology in the University of Jyväskylä, Finland, for their encouragement to host the conference and for facilitating its practical arrangements.

14 January 2020, in Jyväskylä
Tuuli Lähdesmäki, Eerika Koskinen-Koivisto,
Viktorija L.A. Čeginskas and Aino-Kaisa Koistinen

# INTRODUCTION: ETHNOGRAPHY WITH A TWIST

*Eerika Koskinen-Koivisto, Tuuli Lähdesmäki and Viktorija L. A. Čeginskas*

### Why do we need ethnography with a twist?

Ethnography aims at understanding people and their activities from their own perspectives. It is based on the researcher's presence and participation in the daily lives of people and communities, thereby offering various possibilities for encountering and understanding different ways of life and thinking. By engaging in participant observation, the ethnographer enters everyday life and life-worlds and can have access to hidden meanings, nuances and affective realms that are not visible or understandable at first sight. Ethnography as a research method and a mode of knowledge production has its roots in anthropological and sociological studies, seeking to understand – through a Western gaze – foreign cultures and distinct communities. Ethnography has since developed into a broad research field with a wide range of methodological emphases. Today, ethnographic research methods are used in a variety of disciplines for scrutinizing human interaction and experience.

Complex political, environmental, and social developments in rapidly changing global and multicultural societies and the digitalized world have created new kinds of research environments and challenges for ethnographic research. For example, rapid communication and mediation bring to our awareness global and local humanitarian and environmental crises that call for joint action beyond established institutions. Interconnected digitalized environments can bring people from various locations and backgrounds together, offering multiple ways to express their thoughts and creativity. In order to grasp the multiplicity and agency of individual people and collectivities, ethnographers need to find ways to work with not only scholars in other fields, but also with civil organizations and activists outside of academia. These new research environments and challenges require ethnographers to think 'outside the box' of their methodology and its previous tradition in order to critically discuss the core of ethnography: ethics, subjectivity, and the role of the researcher in ethnographic research.

As ethnography expands into multiple fields and is applied in new contexts, scholars across disciplines have created innovative methodological tools and novel approaches to ethnographic inquiry. The volume at hand introduces discussions and examples of the new twists in multidisciplinary ethnographic research. By twists we mean both a) an intentional aim to conduct ethnographic research with novel approaches and methodological tools, and b) sensitivity to recognize and creativity to utilize different kinds of 'twist moments' that ethnographic research may create for the researcher. These sudden 'twist moments', aroused by unexpected incidents *in situ* and related to serendipity, unpredictability, immediacy of embodied experiences, affects or cognitive confusion, can serve to generate new insights for the ethnographer and can be turned into a means for gaining ethnographic knowledge.

In addition to new ways of conducting ethnography and producing research material, ethnographers have actively sought new ways of writing and distributing ethnographic research results. These often include collaboration with other professionals: artists, filmmakers, actors, programmers and game designers as well as non-professionals and the research participants who have an equally central role in the new twists.

## Current trends and experiments

Even though critical, feminist and postcolonial approaches in ethnographic research have sought to deconstruct and dismantle its former ethnocentric and normative bases, various kinds of unbalanced power hierarchies, for example in economic terms, continue to pose challenges for academic researchers and their collaborations. Therefore, we need to critically evaluate the new methodological tools and their ability to tackle issues of power difference and access to resources and knowledge. One solution dealing with these challenges is the use of collaborative methods in ethnography that allow for co-production and co-creation of research material, as well as shared conceptual work and wider distribution of knowledge.

Participatory research enables ordinary people to play an active and influential part in research processes. It has been one of the methodological trends in qualitative research of the 2000s (e.g. Gubrium and Harper 2013, 29). While there is a long tradition of using participatory and collaborative practices in ethnographic research for creating intimate research relationships with individuals and communities, collaborative ethnography emphasizes deep, interactive collaboration in research design, dissemination of research results, and knowledge production (Lassiter 2005). In collaborative ethnography, the researcher invites commentaries from the studied people from the beginning of planning the research project and throughout the fieldwork and writing process. Ethnographer(s) and participants discuss the interpretations together, which are then reintegrated into fieldwork and ethnographic analysis. The results are reciprocal, co-conceived or co-written with local communities of collaborators and thus consider multiple audiences outside the confines of academic discourse, including local constituencies (ibid.). The model of reciprocal collaborative ethnography evolved among studies of indigenous communities, minorities and other vulnerable groups. Other participatory ethnographic approaches, especially participatory action research, a method that evolved in sociology, have been applied and used, for instance, in design research (e.g. Simonsen and Robinson 2012), examinations of everyday lives in urban contexts (e.g. Suopajärvi 2016), studies of health and culture (e.g. Averill 2006) and analyses of activists and civic groups (Hemment 2007).

Traditionally, ethnography has been a relatively lonely research practice, in the sense that ethnographers have worked and written alone (Clerke and Hopwood 2014). In this volume, many texts are based on the collaboration of research teams and other academic collectives and involve reflections on the process of methodological experiments of co-creating knowledge. Along with joint fieldwork, shared conceptual work can offer ground for developing theories through sharing preliminary ideas and intuitive knowledge. Writing ethnography can be a joint creative process that happens both in situ and online. Many ethnographers think that new experimental and creative collaboration is needed that bend the conventions of academic writing and the domination of journal articles (e.g. Marcus 2007; Stavrianakis, Rabinow and Korsby 2017)

This volume also draws on other influential, but more theoretical than practical trends included in the so-called affective turn, which has brought attention to impulses, attitudes, emotions and feelings as sources of knowledge and knowledge production by acknowledging the embodied nature of sensing the world as a basis of human interaction (Ahmed 2004; Thrift 2004; Frykman and Povrazanović Frykman 2015). Ethnography is a valid method for studying the affective, as it encourages the researchers' reflexive attitude and emphasizes the subjective experience of the ethnographer. Furthermore, ethnographic writing that draws on narrativizing the fieldwork experience and reflexivity, offers a fruitful forum for expressing and analyzing affective experiences. Despite these potentials, the study books of ethnographic methods hardly pay attention to the embodied researcher, or to the articulation of emotions, sensing atmospheres or embodied experiences in the text (see Pink 2009 for exception). Experimenting with artistic expression and visual or multimodal forms of representing research results, such as drawings, ethnographic film or theatre performances, can bring about silent and embodied forms of knowledge that would otherwise remain unspoken (ibid.). In recent years, many ethnographers have also made conscious experiments with ethnographic fiction (e.g. Cantú 2019; Silow Kallenberg and Ingridsdotter 2017). Ethnographic fiction affords the author-researcher freedom from normative academic forms of writing and offers possibilities to combine different case studies and to play with temporalities and possible scenarios. Fiction can also facilitate the exploration of sensitive and intimate issues without revealing personal information and offer a channel for articulating the researcher's inside/emic knowledge (e.g. Pohtinen 2019).

## Questions that remain: research ethics and reflexivity

Research ethics is a cornerstone of working closely with people and within the studied field. As each ethnographic research includes unique ethical questions, practices and solutions must always be negotiated case by case with regard to existing guidelines and legislation. Recently, digital realms have raised new challenges of data protection and copyrights. In addition to practical questions that have to do with consent and identification of research subjects, research ethics contain a myriad of complex moral questions about the aims and means of ethnographic research. Many of these questions have to do with understanding the basis of different ways of thinking. For example, when planning collaborative research, it is important to reflect on the issue of reciprocity from the perspective of the participants: what do participants gain when they commit to a collaborative research process? Does participation really open a space for co-production and fruitful negotiation over alternative epistemologies and different ways of knowing, or does it merely reinforce a hegemonic and/or academic theoretical framework upon the experiences of the participants? It is important to bear in mind that often the coproduction of knowledge is an ideal set by the academic community (Mosse 2007). Too often, the research agenda and the interactions with participants and communities are tied to project cycles and research funding, which makes long-term collaboration and evaluation of the impacts of the research challenging (Byrne et al. 2009).

It is often said that the ethnographer is the main tool in ethnographic research and thus, subjectivity is embedded in all ethnographic research practices (e.g. Murchison 2010, 13–14). Critical evaluation of the role of the researcher(s), her position with regard to the research field, politics and epistemologies is a fundamental part of creating validity in ethnographic research (Davies 2002, 3–4). Reflexive attitude needs to run through the whole research process, during which the researcher critically reflects on her own position and presumptions, political engagements in the research, as well as methodological choices. Critical reflection and articulation of positionality become even more crucial when developing and experimenting with new methodological tools.

## Ethnography with a twist in action

This book draws together 13 chapters that reflect the great diversity of approaches, methods, and practices, as well as ethical challenges in current ethnographic research. Our contributors use ethnography to explore various cases and phenomena, which range from heritage sites to slums, and from artistic projects to researcher communities. The cases deal with people of various social backgrounds, from societal elites to migrants and refugees, and include people of different ages, ranging from young children to elderly people. The interaction between the researched and researchers in the exploration of these cases has taken place through different modes of communication and forms of expression, such as story-crafting, drawing, and participant-induced elicitation interviews.

The amalgamating factor among the diversity of topics and themes explored in the chapters stems from their contributors' interest to rethink ways of 'doing' ethnography and their openness to develop new methodological practices, concepts, or tools. The chapters critically discuss keystones of ethnography; ethics, subjectivity, human interaction, the role of ethnographer and the researcher-researched relationship in the ethnographic research process, and the translation of experiences in the procedures of ethnographic knowledge production. Through the variety of explored cases and phenomena, the book enlightens different aspects of 'ethnography with a twist' and demonstrates how it can be understood in action. The focus on 'twists' is reflected also in the ways, in which our contributors discuss and write about them in the book. Several chapters manifest the experimental and alternative take, based on creative, artistic, and narrative modes of presenting thoughts and findings.

The contributions in the volume are structured in four interlinked thematic Parts. Besides the themes of these Parts, individual chapters in each bring forth various theoretical and methodological bridges to chapters from other Parts. Part I discusses the challenges of producing ethnographic knowledge in a research team and in close interaction with other researchers. Its 'twists' in ethnography stem from exploring new collaborative practices, which emphasize intersubjectivity in research, the sharing of sensory experiences, and negotiating interpretations in an ethnographic research process. Part I starts with the chapter of Johanna Turunen, Viktorija L.A. Čeginskas, Sigrid Kaasik-Krogerus, Tuuli Lähdesmäki, and Katja Mäkinen that discusses collaborative and interpretive reflexivity in doing ethnography in a research group. They describe how they implemented their ethnographic fieldwork at 11 heritage sites and how their ethnographic process included not only the sharing of data, such as interviews with various informants, but also the researchers' own experiences through intensive dialogue and exchange of views. They claim that this kind of affective sharing of experiences among researchers goes beyond traditional conceptualizations of team ethnography. As a result of their collaborative and interpretive reflexivity, the authors developed the concept of poly-space – a concept that describes the entanglement of multiple moments and different spatial, temporal, affective, and cognitive experiences in one physical place, such as at a heritage site in their case. Instead of being neutral sites in the authors' memos, their oral communications, exchange of experiences, and sharing of emotions turned these sites into inter-personal space, filled with emotional and affective meanings.

The second chapter in Part I continues the discussion on the role of the researchers' experiences and emotions in ethnography. Eerika Koskinen-Koivisto and Tytti Lehtovaara scrutinize the process of doing sensory ethnography based on sensory observations and interventions in writing. The challenge of sensory ethnography stems from difficulties in documenting and cognitively transmitting the embodied knowledge, sensory experience and memory, which directs our attention, often unconsciously, and may disappear within seconds. In the chapter, this challenge is explored through experiments conducted collaboratively in a workshop in the Ethnography with a Twist Conference at the University of Jyväskylä in 2019. The authors approach the experiences of sensory ethnography as 'twist' moments of ethnographic research, which transformed their understanding of doing ethnography and opened new views of engaging in reflexive ethnographic knowledge production.

The third chapter in Part I stems also from a collaborative and experimental workshop in the same conference. Matthew Cheeseman, Gautam Chakrabarti, Susanne Österlund-Pötzsch, Simon Poole, Dani Schrire, Daniella Seltzer, and Matti Tainio explore a series of walking experiments that took them outside the conference venue to experience the environment through walking in it. These walking experiments and the shared experiences created by them are approached in the chapter as a mode of collective understanding. The authors return in their text to their shared walking experiment and re-embody this moment by continuing walking together, writing together, and engaging their understanding of self and their experiences of walking. Through ethnographic and artistic responses to each-others' walking practices, the authors open their experimentation to the reader and invite her to travel with the authors through the process of ethnographic knowledge production.

Part II discusses visual ethnography and visuality and multimodality as research methods as well as their possibilities and limits to produce ethnographic knowledge. It also explores new visual technologies and ethics related to their uses. The 'twists' in Part II connect to the critical exploration of the roles of images, multimodal items, practices of visualization, and the engagement of the researched and the researcher in an ethnographic research process. Riitta Hänninen opens Part II by discussing participant-induced elicitation interview in two very different contexts: Finnish lifestyle blogging and older adults using digital technology. She claims that participant-induced elicitation broadens the scope of thematic interview and enables gaining a deeper understanding of the object of research by encouraging the interviewees to actively collaborate with the researcher. Hänninen's research on bloggers and older adults demonstrates how the use of multimodal items in interviews, such as blog posts, smartphones, and various ICT applications, may open up a new kind of methodological access to the communities and phenomena under research and provide a versatile extension to the traditional interview as a part of ethnographic field research.

Marina Everri, Maxi Heitmayer, Paulius Yamin-Slotkus, and Saadi Lahlou continue the discussion on the uses of digital technology in ethnography. Their chapter focuses on video-ethnography and qualitative research designs based on video data and examines what kinds of ethical challenges are related to these designs and data. The authors' core concern is the lack of solid ethical regulations and guidelines for using video data in ethnographic research. The chapter provides a systematic review of current research ethics guidelines for using video data, identifies critical issues and gaps related to researcher-researched rapport, informed consent, and participants' rights in video-ethnography, and explores the parameters of ethical research design in such studies. Based on these explorations, the authors provide practical advice for an 'ethical twist' in video-ethnography by looking at the future of ethical regulations for qualitative research designs based on video data.

Multimodality in ethnography and challenges of the researcher-researched relationship are also discussed in the chapter by Pihla Maria Siim. She explores children's experiences and understandings of mobility and describes how the challenge to research young children led her to apply alternative fieldwork methods, including story-crafting and drawing with the children. In their research, Siim and her colleague asked the researched Estonian children to tell a story of a child who moves from Estonia to Finland. The researchers wrote the story down and read it aloud to the children who then were able to correct the story for as long as was needed until they were content with the outcome. The children were also asked to draw things that they missed from Estonia and liked in Finland. The chapter explores these drawings as a dialogue between the 'marks on paper' and the children's thoughts, which enables the researcher to better understand children's experiences with mobility. Siim claims that story-crafting is a method that innovatively combines the real and the imaginary by offering both a space to negotiate experiences and a methodological tool to explore emotions related to them.

Part II ends with an experimental chapter by Marika Tervahartiala. She is a drawer, art educator, and researcher exploring autoethnographic drawing as a method in a post-structuralist framework. Her chapter focuses on discussing the complex relationships between drawing as an act, the drawer-artist, and the drawing as a result of this act. Tervahartiala also explores the ethical challenges of autoethnographic agency when the drawing is not only understood as a research object but rather as an active entity or being. This chapter combines visual, artistic and creative research to discuss how autoethnographic knowledge and understandings can be produced in the process of drawing. It challenges the established and conventional role of the visual in research and criticizes the text-based formats of academic publications.

Part III focuses on the ethnography of power dynamics in challenging contexts ranging from extreme poverty in Africa to power elites in Northern Europe. The chapters explore the power included in the interaction between the researcher and the researched and in the creation of data in ethnographic fieldwork in such contexts. Moreover, its 'twists' stem from various ethical challenges included in these contexts. In the first chapter, Marie Sandberg explores volunteer initiatives for refugee reception in Denmark, Germany and the Netherlands after the increased refugee arrivals to Europe in 2015. Her work applies retrospective ethnography focusing on volunteers' memories of the events in 2015 and their attempts to help the refugees. These memories are not only a result of subjective experiences but rather the effects of collaborative efforts jointly produced between volunteers and the researcher during the researcher's field visits. Sandberg claims that retrospective ethnography should have an inbuilt sensitivity towards 'twisting moments' that enhance ethnographically informed knowledge production as a collaborative endeavour.

Laura Stark's chapter explores urban poor communities in the global South and the methodological and ethical challenges included in ethnographic research of them. In her research, Stark interviewed approximately 300 people in low-income neighbourhoods of Dar es Salaam, Tanzania, some of them through Skype calls. The core challenge of her research arose from various difficulties in encountering the interviewees who struggle with their basic needs on an everyday basis. These difficulties included, for instance, understanding the expectations of people coming from a very different reality than that of the researcher, the effects of poverty and stress on participants' memories, and several research technical issues, such as providing and receiving informed consent from people with a low education level and gathering personal data among those with meagre identity documentation. Stark proposes third-person elicitation and perceived causation as methods that can be used to circumvent some of these challenges.

Part III ends with the chapter written by Lotta Lounasmeri. Here, a twist in ethnographic research arose from the researcher's experiences of the expression of power in terms of societal position and status in interviews of people belonging to societal elites in Finland. Moreover, Lounasmeri explores how gender plays a role in these situations and explores her experiences in a critical feminist framework. The interviewed people in her research worked as chief editors, media executives, public relations and public affairs consultants, decision-makers in the energy sector, and senior officials in the political and civil administrative sectors (if they were not already retired) – most of them were men. Lounasmeri discusses her uncomfortable feelings and her sense of vulnerability, even fear, when facing patronizing attitudes during the interviews and ponders what is the correct ethical reaction to such attitudes. As a conclusion, she suggests seeking to create mutual trust and respect but also maintaining one's own dignity and personality and to giving space for the behaviour of others in order to make it visible and recognizable to them.

Part IV explores affect and embodiment as ethnographers' means for gaining understanding and producing knowledge, the relationship between embodiment and language, and the challenges of wording the affective and embodied experiences and emotions. In the first chapter, Marija Dalbello and Catherine McGowan develop 'aggregative' reading of oral history interviews of people who arrived in America from Europe during the Great Migration at the beginning of the 20th century. The authors interpret the sensorial-affective dimensions of migration through coding from the interviews the narrations of the memories of smell, sight, sound, taste, touch, or synesthetic imagining and representation of physiological and affective issues. As the interviews have been conducted a long time ago by other researchers, Dalbello and McGowan set a goal to develop a methodology for the study of pre-elicited archives and to reflect on pre-elicited interviews as a source for historical ethnography. They also discuss how to respond to different temporal contexts in historical ethnography in order to understand the shared structure of feeling of a historical sensorium. They claim that the research of historical sensorium is both a phenomenological and epistemological project involving sensory knowing and intertwined sensoria of the interviewees and the researchers who coded and interpreted the interviews.

Sofie Strandén-Backa's chapter continues the discussion on affective dimensions of ethnography by telling a story of her encounter with a Finnish Romany woman when washing carpets in her house's laundry room. This unexpected moment created a relationship between the Romany women and the researcher and triggered a series of events that made Strandén-Backa an 'involuntary ethnographer', as she describes her position. In this position, she experienced various emotions ranging from enthusiasm to confusion. In her chapter, Strandén-Backa reflects on her experiences and emotions and explores the factors that make this case of ethnography difficult and uncomfortable. The chapter brings forth how ethnographic cases may accidentally occur and come along unexpectedly for an ethnographer – how 'ethnography is seeking its ethnography', as she notes. The chapter also demonstrates how ethnography can be about 'living' through an ethnographic process that is not linear, foreseeable, or controllable.

Part IV ends with Jessica Bradley's chapter in which she explores how ethnographic research of creative practices may enable new understandings of communication. Her research focuses on the implementation of a street art project in Slovenia and how people participating in it draw on their communicative repertoires to produce creative work. Bradley utilizes in her exploration theories of dynamic multilingualism, applying particularly the concept of translanguaging that draws attention to multimodality and materiality in communication. Her chapter shows how language use is related to bodies, objects, and space, and how ethnographic research can be perceived as transdisciplinary dialogue between different scholarly approaches, including arts-based research and applied linguistics.

The book ends with Tom Boellstorff's epilogue that draws together core themes and challenges examined in the chapters and discusses the state of current ethnographic research and the need for rethinking its methodological and ethical takes. Boellstorff emphasizes the importance of critical approaches in ethnography and developing its methods and conceptual understanding through various 'twists' discussed in this book. He adds to the book's discussion on 'twists' themes and topics that were not covered by its other contributors. These themes include digital and virtual ethnography. The epilogue ends the book by discussing its methodological implications for current research and envisaging future prospects of 'twists' in ethnography.

This book seeks to offer new methodological and conceptual ideas and tools for the continuously evolving field of ethnography by rethinking it as a method and a mode of knowledge production. The chapters in the book demonstrate in numerous ways how 'twisting' the ways of thinking, practicing, and dealing with ethnography opens up new ideas, views, and understandings of the researched cases, objects of study, and most importantly, the researchers themselves and their position as knowledge producers. This book does not seek to close the discussion on 'ethnography with a twist' but rather stimulate further debate and conversation of its usefulness, applicability, and possibilities as well as its limitations. We hope our book also gives new insights and ideas to those who seek new angles to ethnographic methods and who teach and advise students on their way to becoming future ethnographers.

## Bibliography

Ahmed, S. 2004. *The Cultural Politics of Emotion*. Edinburgh: Edinburgh University Press.

Averill, J. B. 2006. "Getting started: Initiating critical ethnography and community-based action research in a program of rural health studies." *International Journal of Qualitative Methods*, 17–27. https://doi.org/10.1177/160940690600500206

Byrne, A., Canavan, J. and Millar, M. 2009. "Participatory research and the voice-centred relational method of data analysis: Is it worth it?" *International Journal of Social Research Methodology* 12 (1): 67–77.

Cantú, N. E. 2019. *Cabañuelas: A Love Story*. Albuquerque: University of New Mexico Press.

Clerke, T. and Hopwood, N. 2014. *Doing Ethnography in Teams. A Case Study of Asymmetries in Collaborative Research*. Cham, Heidelberg, New York, Dordrecht and London: Springer.

Davies, A. C. 2002. *Reflexive Ethnography: A Guide to Researching Selves and Others*. London: New York.

Gubrium, A. and Harper, K. 2013. *Participatory Visual and Digital Methods*. Walnut Creek, California: Left Coast Press Inc.

Frykman, J. and Povrzanović Frykman M., eds. 2015. *Sensitive Objects. Affect and Material Culture*. Lund: Nordic Academic Press.

Hemment, J. 2007. "Public anthropology and the paradoxes of participation: Participatory action research and critical ethnography in provincial Russia." *Human Organization* 66(3): 301–314.

Lassiter, L. E. 2005. *The Chicago Guide to Collaborative Ethnography*. Chicago: The University of Chicago Press.

Marcus, G. 2007. "Ethnography two decades after writing culture: From the experimental to the Baroque." *Anthropological Quarterly* 80 (4): 1127–1145.

Mosse, D. 2007. "'People's knowledge', participation and patronage: Operations and representations in rural development." In *Participation: The New Tyranny?*, edited by B. Cooke and U. Kothari, 16–35. London: Zed Books.

Murchison, J. 2010. *Ethnography Essentials: Designing, Conducting, and Presenting Your Research*. San Francisco: Jossey-Bass.

Pink, S. 2009. *Doing Sensory Ethnography*. London: Sage.

Pohtinen, J. 2019: "From secrecy to pride: Negotiating the kink identity, normativity, and stigma." *Ethnologia Fennica* 46: 84–108. https://doi.org/10.23991/ef.v46i0.74306

Silow Kallenberg, K. and Ingridsdotter, J. 2017. "Etnografisk fiction. Introduktion." *Kulturella perspektiv* 2 (26): 2–10.

Simonsen, J. and Robinson, T., eds. 2012. *Routledge International Handbook of Participatory Design*. London: Routledge.

Stavrianakis, A., Rabinow, P., and Korsby, T. M. 2017. "In the workshop. Anthropology in a collaborative zone of inquiry." In *The Composition of Anthropology. How Anthropological Texts Are Written*, edited by M. Nielsen and N. Rapport, 179–192. London and New York: Routledge.

Suopajärvi, T. 2016. "Knowledge-making on 'ageing in a smart city' as socio-material power dynamics of participatory action research." *Action Research* 15(4): 386–401. https://doi.org/10.1177/1476750316655385.

Thrift, N. 2004. "Intensities of feeling: Towards a spatial politics of affect." *Geografiska Annaler* 86(1): 57–78.

# PART I
# New collaborative practices in ethnography

# 1
# POLY-SPACE

## Creating new concepts through reflexive team ethnography

*Johanna Turunen, Viktorija L. A. Čeginskas, Sigrid Kaasik-Krogerus, Tuuli Lähdesmäki and Katja Mäkinen*

### Introduction

Ethnographic research always contains an element of surprise (Malkki 2007). In this chapter, we engage with a process of knowledge production and collaborative sense-making that grew out of such unexpected elements. At the core of this chapter are the short "bizarre" moments that the EUROHERIT[1] research team felt when conducting ethnographic fieldwork at selected heritage sites that the European Union (EU) has awarded with the European Heritage Label. These "bizarre" moments occurred to us unexpectedly and outside our planned observation agenda, when our attention shifted to some secondary or minor details or trivial events, which suddenly became very meaningful for understanding the world(s), people and life entangled with the heritage site.

Although usually lasting only a short time, between a flash of surprise and a short discussion, these moments often had continuing effects throughout the remainder of the fieldwork. When viewed separately, the moments seemed deeply personal and disconnected. It was only in retrospect, when viewing them jointly, that we came to perceive their importance for understanding something new about heritage sites and the idea of heritage itself. As we have come to realize, these experiences and the insights they brought about may change the ways in which we relate to heritage and perceive its meanings.

To better grasp these experiences, we propose that heritage sites can be approached as poly-space in the sense that they enable and contain different spatial, temporal, affective, sensory and cognitive experiences in one physical place, the heritage site. Poly-space includes four distinct aspects that are in continuous flux, processual and interrelated: 1) an element of suddenness and surprise, 2) experience of bizarreness, 3) social agency and interaction and (4) affect, emotion and empathy. The concept of poly-space encourages (self-)reflection and enables discussion of the various temporal and spatial dimensions included both in the heritage narratives and practices and in individual experiences felt at the heritage site (for a more detailed definition, see Lähdesmäki et al. 2020).

In this chapter, we outline how we developed the concept of poly-space by discussing our fieldwork experiences and making sense of them through the process of "interpretive reflexivity" (Lichterman 2015) and affective sharing. Approaching methodology through the lens of knowledge co-creation, according to Boyer and Marcus (2015, 3), can be considered as an enabler of epistemological critique. Poly-space can be used to re-evaluate the depth of ethnographic knowledge even when the duration of fieldwork is not long: affective, unconscious experiences inspire, trigger and entangle with interpretive and cognitive processes, to mutually create new insights and knowledges. As Dalsgaard and Nielsen (2013, 3) note, "the length of the fieldwork period has constituted a central albeit much contested factor for determining the quality of collected ethnographic data". Spending months or years in the field has become problematic due to the fast pace of academic research today; emphasizing duration is ill-suited for mobile and team-based ethnographic approaches. Extensive fieldwork periods are connected with the "chances of serendipitous findings or surprises, which will supposedly destabilize the researcher's prior understandings and generate new insights" (ibid.). However, we argue, emphasis on duration can be (partially) remedied by enabling ethnographers "to take often marginalized forms of embodied affective, imaginative and creative knowledge seriously" (Culhane 2017, 7), which allows us to challenge how we come to know the things we know.

Although we mainly engage here with the theory and methodology behind our collaborative work and conceptual innovation, a short introduction to our fieldwork is needed before we enter these debates. The European Heritage Label (EHL) is the EU's heritage action initiated in 2011 to highlight the so-called European significance (see Lähdesmäki and Mäkinen 2019; Turunen 2019) of heritage sites across Europe. Creating an idea of joint European cultural heritage is fundamentally a political act. The EUROHERIT researchers are most interested in this political nature of the production of ideas and practices of "European heritage" and its identity-political relevance. To access these politics, discourses and practices of heritage, the EUROHERIT team conducted ethnographic fieldwork at 11 EHL sites[2] and at the European Commission in Brussels in 2017 and 2018. The duration of each visit ranged between four and six days. All researchers participated in the data collection. The fieldwork at each site was primarily carried out by one researcher, although some sites were visited by several members of the project, either before or after the actual fieldwork. Native-speaking research assistants were used at some of the sites, especially for the visitor interviews.

During the fieldwork, we collected a broad range of data both on and off the site through participant observation, interviewing and going through documentary, archival and academic literature (e.g. Clifford and Marcus 1986; Culhane 2017). This data includes extensive interviews with both heritage practitioners and visitors to the sites, as well as the use of a broad range of visual and written materials related to the sites and their exhibitions. Our analysis of different aspects of this data has been published elsewhere (e.g. Lähdesmäki et al. 2019; Lähdesmäki et al. 2020). In this chapter, we focus on material produced by the team members during and after the fieldwork. These include fieldwork memos and journals, notes from project meetings, email exchanges and informal conversations. These different forms of communication between the project researchers form the core empirical data used here to decipher the dynamics of collaborative knowledge creation and collective sense-making practices.

## Towards collaborative ethnography and collective interpretive reflexivity

Ethnographic research has evolved from its roots in cultural anthropology and the colonial entanglements that the discipline had in its early forms (e.g. Stocking 1991; Comaroff and Comaroff 1992). This overcoming of historical legacies has not been an easy or simple process. As the vast literature on ethnographic research methodologies shows, the practice and ethics of ethnographic research has gone through several cycles of reinterpretation. It has come a long way from classic anthropological ethnographies, often conducted in colonial settings (e.g. Malinowski 1922/1972; Evans-Pritchard 1940) or the early works of scholars of the Chicago School of Sociology, who used ethnographic approaches to study cultures of disenfranchised minority groups in urban environments (e.g. Park, Burgess, and McKenzie 1926; Blumer 1933). Influenced by the reflexive turn and increasing postcolonial critique of the 1980s (e.g. Geertz 1973; Clifford and Marcus 1986) ethnography has developed into a widespread approach that endorses reflexivity and co-production of knowledge as the crucial elements of research practice and analysis. The steady flow of literature on the relationships between fieldwork practices, methodology and theory (e.g. Cerwonka and Malkki 2007; Puddephatt et al. 2009; Burgess and Murcott 2014), the social nature of ethnographic knowledge (e.g. Katz 2012), ethnographic writing (e.g. van Maanen 2011), reflexivity (e.g. Davies 2008) and new alternative and multi-faceted approaches to ethnography (Hämeenaho and Koskinen-Koivisto 2014; Elliott and Culhane 2017), all show that the development of ethnographic practices is ongoing. In this process, the role of interdisciplinary knowledge production, intersectional social positions and new arenas of ethnographic research, such as online environments, are emerging areas of debate.

Moreover, in recent years, there has been a shift towards collaborative team ethnographies (e.g. Spiller et al. 2015), multi-sited approaches (e.g. Marcus 1995; Falzon 2009) and mobile ethnographies (e.g. Jarzabkowski et al. 2015). This multi-sitedness has arisen from changing cultural mobilities that have "transformed locations of cultural production" (Marcus 1995, 97) forcing ethnographers to focus on connections or associations between separate places, rather than on a single site or entity. These mobile research approaches (see also Büscher and Urry 2009) aim to trace or follow their ethnographic object through multiple locales. The aim of multi-sited approaches is not to produce "thick descriptions" (Geertz 1973) of single sites or precise cultural practice, but rather to engage with complex transnational cultural phenomenon that "cannot be accounted for by focusing on a single site" (Falzon 2009, 1).

This mobility, scale and transnational nature of contemporary cultural transformation has increasingly led researchers to adopt collaborative approaches to both data collection and analysis (e.g. Jarzabkowski et al. 2015). This was also the case in our research process. Tracking and analysing transnational production of the ideas and practices of "European cultural heritage" not only involves numerous research locales and layers of meaning but also requires multiple sets of expertise. The team was able to bring together a broad range of disciplinary backgrounds in the social sciences and humanities, as well as several nationalities and languages. Although most of us had collected data by ethnographic means in previous research, only one of us readily identified herself as an ethnographer. Participating in a reflexive, collaborative ethnography as a form of knowledge production was therefore a new experience for most of us.

The process of bringing different disciplinary viewpoints into a coherent approach has been described in many ways. Franks and colleagues (2007) have characterized this process as "knowledge integration", whereas Spiller and colleagues (2015, 558) have settled on the use of carnival as an allegory for a "transformation, in which the world is turned upside down". As they argue, this space, that is akin to Bakhtin's "place-beyond-place", creates the openness to let go of our disciplinary boundaries and to think again through new perspectives. Moreover, there is an element of serendipity (e.g. Rivoal and Salazar 2013; Hazan and Hertzog 2011) involved in the process of creating new knowledge. This serendipity allows us to relax our conceptions of knowledge, facilitating the emergence of new forms of knowledge out of the combination of different disciplinary backgrounds and our own affective experiences. By affective experiences, we refer here to emotional reactions, sensory experiences, gut feelings and other embodied sensations we experienced during our fieldwork. All knowledge constructed through such experiences challenges the conventional Cartesian division of mind and body and enables us to "articulate a realm of experience, thinking and being; one that has formerly been considered as inarticulatable" (Tolia-Kelly, Waterton and Watson 2017, 1). By making inarticulatable knowledge articulable, we acknowledge the subjectivity and plurality of the knowledges that surround us. They overlap, entangle and build in relation to other forms of making sense of the world, and testify against ideas of universal truth or knowledge.

As it is often stated, all knowledge gained through ethnography is, in many senses, partial (Clifford 1986), situated (Haraway 1991) and plural (e.g. Fenske and Davidovic-Walther 2010). Acknowledging this incompleteness highlights our own limitations as ethnographers and producers of knowledge. Focusing on the "inarticulatable" in team ethnography, however, means that our collective embodied knowledges include hidden, silent and tacit observations of multiple researchers that exist rather in terms of affects, interpretive insights and shards of wisdom than in a form of easily sharable knowledge. Then the main question, brilliantly framed by Jarzabkowski, Bednarek, and Cabantous (2015, 7), is "how [do] we make such ethnographies 'whole' given that the ethnographic experience of 'being there' is said to be intrinsically personal"? In other words, how can we share the (embodied) experiences and insights of being there when we have each conducted our fieldwork alone? The "whole" in this context does not relate to definite, true knowledge, but to the collective sum of our subjective observations, their internal relations and what they tell us about our subject – European cultural heritage.

To understand our experiences and allow affective knowledge to emerge, we needed to think beyond our positionalities as academics relating to our research subjects (see Bourdieu and Wacquant 1992) and to practice active reflexivity in terms of our positionalities within the team. As Creese and colleagues state, building on the work of Jones and his co-authors (2000), the team dynamic of ethnographic research requires the "interpretive knowledge building exercise to be explicitly interactive and negotiated" (Creese et al. 2008, 200). This negotiation is formed through the "interaction of different identities/values/histories that are brought directly into the research process by different team members" (ibid.). For us, negotiation of viewpoints within the team has been a continuous process. Although there are many similarities between the team members – all of us are white, able-bodied, European women with higher education and a certain level of privilege – we are also different in terms of our nationalities, cultural backgrounds, family status, mother tongues and language skills, disciplinary identities, areas of interest and more. Balancing these intersectional differences and deciphering their many influences on our dynamics of knowledge production is not easy; for example, notions of class status differ in our respective native countries and many of these differences have both historical roots and contemporary manifestations. Moreover, all of us (on the team and in general) have different affective capacities and registers (Tolia-Kelly 2006, 213) which actively influence the way we perceive and interpret our surroundings. For Tolia-Kelly, discussing affective capacities is a way to promote a "non-universalistic understanding of emotional registers" (216). This highlights how individuals not only perceive affective geographies differently due to intersectional dynamics of social positioning and associated power hierarchies (see also Haraway 1991), but also respond and react differently to affects. Although not always actively acknowledged, all these aspects were entangled in every phase of planning and conducting our joint ethnographic fieldwork.

We have attempted to counteract this disjointedness of ethnographic knowledge that has resulted from a collaborative approach, by practising what Lichterman (2015) has conceptualized as "interpretive reflexivity", a process of not only figuring out our own positionalities but trying to understand "how we came up with our interpretations" (ibid., 38). As we embarked on this reflexive process together, we needed to figure out our roles as co-producers of knowledge and how we collectively come to know "something". This practice has a direct impact on the more epistemological conditions that influence our knowledge production and the way we know what we know as individual ethnographers and as a team. By practising interpretive reflexivity, it is possible to "show how we came up with the patterns we call meaningful or cultural" (ibid., 42), and more importantly, as we will show, to create knowledge that is beyond the scope of a single ethnographer.

## Practices of sharing knowledge

There are different modes of sharing in ethnographic teamwork (e.g. Jarzabkowski et al. 2015, 19). These sharing practices can be conducted face-to-face or via virtual tools and at different stages of research, whether before, during or after fieldwork. Our collaboration entailed multiple forms of sharing, including sharing the entire data with all team members, analysing data together, cross-commenting on academic articles and co-authoring a book based on our fieldwork (Lähdesmäki et al. 2020). In this chapter, we focus on the relationship between emotional and empirical sharing as a form of conceptual development. Through practising interpretive reflexivity, we analyse how different processes of sharing emotions, experiences, ideas and insights enabled new forms of knowledge to emerge and how these were used to develop the concept of poly-space.

We used various tools to communicate in our team. Face-to-face meetings are crucial for sharing experiences but since we neither live nor work close to each other, the use of virtual tools was key to our cooperation. We used Skype video conference calls, collaborative writing on virtual platforms and chat platforms, Whatsapp group messages and a lot of email exchanges. Many emails focused on the practical aspects of teamwork, but early on, these emails also contained "emotional labour". By sharing anecdotes from the conferences, fieldwork experiences and frustrations of academic work, the team members settled into their own sharing habits. Some focused mainly on meetings in person, whereas others shared more online. For example, Johanna and Sigrid accidentally found themselves sharing long, meandering emails, resembling free writing or a stream of consciousness, which allowed them to go through their emotions, but also work on unfinished thoughts and emerging ideas in a pressure-free environment. Viktorija and Katja worked a lot through discussions on Skype, while Viktorija and Sigrid found conversations and emails in their Estonian mother tongue a more natural way to make sense of their ideas and experiences.

These multiple ways of sharing constructed what Wasser and Bresler (1996, 6) have conceptualized as a "[p]owerful interpretative zone". For them, multidisciplinary teams create an affective space "where multiple viewpoints are held in dynamic tension as [the] group seeks to make sense of fieldwork issues and meaning" (ibid.). Crossing the boundaries of one's own discipline and knowledge is crucial. Within our team these multidisciplinary tensions not only started to dynamically provoke our thinking, but also helped to entangle our disciplinary and cultural knowledges into new forms of conceptualizing the realities and imaginaries embedded in our vast research data.

Emails between members of the research group were a crucial tool in coping with the fieldwork and the many emotional reactions it sparked in us. Viktorija, as the first to go into the field, started this tradition but sharing experiences from the field became a habit for the rest of the team as well. For example, Johanna, the most junior member of the team who had very limited experience of ethnographic fieldwork, wrote a long email after her first day of the field in Camp Westerbork, the Netherlands, a former transit camp for Jews, Roma and Sinti during the Second World War.

> **From: Turunen, Johanna**
> **Sent: 27 January 2018 7:08 PM**
> **To:** Čeginskas, Viktorija; Lähdesmäki, Tuuli; Mäkinen, Katja; Kaasik-Krogerus, Sigrid
> **Subject:** So this is field work?
>
> Hi all and greetings from Westerbork.
> Day one is done and although as an eternal internal critic there were some things I should have done better (I think I rushed too much in the interviews), I think overall, we already got more than we bargained for and even though I had a really nice day I am not sure I was truly prepared for all of this. I almost cried in one of the interviews … but I will get back to that.

Johanna goes on to give a long and detailed record of her observations at the site, as well as a summary of a very touching interview with one of the visitors – a person who had lost almost his entire family during Holocaust. In her email, Johanna also recounts a second chance encounter, which in fact came to characterize her stay in Camp Westerbork and evolved in her field journals into a key element of her experience of poly-space at this site, although she did not have words or concepts to describe it as such at this point. This was an encounter with another phase of the camp's history. For approximately 20 years, it served as a resettlement camp for a group of Moluccan refugees. As she continues in the same email:

> Already in the morning, it turned out that our cab driver had been born at the camp. His parents had arrived there as refugees after the end of the Dutch colonial rule and he had lived the first 11 years of his life there at the camp. He talked of how he feels really torn when going there. For him it was a happy place. He was happy as a child. Playing in the forests. No-one in the community told the children what the place had initially been used for. He only found out much later when he was older.

This email sparked words of encouragement but also interesting reflections from the team members. After the fieldwork, Johanna recounted the effects of the experience with the Moluccan taxi driver once more in her notes. This time she put her experience into the perspective of her whole research stay. The excerpt brings out the powerful impact that this early encounter had and the time-bending effect it seemed to produce.

> Later when walking in the museums, the forest and around the now demolished camp and reading and hearing the heartbreaking personal stories of the people who had passed through it, in the back of my mind I kept hearing laughter. It was the laughter of the Moluccan children whose families had been forced out

**FIGURE 1.1** Part of the forest around the former campground in Camp Westerbork has been cleared for a field of radio telescopes. These telescopes, placed next to the memorial to the camp's victims, are visible from the site of the former camp, contributing to the bizarre experience of different worlds meeting. Copyright: EUROHERIT

of their home in Indonesia, but who managed to turn the transit camp into a happy home for themselves. Although the memories of the site were quite different for their parents who carried the trauma of leaving Indonesia and who knew the history of the place they were living in, the memories of the happy, innocent childhood lingered and almost haunted me throughout my visit. However, it was not a terrifying haunting, but a haunting of hope. A sign that even in the saddest of places, we can find happy memories.

Although the mixing layers of the Holocaust, the Moluccan child and the contemporary moment of the fieldwork already had some of the seeds of the idea of poly-space, this flux of temporalities was something Johanna initially felt to be just a silly trick of her mind and therefore she did not share this part of the experience with the team. Later on, as our team started to share stories and experiences more intensely, they started to become increasingly meaningful for us all and, through focusing on the small, the irrelevant and the banal, we were able to create space for new conceptual innovations.

## Constructing poly-space

In spring 2017, when planning our fieldwork, we were seeking to investigate the multitemporality of heritage and the relationships between the past, present and future. Although this was a central interest of the project, it was only during and after the fieldwork in spring 2018 that the need for new concepts started to emerge. This quest for a conceptual tool that would allow us to make sense of our fieldwork experiences started as a theoretical one. We explored concepts like Foucault's (1997) "heterotopia", Turner's (1974) ideas on liminality and the liminoid, and Massey's (2005) work on "time-space compression". Next, we turned to memory and heritage studies and tried to think through Macdonald's (2013) "past presencing", Rothberg's (2009) "multidirectional memory" and Hirsch's (2012) idea of "post-memory". While none of these seemed to fully capture our need, we looked outside the Western tradition of knowledge. Viktorija pondered on the idea of "time-knots" developed by Chakrabarty (2000) and Johanna read up on conceptualizations of time in Yoruba culture (e.g. Kazeem 2016).

While all this theoretical work was underway, we also turned inwards and started to look more into our own experiences. How did we experience time during our fieldwork? If and when temporalities mixed, what initiated that experience? The idea behind poly-space started to finally take shape after Viktorija shared her experience of one moment characterized by a sudden flux or overlapping of multiple layers of time and space, or a "flash of surprise". This happened in the Archaeological Park Carnuntum, Austria, an open-air reconstructed Roman site rebuilt using Roman techniques on the excavated remains of the original site.

> I went alone to visit again the kitchen of the Villa Urbana. It was in the late afternoon and the late sun was shining into the otherwise rather dark kitchen.

> I surprised two small birds, which had flown in and were picking at bread. The bread is part of the fresh props lying in the reconstructed buildings with the intention to create an "authentic" experience of inhabited space and of travelling through time for the visitors. It then suddenly occurred to me that such situations had happened at precisely the same spot but some 1700 years ago, when birds flew into the kitchen to pick at food leftovers on the bare ground and were startled by the entrance of a slave, a servant, or the mistress of the house. This realization came as a surprise and made me feel closer to the situations that happened in the past. It helped me to reimagine or see the past with different "eyes", making it also part of a personal experience for me and imagining it as a personal experience for people unknown to me who had lived almost 2000 years ago. It made the otherwise still and material sites be filled with life and people.

When we started to think about poly-space through connecting it to some kind of external, interactive and affective catalysts – like Viktorija's birds or Johanna's taxi driver – we were able to see the relationships between our individual experiences as interrelated and embedded in the nature of heritage sites. While doing her fieldwork in the Great Guild Hall in Tallinn, Estonia, Sigrid had a sensation of the histories narrated in the museums entangling with contemporary realities beyond its doors. The permanent exhibition of the Great Guild Hall positions the Germans and Russians as both the main historical "Others" and as important past and contemporary minorities in Estonian society. The ambivalence of these historical and intercultural relations was mirrored in the social landscape that surrounded the museum – in a way expanding the narrative of the museum to the everyday practices of the old town of Tallinn. Sigrid, herself Estonian, explained this in her field journal.

> On my very first fieldwork day, I experienced how this ambivalent relationship was performed there in the neighbourhood of the Great Guild Hall. On Wednesday afternoon, I heard shouts and noise from outside until the museum staff closed the large front door. I asked about this noise the next day during one of my interviews. It turned out that it was a protest in front of the Russian embassy [located just next to the museum], as my interviewee captured it, "against Russia, for Ukraine". This weekly protest is repeated every Wednesday afternoon, so according to the museum practitioner, it helps them to recall that, "oh, it is Wednesday again". This experience made me feel that the past, present and the future are indeed entangled and also very much "alive" and "in action" in heritage sites, sometimes in a rather surprising way.

This experience shows that the existing interaction with the social forces beyond the museum seemed to highlight and interlink continuities between the past and the present at the site, thereby creating a space where past and present coexisted in the same physical space of the museum and its immediate surroundings. In contrast, the fieldwork in the Franz Liszt Academy of Music in Budapest, Hungary, illustrated how the past and the present may exist in the same space but, as Tuuli notes, still be totally disconnected from each other.

> I felt it was a big contrast to stand in Liszt's living room surrounded by his pianos, paintings of him made by famous Hungarian painters, marvellous old furniture, decorative wall paper, chandeliers and so forth, to listen to his music through an audio guide, and at the same time to look from the balcony window to the Vörösmarty utca metro station and see today's people walking and hanging around the metro station. For example, two black young men wearing trendy street clothes and headphones passed the windows while I looked out. They seemed to be so far from the reality of the room, although just some metres away. It felt that the past and today's world were there in this quarter at the same time, but without any connection to each other.

After coming up with these initial experiences, we started to see aspects of poly-space in our broader data. Going through the vast data we had collected, we often marked out issues related to poly-space and shared them with the team, as the next email from Sigrid demonstrates.

> **From:** Kaasik-Krogerus, Sigrid
> **Sent:** 11 January 2019 3:21 PM
> **To:** Čeginskas, Viktorija; Lähdesmäki, Tuuli; Mäkinen, Katja; Turunen, Johanna
> **Subject:** Some more poly-space
>
> Dear all,
> I started to go through the expert interviews and the data is very rich and inspiring indeed!
> Although I try to focus on the centre-periphery aspect, I could not help other associations evoking while reading the interviews. I wrote down some ideas related to poly-space that may be relevant from the perspective of the article.

## Integrating senses and affects

As more and more material related to poly-space emerged in our data, we started to pay more attention to the sensory and affective elements of our experiences with poly-space. It was clear that our insights were not gained by knowledge or cognitive work but through sensory experiences, emotional reactions and gut instincts – in other words, through our varied affective experiences. Our understanding of poly-space therefore encompasses an embodied element – the feeling of being swept out of time and place. Although often connected to the cognitive meaning-making practices around heritage, the sensorial and physical element of experiencing poly-space was crucial in terms of thinking heritage sites not only through poly-space, but also inherently as poly-space – as places where several histories and temporalities are layered and active.

**FIGURE 1.2** The view from the living room in the Franz Liszt Memorial Museum in Budapest. Copyright: EUROHERIT.

To include this affective, sensory experience in our elaboration of poly-space, our research draws from the affective turn in scholarship, which considers the body as a vehicle in creating "authentic" knowledge (e.g. Crang and Tolia-Kelly 2010; Waterton 2014). As Sather-Wagstaff (2017, 13) notes, "[a]ffective experiences translate into multiple effects, one being knowledge [...] and the other an excess residual that may never be fully categorized cognitively". There is a sociocultural, but also biological, aspect to these senses, which points towards the need to overcome the Cartesian separation of mind and body, or knowledge and feeling, in order to move towards an approach that celebrates and encompasses both aspects of our sense-making capabilities.

When debating the sensory experiences related to heritage, the visual aspects are often emphasized, because Western cultures tend to value sight as the highest of our senses. At times sensory experiences are more comprehensive, or to borrow from Sather-Wagstaff (2017), polysensory. This was the case in our fieldwork in Sagres Promontory, Portugal. Johanna described this in her field journal.

> The most influential experience was the "Voice from the Sea" installation that was also known as the dragon's breath. It was a spiral shaped echo chamber built on top of the caves, which connect the promontory to the sea tens of metres below. In the chamber, you can stand on metal crates built on top of the cave entrance and feel "the dragon breathe". As the waves rush into the caves, a surge of warm air gushes through the caves and surrounds you with an explosive wind that shoots your hair up and roars around you. The bigger the wave, the louder the roar. Because of the rhythm of the waves, the gusts of wind come up and through the caves in a rhythm of someone breathing.

The power was so intense that my research assistant had to leave. It all made her feel physically uneasy. I stayed behind and suddenly I was overwhelmed with the stories we had heard the day before from the staff. Stories of the promontory having been an ancient sacrificial site belonging to the gods and more importantly the story of Henry the Navigator, the Portuguese prince who had built his personal fortress on the Promontory. Henry's emblem was the black dragon and as I sat, listened and felt the dragon breathe around me, my mind travelled to the past, to people who came to the promontory, under the dark sky, with wooden torches in their hands to meet the dragon the fortress owner had locked up in the caves below.

This last excerpt from our field journals shows the complexity of the relationship between our sensory experience, the physical place of the heritage site and the narratives used to make sense of the many layers of history that the site encompasses. Ingold (2008) has explained how ethnographic research is about figuring out the "entangled relationships" between humans and non-humans and the natural, social and cultural environments that they inhabit. According to Ingold, these environments are not merely the "surroundings of the organism but a zone of entanglement" (ibid., 1797). Hence, poly-space became one way for us to make sense of the zone of entanglements that existed in and around the heritage sites we were researching. Our experiences and engagements all contained an element of memory, as they were in one or more ways embedded in our own past experiences, as well as the histories and narratives of the site. As such, it is easy to agree with Seremetakis (1994, 9, quoted in Sather-Wagstaff 2017, 19) who states that memory "as a distinct meta-sense transports, bridges and crosses all the other senses". We do not want to claim that poly-space is an element

**FIGURE 1.3** Johanna at the *Voice from the Sea* sound installation in Sagres Promontory
Copyright: EUROHERIT.

exclusively reserved for heritage sites. Rather, we see it as an experiential moment that can emerge in a multitude of surroundings. Nevertheless, the central role of memory in our meaning-making practices suggests that heritage sites as places that "materialize memory" are particularly active poly-spaces – physical places that make the entanglements of multiple moments and experiences of layered histories visible and tangible.

## Conclusions: how do we know what we know?

There is an epistemological elephant in the room when talking about poly-space: it is always experienced subjectively. Since it builds on personal experiences, memories, senses, affective capacities and social awareness of the individual and the social surrounding in which the experiencer is located, it is always different. Two people visiting the same site will not experience it in the same way, neither will a person visiting the same site again experience it in exactly the same way as they did before. Therefore, the whole idea of taking poly-space seriously breaks a foundational rule of scientific knowledge – its repeatability.

Moreover, our insights were not gained by knowledge or cognitive work alone but through the entanglements of sensory experiences, affective reactions and intuitive knowledge that sparked a cognitive process. Allowing these sensory elements to play a role in our collaborative sense-making practices has been a form of epistemological critique or a challenge to the status quo of scientific knowledge. As Culhane explains:

> Academic conventions reflect this culturally and historically specific approach to knowledge where sights, words, and text are privileged, whereas dynamic interactions among sounds, tastes, odors, touches, senses of place and of belonging and exclusions, and the extrasensory are often ignored or dismissed as irrelevant to social life and the study of knowledge. To take sensory experience, like imagination, as significant in knowledge co-creation constitutes a practice of epistemological and political critique. (Culhane 2017, 11)

It is precisely because of these sensory aspects of knowledge that "one cannot reduce understanding to a method, [...] the fusion at the center of understanding means that we must see knowledge production as a flexible, creatively, historically influenced process" (Cerwonka 2007, 23). Both understanding and knowledge are always partial and situated (Haraway 1991) and to a significant degree also conditioned by our own personal histories which "shape our capacities for affect as well as interpretation of affective experiences" (Sather-Wagstaff 2017, 23). Acknowledging and interpreting these situationalities needs to be at the core of reflexive work around knowledge production, as it allows us to map the boundaries, overlaps and conflicts in and between our cognitive processes.

As we have argued in this chapter, collaborative reflexive work can allow new forms of knowledge to emerge from affective encounters in the field. Poly-space would not have developed as a concept without our team engaging in interpretive reflexivity and affective sharing of the inarticulatable. Our embodied experiences, taken individually, seemed initially rather personal and irrelevant to academic knowledge. Yet they made sense when connected with other similar experiences. Only through this merging or integration of diverse experiences and perspectives were we able to produce knowledge that we could not have created as individual ethnographers. We co-constructed this knowledge through our collaborative meaning-making practices. For the researchers, engaging in this type of emotional and intellectual sharing demands profound openness, reflexivity, empathy and, ultimately, courage.

## Acknowledgements

This work was supported by the European Research Council (ERC) under the EU's Horizon 2020 Research and Innovation Programme under Grant 636177 (EUROHERIT). The content of this chapter does not reflect the official opinion of the European Union. Responsibility for the information and views expressed in the chapter lies entirely with the authors.

## Notes

1. Legitimation of European cultural heritage and the dynamics of identity politics in the EU, European Research Council, H2020, 2015–2020.
2. Alcide De Gasperi's House Museum, Italy; Archaeological Park Carnuntum, Austria; Camp Westerbork, The Netherlands; European District of Strasbourg, France; Franz Liszt Academy of Music, Hungary; Great Guild Hall, Estonia; Hambach Castle, Germany; Historic Gdańsk Shipyard, Poland; Mundaneum, Belgium; Robert Schuman's House, France; and Sagres Promontory, Portugal.

## Bibliography

Blumer, H. 1933. *Movies and Conduct*. New York: Macmillan and Company.
Bourdieu, P., and L. Wacquant. 1992. *An Invitation to Reflexive Sociology*. Chicago: Chicago University Press.
Boyer D., and G. Marcus. 2015. "Introduction". In *Theory Can Be More Than It Used to Be: Learning Anthropology's Method in a Time of Transition*, edited by D. Boyer, J. Faubion, and G. Marcus, 1–12. Ithaca, NY: Cornell University Press.
Burgess, R., and A. Murcott. 2014. *Developments in Sociology*. Hoboken: Taylor and Francis.
Büscher, M., and Urry, J. 2009. "Mobile methods and the empirical". *European Journal of Social Theory* 12 (1), 99–116. https://doi.org/10.1177/1368431008099642
Cerwonka, A. 2007. "Nervous conditions: The stages in interdisciplinary research". In *Improvising Theory: Process and Temporality in Ethnographic Fieldwork*, edited by A. Cerwonka and L. H. Malkki, 1–40. Chicago: University of Chicago Press.
Cerwonka A., and L. H. Malkki, eds. 2007. *Improvising Theory: Process and Temporality in Ethnographic Fieldwork*. Chicago: University of Chicago Press.
Chakrabarty, D. 2000. *Provincializing Europe: Postcolonial Thought and Historical Difference*. Princeton, NJ: Princeton University Press.

Clifford, J. 1986. "Introduction: Partial truths". In *Writing Culture: The Poetics and Politics of Ethnography*, edited by J. Clifford and G. Marcus, 1–26. Berkeley: University of California Press.
Clifford, J., and G. Marcus. 1986. *Writing Culture: The Poetics and Politics of Ethnography*. Berkeley: University of California Press.
Comaroff, J., and J. Comaroff. 1992. *Ethnography and the Historical Imagination*. Boulder: Westview.
Crang, M., and D. Tolia-Kelly. 2010. "Nation, race, and affect: Senses and sensibilities at National Heritage sites". *Environment and Planning A* 42 (10): 2315–2331.
Creese, A., A. Bhatt, N. Bhojani, and P. Martin. 2008. "Fieldnotes in team ethnography: Researching complementary schools". *Qualitative Research* 8 (2): 197–215.
Culhane, D. 2017. "Imagining: An introduction". In *A Different Kind of Ethnography: Imaginative Practices and Creative Methodologies*, edited by D. Elliott and D. Culhane, 1–21. North York, Ontario, Canada: University of Toronto Press.
Dalsgaard, S., and M. Nielsen. 2013. "Time and the field". *Social Analysis* 57 (1): 1–19. doi:10.3167/sa.2013.570101
Davies, C. A. 2008. *Reflexive Ethnography: A Guide to Researching Selves and Others*. 2nd ed. London: Routledge.
Elliott, D., and D. Culhane, eds. 2017. *A Different Kind of Ethnography: Imaginative Practices and Creative Methodologies*. North York, Ontario, Canada: University of Toronto Press.
Evans-Pritchard, E. E. 1940. *The Nuer: A Description of the Modes of Livelihood and Political Institutions of a Nilotic People*. Oxford: Clarendon Press.
Falzon, M-A. 2009. *Multi-Sited Ethnography; Theory, Praxis and Locality in Contemporary Social Research*. Farnham: Ashgate Publishing.
Fenske, M., and Davidovic-Walther, A. 2010. "Exploring ethnological knowledges". *Journal of Folklore Research: An International Journal of Folklore and Ethnomusicology* 47 (1–2): 1–5. doi:10.2979/JFR.2010.47.1-2.1
Foucault, M. 1997. "Of other spaces: Utopias and heterotopias". In *Rethinking Architecture: A Reader in Cultural Theory*, edited by N. Leach, 330–336. New York: Routledge.
Franks, D., P. Dale, R. Hindmarsh, C. Fellows, M. Buckridge, and P. Cybinski. 2007. "Interdisciplinary foundations: Reflecting on interdisciplinarity and three decades of teaching and research at Griffith University, Australia". *Studies in Higher Education* 32: 167–185.
Geertz, C. 1973. *The Interpretation of Cultures: Selected Essays*. New York: Basic Books.
Haraway, D. J. 1991. "Situated knowledges: The science question in feminism and the privilege of partial perspective". In *Simians, Cyborgs and Women: The Reinventions of Nature*, by D. Haraway, 183–201. New York: Routledge.
Hazan, H., and E. Hertzog, eds. 2011. *Serendipity in Anthropological Research: The Nomadic Turn*. Farnham: Ashgate.
Hirsch, M. 2012. *The Generation of Postmemory: Writing and Visual Culture after the Holocaust*. New York: Columbia University Press.
Hämeenaho, P., and E. Koskinen-Koivisto. 2014. *Moniulotteinen etnografia* [Multidimensional Ethnography]. Helsinki: Ethnos.
Ingold, T. 2008. "Bindings against boundaries: Entanglements of life in an open world". *Environment & Planning A* 40 (8): 1796–1810.
Jarzabkowski, P., R. Bednarek, and L. Cabantous. 2015. "Conducting global team-based ethnography: Methodological challenges and practical methods". *Human Relations* 68 (1): 3–33.
Katz, J. 2012. "Ethnography's expanding warrants". *The Annals of the American Academy of Political and Social Science* 642 (1): 258–275. doi:10.1177/0002716212437342

Kazeem, F. A. 2016. "Time in Yorùbá culture". *Al-Hikmat* 36: 27–41.
Lichterman, P. 2015. "Interpretive reflexivity in ethnography". *Ethnography* 18 (1): 35–45.
Lähdesmäki, T., and K. Mäkinen. 2019. "The 'European significance' of heritage: Politics of scale in EU heritage policy discourse". In *Politics of Scale. New Directions in Critical Heritage Studies*, edited by T. Lähdesmäki, S. Thomas, and Y. Zhu, 36–49. New York: Berghahn Books.
Lähdesmäki, T., L. Passerini, S. Kaasik-Krogerus, and I. van Huis, eds. 2019. *Dissonant Heritages and Memories in Contemporary Europe*. New York: Palgrave Macmillan.
Lähdesmäki, T., V. L. A. Čeginskas, S. Kaasik-Krogerus, K. Mäkinen, and J. Turunen. 2020. *Creating and Governing Cultural Heritage in the European Union: The European Heritage Label*. London: Routledge.
Macdonald, S. 2013. *Memorylands: Heritage and Identity in Europe Today*. New York: Routledge.
Malinowski, B. 1922/1972. *Argonauts of the Western Pacific: An Account of Native Enterprise and Adventure in the Archipelagoes of Melanesian New Guinea*. 8th edn. London: Routledge and Kegan Paul.
Malkki, L. 2007. "Tradition and improvisation in ethnographic field research". In *Improvising Theory: Process and Temporality in Ethnographic Fieldwork*, edited by A. Cerwonka and L. H. Malkki, 162–188. Chicago: University of Chicago Press.
Marcus, G. E. 1995. "Ethnography in/of the world system: The emergence of multi-sited ethnography". *Annual Review of Anthropology* 24: 95–117.
Massey, D. 2005. *For Space*. London: Sage.
Park, R. E., Burgess, E. W., and McKenzie, R. D. 1926. *City*. Chicago: Chicago University Press
Puddephatt, A., W. Shaffir, and S. Kleinknecht. 2009. *Ethnographies Revisited: Constructing Theory in the Field*. Milton Park: Routledge.
Rivoal, I., and N. B. Salazar. 2013. "Contemporary ethnographic practice and the value of serendipity". *Social Anthropology/Anthropologie Sociale* 21 (2): 178–185.
Rothberg, M. 2009. *Multidirectional Memory: Remembering the Holocaust in the Age of Decolonization*. Stanford, California: Stanford University Press.
Sather-Wagstaff, J. 2017. "Making polysense of the world: affect, memory and heritage". In *Heritage, Affect and Emotion. Politics, Practices and Infrastructures*, edited by D.P. Tolia-Kelly, E Waterton, and S. Watson, 12–29. Abingdon: Routledge.
Spiller K., K. Ball, E. Daniel, S. Dibb, M. Meadows, and A. Canhoto. 2015. "Carnivalesque collaborations: Reflections on 'doing' multi-disciplinary research". *Qualitative Research* 15 (5): 551–567.
Stocking, G. W. ed. 1991. *Colonial Situations: Essays on the Contextualization of Ethnographic Knowledge*. Madison, Wis.: University of Wisconsin Press.
Tolia-Kelly, D. P. 2006. "Affect – an ethnocentric encounter? Exploring the 'universalist' imperative of emotional/affectual geographies". *Area* 38 (2): 213–217.
Tolia-Kelly, D. P., E. Waterton, and S. Watson 2017. "Introduction: Heritage, affect and emotion". In *Heritage, Affect and Emotion. Politics, Practices and Infrastructures*, edited by D. P. Tolia-Kelly, E. Waterton and S. Watson, 1–11. New York: Routledge.
Turner, V. 1974. "Liminal to liminoid, in play, flow and ritual: An essay in comparative symbology". *Rice University Studies* 60 (3): 53–92.
Turunen, J. 2019. "A geography of coloniality: Re-narrating European integration". In *Dissonant Heritages and Memories in Contemporary Europe*, edited by T. Lähdesmäki, L. Passerini, S. Kaasik-Krogerus, and I. van Huis, 185–214. New York: Palgrave Macmillan.
van Maanen, J. 2011. *Tales of the Field: On Writing Ethnography*. 2nd edn. Chicago: University of Chicago Press.

Wasser, J. D., and L. Bresler. 1996. "Working in the interpretive zone: Conceptualizing collaboration in qualitative research teams". *Educational Researcher* 25 (5): 5–15.

Waterton, E. 2014. "A more-than-representational understanding of heritage? The 'past' and politics of affect". *Geography Compass* 8 (11): 823–833.

# 2

# EMBODIED ADVENTURES

An experiment on doing and writing multisensory ethnography

*Eerika Koskinen-Koivisto and Tytti Lehtovaara*

## Introduction

> I walk up the red-brick stairs through a dim stairway, take a turn to the left and come to a medium-sized auditorium with similar red-brick walls. The room is full of warm light. I can hear the air-conditioning and sense the cool dry air. There are already some people in the room when I enter. I look around and greet them, recognizing a few familiar faces. I walk to the stage where my co-chair is waiting for me. I feel excited that our workshop will finally take place. I sense the excitement as alertness in my body, but I do not have time to reflect on it further since we need to set our presentation and start the workshop. (Field diary, Eerika)

When reading through scattered notes about a situation that took place months ago, like the one described above, it is often difficult to remember what happened and how it felt. Most often, notes entail fragmented details of the environment and atmosphere, descriptions of the space and people there. In the beginning, the researcher often notes her own sentiments, but as soon as participation and social activities begin, there is no time for taking notes nor reflection. General textbooks and guides about ethnographic methods encourage the researchers to pay attention to details and to include "as much of the sensory experience of participant observation as possible" (Murchison 2010, 72). The textbooks seldom give any further advise on how to make sensory observations. This strategy of turning our attention to sensory perceptions and embodied being in the world has developed into the more specific and increasingly popular approach of sensory ethnography. Sensory ethnography is a different mode of *doing* ethnography. It is not a single method, but rather a critical methodology, a reflexive and experiential process in which the role of the researcher as embodied subject is crucial (Pink 2009, 8). It is based on the idea that all human beings are connected to materiality and the physical environment through their sensing bodies (Pink 2009, 8–9). At the core of sensory ethnography are sensory experiences (sight, hearing, taste, smell and touch), and their role in social practices and relations (Pink 2009, 12–15, 25–26). By studying sensory experiences, one can find nonverbal and seemingly meaningless and self-evident information that affects our everyday life and daily practices (Bendix 2000, 41; Ingold 2000, 285; Pink 2009, 8, 12).

It is crucial to note that sensory and embodied knowledge is not a language-centered experience, and often not spoken (Bendix 2000, 41). Therefore, in order to interpret the embodied experiences and analyze the co-produced data, sensory knowledge must, like any other ethnographically produced data, be verbally processed by the ethnographer and collaborative participants. Thus, the methodological challenge of sensory ethnography lies not only in identifying sensory knowledge, but also in rendering our interpretations into words and communicating them in a way that other people can understand and imagine the situations and circumstances we experience (Pink 2009, 132). In this chapter, we turn our attention to this process of gaining and sharing sensory knowledge. We approach this knowledge as embodied, intersubjective and dialogic (Csordas 1999; Coffey 1999, 59; Pink 2009, 25). Anthropologist Thomas Csordas, for instance, argues for the integration of an embodied perspective in ethnography because representation (language) and being in the world are dialogic partners in knowing about the world (Csordas 1999, 147). We scrutinize a collaborative process of learning sensory ethnography and sharing the experience in written and verbal form. This process took place in an experimental workshop in the conference "Ethnography with a Twist" in Jyväskylä in 2019. We invited participants to work as ethnographers with us to explore and to reflect on how we could use our senses to study the entire conference setting "by moving in different spaces indoors and outdoors, turning our attention to our sensory perceptions and documenting them with the help of audio, video, GPS, and other technologies on our mobile phones" (Workshop proposal). Our aim was not only to make sense of the surrounding physical environment and people's activities therein, but also to analyze the encounters between the people and matter.

The participants of the workshop were all scholars with varied multidisciplinary backgrounds. We have decided to call them participants instead of using their names or pseudonyms, since we wish to represent them as equal participants in a shared experiment. Some of them had more experience in ethnographic fieldwork than others and are also more advanced in the academic hierarchy. All participants gave us permission to study their participation and outcomes of the workshop and signed consent forms allowing us to use the raw data we produced together in the workshop, including their co-produced writings, photos and videos. In addition to this, we used our own notes about the contents of the workshop and the discussions we had in the classroom. This text features excerpts from both authors' notes.

In this text, we scrutinize the process of doing sensory ethnography from sensory observations and interventions to writing. Our interest in sensory ethnography arose from our individual research projects in which we have studied everyday materiality and sensory memory. We have struggled with both documenting and writing about sensory experiences and embodied knowledge. Often the sensations that we gain through being outdoors and indoors, visiting different places and people are intense situations in which many things happen and there are many details to observe. Smelling the air or touching a piece of cloth are *fleeting moments* (Murchison 2010, 70) that direct our attention unconsciously and disappear within seconds. In this text, we ask how can we become aware of them, document them and verbalize them in a way that would allow us to analyze this information? We scrutinize the holistic process of sensory ethnography, and the different phases it includes: How to begin the sensory observations? Which are the challenges of identifying sensory knowledge and possible solutions to these? These questions inspired us to plan the experimental workshop on doing sensory ethnography and to engage in these questions collaboratively. We approach the experiences of sensory ethnography as "twist" moments of ethnographic research which transformed our previous understanding of doing ethnography and engaging in reflexive ethnographic knowledge production.

## The sensory ethnography workshop

Our workshop encompassed two collaborative and reflexive exercises, and was divided into three sections: 1) Introduction to sensory ethnography and instructions of how to do the experiment, 2) Exercise of doing sensory ethnography (observation within the conference site), 3) Writing Exercise and reflection: joint writing in a shared online platform (GoogleDocs) and discussion about the experiment. At the end of the workshop, we discussed our experiences and thoughts together.

> When the participants began to arrive in the classroom, they chose their sitting places quite close to us. We were happy about that because we wanted to build an intimate and reliable atmosphere. The participants sat relatively close to each other and formed a semi-circle. Later on, this proved to be an important thing because it was easier for the participants to talk together when they not only heard but also saw each other. (Field diary, Tytti)

Participants were from the following fields: geography, oral history, music studies, political sciences, social work, anthropology and sociology. Their specializations included soundscape and landscape studies, urban and consumption studies, study of youth cultures and anthropology of money. Many of them had used ethnography in scrutinizing various groups of people, for example, practitioners of martial arts, homeless people, and transnational families. The varied cultural and geographical backgrounds (e.g. urban/rural) led to discussions about the different perspectives on interpreting sensory experiences in the workshop. The participants' backgrounds provided a good picture of how sensory ethnography is a necessary method for many different science fields. Many of them had done research that focused on one sensory aspect (e.g. soundscapes) but needed a broader view of multisensory approach. Others wanted to learn new methodological tools that could be used in teaching.

Step one of the experiment was a practical exercise in doing sensory observations in the conference setting. We asked the participants to move around in the conference hall, taking notes for an estimated period of 30 minutes. We suggested that the participants document their observations by using different tools such as pictures, drawings, maps, videos and GPS technology. The experiment was done in pairs so that they could plan the experiment together and engage in a dialogue while observing. Social contacts and encounters were encouraged.

After the observation exercise, the experiment continued with a joint writing session of approximately 20 minutes. The idea was to write down experiences and perceptions. After writing, we had a brief discussion of each pair's thoughts about the experiment. Our analysis in this text focuses on the challenges that the participants met during the experiment and the ways in which they think sensory ethnography differs from regular ethnographic fieldwork. We also wish to evaluate the knowledge we gained and to make suggestions about how an experimental workshop on sensory ethnography could be developed.

## Putting on new lenses and *doing* in the field

Anthropologists David Howes and Constance Classen who have studied cultural orders and hierarchy of senses (sensorium) suggest that researchers who engage in sensory ethnography, should first take exercises to overcome their own culture-oriented sensory biases (Howes and Classen 1991; Pink 2009, 51–52). Even if these biases are difficult to detect, it is important to note that senses are valued differently, and in different social and cultural contexts, some senses gain more emphasis than others (e.g. Classen 2012). In the workshop, we asked the participants to reflect on the sensory hierarchies and intentionally engage with sensory dimensions that are often ignored. In order to prepare and orient the workshop participants to sensory observation, we prepared a brief list of possible sensory dimensions that they could pay attention to:

SOME HELP FOR THE EXPERIMENT

Different sensory/bodily information:
AUDITIVE: voices/noise/silence/echoes
VISUAL: lights/shadows/colours/shapes/aesthetics
TOUCH and SPATIAL issues: temperature/air/materials/furniture/architecture/layout/texture
KINESTHETIC: rhythm/movements/practices/gestures
OLFACTORY/TASTE: smells, scents and tastes

In addition to this list, we also suggested some behaviours or motions that would help in order to make perceptions of senses that we might not usually pay attention to: close one's eyes, sit in unusual places, and touch and smell things. In some situations and places, these actions might have seemed out-of-place, odd or inconvenient, but in our view, these small interventions were crucial in conducting multisensory ethnography, as they made us perceive the world differently and reorient our ways of being in the world. The participants of our workshop seemed to embrace the idea of engaging with the environment and doing unusual things:

> Most of the pairs went outside the classroom and the conference venue (the main building of University of Jyväskylä). They went to the lobby, to the bathroom area or to other classrooms. One pair stayed in the lecture room and one navigated out of the main building to the nearby area of the campus elementary school. Participants in the lobby walked, looked around, sat down in different places and listened, smelled and touched the materials of the environment with their different body parts, for example with their hands, feet, bottoms and backs. Most of them took notes, photos and videos, but most of all, they seemed to fully engage in sensory knowledge through their bodies and minds. (Field diary, Tytti)
>
> When starting the observation experiment, the participants did not directly leave the room in haste and head somewhere, but moved more slowly, looking around as if seeing the room for the first time, alert and open, and paused at the doorway touching the door and the walls surrounding it, more aware of the space and its functions. I also noticed that the pairs who stayed in the classroom moved more slowly than usual to the back of the room, approached the back wall and last seats, sitting down and standing up, and touching the surfaces of seats and walls. They seemed to notice things that they would usually ignore and, above all, to approach the space and movement in the space differently. (Field diary, Eerika)

When observing the environment, the workshop participants sometimes decided to use a particular sense and other times engaged multiple senses. A few participants decided to conduct exercises of *touching* things. Touching is deeply affective; it is the first sense through which we develop the sense of care and connection (Classen 2012; Kinnunen and Kolehmainen 2019, 30). Furthermore, touch is crucial for many everyday life activities such as cooking and building, and for the acquisition of knowledge and creativity in science and art. The workshop participants described the experience of touching things as *emotional* and mostly positive:

> It's a *funny feeling* to touch across the brick-walk, it feels so *rough*, particularly where brick and mortar meet. I sit on the wooden bench – and like usually I can't help touching the wooden bench – I love touching wood. It is so *soothing, calm, nice,* I don't know why. Gives me an idea, I move back towards the reception, touch the walls, the different materials – some are cold, some are warm – some sensations are *nice*. (Participant 2, 2019)

Most participants seemed to enjoy touching materials such as wooden details and the red brick walls. Often, the act of touching was combined with moving in space. Motion is multisensory, an interplay of tactile, sonic, and visual senses that fuel the

**FIGURE 2.1** Conference venue. Photo by Tytti Lehtovaara.

perceptual engagement of emplacement (Feld 2005, 181; Österlund-Pötzsch 2008, 117). It also forms kinesthetic (sensation of movement) and proprioceptive (awareness of the position of one's body) knowledge that constitute many everyday-life routines and tasks (see e.g. Tiili 2016, 34; O'Dell 2004). One means of doing sensory ethnography is to walk specific routes and perceiving the environment (e.g. Österlund-Pötzsch 2008), or to practice accompanied *walk-along-ethnography* in the form of a *sensory memory walks*, during which the participants share *sensory memories* attached to place (e.g. Järviluoma and Vikman 2013; Aula 2018). We encouraged the workshop participants to reflect on their memories, and a few of them mentioned that sensory perceptions triggered memories of similar places:

> For [my workshop partner], the first thing that these bricks remind her of is primary school, standing outside of the entrance door where she used to (strangely) smooth out a bitten section of her apple, which she used to eat at break time. (Participants 6 and 7)

By moving in the space and testing different routes, the conference participants explored *the cultural kinesthesia,* culturally specific set of movements that are formed through everyday life practices of using and navigating particular spaces (O'Dell 2004). It is interesting how the workshop participants, most of whom were not familiar with the conference building and campus before, analyzed the constraints of moving in its space:

> To our left there was a door leading to a video conference section. You could not see through the door – we wondered if it was off limits as it looked like you needed a key card to get into it. We tried the door, which led to a hallway of other doors. The ability to not see through gave a certain impression of "off limits". Materials have a very significant power in the impressions of space and our mobility choices. [...]
> We went through a door leading to a short corridor and the floor changed. As we passed through the door, we walked over a plastic black scratchy mat, intended for wiping your feet. The mat made a *scratchy noise* as we walked over it, which made my partner *feel really uncomfortable*. The floor then changed to tiles, which looked like the bricks on the wall. The space suddenly went from feeling very light and open to *dark and claustrophobic*. It felt prison-like. (Participants 6 and 7, 2019)

In the excerpt above, different embodied sentiments are interlinked, forming an interpretation of a prison-like environment and atmosphere. The situation was a good example of multisensory experiences occurring in specific material environments into which different sensory and bodily dimensions are immersed (Aula 2018, 80–81; Sumartojo and Pink 2019).

Most often, sensory experiences, like smell, and taste, touch and feel are intertwined. The participants noted that distinguishing smell from other senses was challenging.

> The smell of coffee, or is its taste? (Participant 5, 2019)
> We go out – the air smells cold, it is cold but definitely smells cold. (Participant 2, 2019)

In addition to identifying odors, they also struggled to describe them:
> In the open spaces, we didn't detect a significant smell. It felt clear, almost like an invisible sense. As we enter into the side doors and rooms, however, musky smells were evident. It smelt damp, with stale air. (Participant 6 and 7, 2019)

Hearing and sight, by contrast, are sensory dimensions that are well represented in ethnographic inquiry. Sound, combined with an awareness of sonic presence, is a powerful force that shapes our social experience, relation to community and to other people, and the spaces and places we inhabit (Feld 1996). Two participants of the workshop were specialized in the in the study of sound and *soundscapes* in particular environments (Järviluoma and Vikman 2013). One of them taught her partner, who had no prior experience of soundscape studies, to pay attention to the ways in which sounds and echoes move in the space and to the absence of certain expected sounds:

> I immediately check and start to listen to the ventilation system I have not paid attention to yet. No hum of the ventilation system could be heard. Usually this hum is very dominating in the building and lecture halls where I work. I've realized how people pay attention to the changing sounds of the ventilation system when it pauses and starts again during the lectures and seminar just by following their gestures and facial expressions. [...] Going out the hall, I pay attention to the tile wall. A feeling like I was outside. Smelling the street.... The atmosphere changes, acoustics of the space. Nice labyrinth structure makes one need to guess the direction of the sounds. [...] Wide hall, [it's] good to be able to pay attention to its details. In the middle of the hall you can hear [sounds from] three different directions because they have their own sound bubbles: [an] info desk [–], [a] cafe and the brightest corner with a group talking. (Participant 1, 2019)
>
> [My workshop partner] remarks how funny this labyrinth is – how it reflects and changes the noises and what kind of sensations it gives, kind of fortifying the sensations. The noise actually grows stronger – yeah, you hear cups clinking, people talking, laughing, it grows louder. What a difference in the hearing experience – it has grown from silent to louder. (Participant 2, 2019)

These remarks are detailed, and feature special language and vivid expressions describing the acoustics of the place with expressions like "labyrinth" and "sound bubble".

We, the organizers, were familiar with the venue but had never paid attention to its soundscapes. However, we became more aware of them when some participants explained that they had noted how different the audible sensations were inside and outside the building:

> We walked downstairs and straight to the foyer where we had previously been for tea and coffee and food. The sound of dishes being moved in the kitchen was immediately apparent. Clattering of dishes and cutlery against each other. (Participants 6 and 7, 2019)
>
> [We] heard fan noises from the exhaust of the building and smelled the first smell of our journey: heat, smell of burning oil (?). We came upon children laughing and playing with a ball, *sounds of children laughing and playing*, and running through the sun. Then we heard a siren of the police in the distance. [...] *Crunch crunch crunch* on the snow. Birds in the distance singing, every so often [...] Different shades of light in the trees and contrast with the shady areas. [...] Sound of a car slowly slowly moving behind us signalled danger! (Participant 3 and 4, 2019)

In the latter excerpt, the participants try to describe the different kinds of sounds they heard both near and at a distance, including the onomatopoeic "crunch crunch crunch". They documented places they had visited in short videos they displayed in the classroom. Audiovisual materials expand media of documentation and communication in ethnographic practice and can be extremely useful in sensory ethnography because they contain more information than ca be described through language (see MacDougal 2005). In addition to capturing voices, movements, physical environments and gestures, video-ethnography enables both researchers and the research audience to revisit scenes and see them from multiple perspectives (Sumartojo and Pink 2019, 11–12). The making of video ethnography can also enable new kinds of encounters between people and research audience, when films introduce intimate spaces such as people's homes (Pink et al. 2015).

Analyzing and becoming aware of how we see, view and represent things, is central in visual anthropology/ethnography (MacDougal 2005; Pink 2007). Although this field of inquiry connects to sensory ethnography, we, the organizers took sight for granted at first and did not reflect on the ways in which we, as ethnographers, look at things. The participants, however, pondered on the ways in which sensory observation made them aware of how things and space can be viewed differently. Some participants used sight in an interesting way:

> Looking up we saw all the colours painted on the portico (?) when you look up (the pieces that overhang the building) […] brilliant blues, ochre, green, maybe some yellow. […] We re-entered the building talking about scale and how scale matters. We noticed the columns looked like the tree trunks and had the same scalar thing going on […] grooves in the columns like crevices in the trees. (Participant 3 and 4, 2019)

In our discussions after the workshop, we noted that sight dominates the act of observing. It is often argued that at least in Western cultures, sight is the dominant mode of understanding the world (e.g. Howes 1991; Sparkes 2009; Pink 2009, 12). In the workshop, the participants noted that the vocabulary we use in describing sensory experience is also highly metaphorical: when writing about their experiences, participants used expressions such as "the mind's eye". When we write about our sensory experience, we should be aware of this bias and seek ways to overcome it and expand our sensory vocabulary.

## Sensory ethnography as adventure and exposure

As many scholars studying senses have pointed out, in our everyday life the senses work "unconsciously". They are culturally encoded and intertwined with each other (Sparkes 2009; Bendix 2000). Our workshop was multicultural and multidisciplinary, which proved to be a good way to learn how to observe sensory experiences. Even though ethnography can and is often conducted in teams (see e.g. Clerke and Hopwood; Turunen et al. in this volume), ethnographies, especially monographs, are still most often written alone (for an exception, see Stavrianakis, Rabinow and Korsby 2017). In our workshop, we worked in pairs and practiced collaborative writing. When two people from different cultures, or different living and working environments, engaged together in observing and writing, they adjusted to different modes of observing the environment, thus learning from each other. Our participants experienced the pair work and the joint writing session as fruitful.

> Step 2 of the experiment, a joint writing session, began in scheduled time. After a few technical problems, the participants wrote efficiently, and a lot of text, about 9 pages, accumulated quickly. There was few time left for discussion but the debate was expeditious and multidisciplinary, and it was interesting how the observations and topics varied and how different each pairs' and each participant's experience was. (Field diary, Tytti)

During our discussion, the participants reflected on the outcomes of the experiment, and the challenges they faced in doing sensory observation. One of the pairs who participated in our workshops named their notes as follows: "What follows is James' and Harry's sensory adventure" (James and Harry are pseudonyms used by the participants themselves in their text. Participant 3 and 4, 2019). According to them, this title reflects the experimental nature of the workshop, which felt like stepping into an unknown world and sensing its details as an explorer. Many workshop participants felt that doing the sensory observations meant crossing the boundaries of usual conference behaviour. This behaviour did not always feel comfortable, and participants were candid about this:

> Putting our ear towards the door, we could hear a male voice (the programme would have suggested a woman presenting – this is what happens in conferences, things do not happen according to the programme). *Felt like peeping, fear of getting "caught"* or that somebody would open the door and we would be hit by the door. (Participant 8 and 9, 2019)
>
> I don't usually do this kind of stuff. There is no need to say this but I feel a bit strange walking around and touching things. (Participant 2, 2019)

Questions of social courtesy, courage and fears of interrupting the intensity and intimacy of the situation often come up when conducting participant observation. Some ethnographers fear "becoming a spectacle", attracting an onlookers and questions, and generally being in the centre of attention (Murchison 2010, 71). Taking notes and photos, and especially filming, does hinder participation and evokes direct questions. Although cameras, especially mobile phone cameras, have become everyday objects that are used almost anywhere, it is necessary for ethnographers to consider when and where it is appropriate to film and take photos. In many cases, it is necessary to obtain consent.

Another challenge that workshop participants faced in observation was focusing and maintaining continuous attention in the flow of events and thoughts. They often felt that they were drifting away from the moment of perception and had to "return back to the present":

Actually, I get interested in the posters and start reading them – isn't that what you are doing at conferences? You take lots of stuff in. I see [my workshop partner] taking some picture of the ceiling (ceiling? I haven't paid attention to this part. Why – well, it's high, it's there, should I care? I decided I should maybe focus on the work again. (Participant 2, 2019)

By the end of the sensory ethnography workshop, the participants felt that their perception of the senses and the world around them had changed. They had gained new perspectives into their areas of interest and new ideas on how they could expand their own research into the world of senses. The participants discussed how the senses blend with each other and later mix with other perceptions and memories, forming accumulated and situated knowledge. This is why writing about sensory ethnography and sensory experiences can be challenging: even after a few hours, researchers see things differently and begin "losing" bodily experiences. In writing ethnography, researchers can "go back" to the observed situations and spaces, and bring them alive with the help of notes and *sensory memory and imagination* (Pink 2009, 38, 40). In sensory memory and imagination, perceptions, reflections and images intermingle, merging with words, expressions, images, narrative structures, metaphors, theories and concepts. In sensory ethnography, writing needs to express bodily sensations, describe the circumstances and environment vividly in order to enable others to imagine the spaces, narrating subjects, and the situations and emotions the researchers encounter.

The buildings were breathing; the trees were alive with warmth. And [my workshop partner] was freezing. (Participant 3 and 4, 2019)

All of this brings sensory ethnography close to creative writing and fiction. In fact, the line between them is thin (e.g. Clifford 1986). Ethnographic writing is an attempt at narrativizing the process by which the ethnographer gains new perspectives and knowledge. Descriptions of sensory experiences, environments and atmospheres, are the first step in ethnographic writing that was covered by workshop. The next steps include reflexive analysis and comparison of the ethnographer's experiences with notions and interpretations made by other researchers. Ethnographic writing thus includes both descriptive/creative writing and analytical/theoretical discussion. Further, in order to resonate with its readers, ethnographic writing needs to be vulnerable in the ways that challenge the conventions of factuality and neutrality in scientific writing (Gullion 2016, xiii). This means it needs to be evocative, empathetic and reflexive (Pink 2009, 136).

By the end of the workshop, after our joint discussion, we, the organizers, felt that the experiment should have been longer to include more than one writing session. For those who are planning a workshop or a course on mediating sensory ethnography, we thus recommend organizing at least two separate sessions. During the first session, the group could go through the introduction and do the sensory experiment followed by a writing session. During the second session, which could occur a day or week later, the participants could process and analyze the texts, reflect on and interpret their experiences, relate them to research literature, and conceptualize them theoretically.

## Conclusions

In the final discussion that took place at the end of the workshop, all the participants agreed that sensory ethnography is not only a simple tool for producing research data, but also a comprehensive reflexive process that begins with sensory adventures that break the boundaries of social behaviour and extends a process of creative writing which entails analysis and interpretation. The participants reported that even during the short workshop, they had become aware of the way in which senses play a part in interactions with space and time-space relations. One of the major outcomes of the workshop was that we all realized that paying attention to sensory experiences increases the researcher's awareness of his/her embodied being and self-reflection.

During our experimental workshop, our participants learned that engaging in sensory perception and reflexivity presents the challenge of being present and alert in one's mind and body as the moment-to-moment sensory perceptions mix with sensory memories of other situations and places. In fact, continuous observations of subtle nuances without interruption is quite impossible in many social situations. In our experimental setting, our participants were able to test different strategies and carry out small interventions changing their regular social behaviour and movement in space. They noted that paying attention to specific and multiple senses requires unusual behaviour, motions and activities that interrupt and even break social conventions. When these doings feel natural, good, funny, comfortable, soothing, or inconvenient, strange, scary, and disgusting – or mixture of any negative and positive affects – they inform the researcher of sensory and embodied, affective knowledge that informs us.

According to our participants, one of the major challenges in conducting sensory ethnography lies in the intertwining of sensory experiences and embodied knowledge into feelings and sentiments that are difficult to verbalize (see Bendix 2000, 41; MacDougal 2005). We all perceive and experience the environment differently and make different interpretations based on our personal preferences and cultural backgrounds. It is natural that in certain contexts, some sensory dimensions receive more attention than others, and are easier to grasp and document. The context of a scientific conference allowed the participants to pay attention to spatial dimensions such as movements in space, the details of architecture, and sounds within a building. However, writing about sensory experiences – even in those sensory realms that we can document by photographing and videotaping – requires a specialized and creative vocabulary. For example, writing about soundscapes calls for an understanding of the language of acoustics and music. In addition to specific vocabulary, we need to find ways of communicating how we feel, how senses and emotions mix and connect with sensory memories of the past, and how certain situations feel easy and convenient while others feel awkward, confusing and inconvenient. Smell, for example, in the modern West has been ignored as something non-present or neutral (Classen, Howes, and Synnott 1994). To sum up, in order to write about sensory experiences, we need to be able to describe the embodied relationship with the world with an evocative, expressive and creative sensory vocabulary.

In our workshop, we focused on the subjective sensory experiences of the researcher, and the ways in which we can communicate those experiences through writing. Our experiment was just a brief example in which participants could engage in their own sensory and bodily experiences and share them with a partner in a joint writing session. The writing process did not proceed to analysis and theoretical conceptualization, a necessary phase of research that could also be done collectively as a joint process of shared conceptual work (see e.g. Stavrianakis, Rabinow, and Korsby 2017). Furthermore, in our workshop we did not have time to explore other representations of sensory experiences than those rendered into words in the form of notes and immediate free flow writing. Senses and sensory knowledge could be articulated as images and different forms of art, film and performance (see more e.g. Pink 2009, 132–153).

Acquiring and communicating sensory knowledge calls for creative means and new tools. Although senses and sensory experiences are part of everyday life, paying attention to them requires a different mode of being and doing that adds an extra twist to ethnographic research practices. This embodied twist makes the ethnographer an active corporeal explorer rather than passive observer. The sensory and embodied twist thus enables new perspectives on everyday embodied practices, spatiality, and materiality. Sensory ethnography is a constant process of learning by doing which involves various stages: becoming aware of sensory experiences, analyzing and acknowledging the holistic nature of sensory experiences, and seeking new ways of communicating them in words, and other creative modes.

## Sources:

Workshop proposal, published at www.jyu.fi/en/congress/ethnotwist/programme/schedule.pdf
   Notes and Field diary February 12, 2019, Tytti Lehtovaara
   Notes and Field diary February 12, 2019, Eerika Koskinen-Koivisto
   Writings by workshop participants in a shared GoogleDocs file "STEP 2: WRITING".

## References

Aula, I. 2018. "Aistikävely kaupunkimaisemaan – yhteisen tilan kokemus ja joutomaiden polut". *Elore* 25 (1): 74–95. https://doi.org/10.30666/elore.72816
Bendix, R. 2000. "The pleasures of the ear: toward an ethnography of listening". *Cultural Analysis* 1: 33–50. www.ocf.berkeley.edu/~culturalanalysis/volume1/pdf/bendix.pdf (accessed 6 November 2018).

Classen, C. 2012. *The Deepest Sense: A Cultural History of Touch.* Urbana: University of Illinois Press.

Classen, C., D. Howes, and A. Synnott. 1994. *Aroma: The Cultural History of Smell.* London: Routledge.

Clerke, T., and N. Hopwood. 2014. "Ethnography as collective research endeavor". In *Doing Ethnography in Teams,* edited by T. Clerke, and N. Hopwood, 5–17. New York: Springer.

Clifford, J. 1986. "Introduction: Partial truths". In *Writing Culture,* edited by J. Clifford, and G. Marcus, 1–26. Berkeley and Los Angeles: University of California Press.

Coffey, A. 1999. *The Ethnographic Self. Fieldwork and the Representation of Identity.* London: Sage.

Csordas, T. J. 1999. "Embodiment and cultural phenomenology". In *Perspectives on Embodiment. The Intersections of Nature and Culture,* edited by G. Weiss, and H. Fern Haber, 143–168. New York and London: Routledge.

Feld, S. 1996. "Waterfalls of song: An acoustemology of place resounding in Bosavi, Papua New Guinea". In *Senses of Place,* edited by S. Feld, and K. Basso, 91–135. Santa Fe: School of American Research Press.

Feld, S. 2005. "Places sensed, senses placed: Towards a sensuous epistemology of environments". In *Empire of the Senses. The Sensual Culture Reader,* edited by D. Howes, 179–191. Oxford and New York: Berg.

Gullion, J. S. 2016. *Writing Ethnography.* Rotterdam: Sense Publishers.

Howes, D. 1991. "Sense and non-sense in contemporary ethno/graphic theory and practice". *Culture* 11: 51–62.

Howes, D., and C. Classen. 1991. "Conclusion: Sounding sensory profiles". In *The Varieties of Sensory Experience. A Sourcebook in the Anthropology of the Senses,* edited by D. Howes, 257–288. Toronto, Buffalo, and London: University of Toronto Press.

Ingold, T. 2000. *The Perception of the Environment.* London: Routledge.

Järviluoma, H., and N. Vikman. 2013. "On soundscape methods and audiovisual sensibility". In *The Oxford Handbook of New Audiovisual Aesthetics,* edited by J. Richardson, C. Gorbman, and C. Vernallis, 645–648. Oxford Handbooks Online. https://doi.org/10.1093/oxfordhb/9780199733866.001.0001

Kinnunen, T., and M. Kolehmainen. 2019. "Touch and affect: Analysing the archive of touch biographies". *Body & Society* 25 (1): 29–56. https://doi.org/10.1177/1357034X18817607

MacDougal, D. 2005. *The Corporeal Image: Film, Ethnography, and the Senses.* Princeton: Princeton University Press.

Murchison, J. 2010. *Ethnography Essentials: Designing, Conducting, and Presenting Your Research.* 1st edn. San Francisco: Jossey-Bass.

O'Dell, T. 2004. "Cultural kinesthesis". *Ethnologia Scandinavica* 34: 108–129.

Pink, S. 2007. *Visual Ethnography: Images, Media, and Representation in Research.* 2nd edn. London: Sage Publications.

Pink, S. 2009. *Doing Sensory Ethnography.* London: Sage.

Pink, S., K. Leder Mackley, and R. Moroşanu. 2015. "Researching in atmospheres: Video and the 'feel' of the mundane". *Visual Communication* 14 (3): 351–369. https://doi.org/10.1177/1470357215579580

Sparkes, A. C. 2009. "Ethnography and the senses: Challenges and possibilities". In *Qualitative Research in Sport and Exercise* 1 (1): 21–35. https://doi.org/10.1080/19398440802567923

Stavrianakis, A., P. Rabinow, and T. M. Korsby. 2017. "In the workshop. Anthropology in a collaborative zone of inquiry". In *The Composition of Anthropology. How Anthropological Texts Are Written,* edited by M. Nielsen, and N. Rapport, 179–192. London and New York: Routledge.

Sumartojo, S., and S. Pink. 2019. *Atmospheres and the Experiential World. Theory and Methods.* London and New York: Routledge.

Tiili, M-L. 2016. *Ammatillisuuden ankkuripaikat: Kinesteettinen ja kulttuurinen tieto Suomenlahden merivartiostossa.* Kansatieteellinen arkisto 55. Helsinki: Suomen muinaismuistoyhdistys.

Österlund-Pötzsch, S. 2010. "The ephemeral act of walking: Random reflections on moving in landscapes of memory (loss)". *Ethnologia Scandinavica* 41: 111–128.

# 3

# RAMBLINGS

A walk in progress (or the minutes of the International Society of the Imaginary Perambulator)

*Matthew Cheeseman, Gautam Chakrabarti, Susanne Österlund-Pötzsch, Simon Poole, Dani Schrire, Daniella Seltzer and Matti Tainio*

## Preamble

In this paper, seven writers experiment with ethnographic and artistic responses to each other's walking practices. The point of departure is a panel held at a conference at the University of Jyväskylä.[1] In the morning session, five papers were presented and discussed. In the afternoon the panellists and audience engaged in a series of walking experiments that took us outside the confines of the lecture room, and indeed, the conference venue. In this chapter, we (the panel presenters and co-chairs) re-embody this moment by walking together, writing together and engaging our understanding of self and our experiences of walking. This sense of experimentation is open to the reader, to whom we extend an invitation to travel with us through the process of ethnographic knowledge production.

Walking is a pedestrian activity peculiarly elusive to academic categorisation. It engages the emotions, involves the senses, invites creativity, brings forth memories and provokes the imagination. All are notoriously difficult to capture in ethnographic writing. Consequently, some of the questions we approached in our initial meeting were focused on possibilities: how can the intangible experience of walking be conveyed in writing? Can walking be archived? What happens in the process of textualisation? Can genres like creative writing and ethnographic fiction help us understand and communicate the "unwritable", including those emotive, mobile and sensory aspects? Finally, we wanted to know whether walking could be used as a hermeneutic tool – could enactment elucidate that which evades ethnographic description?

Such questions may not be satisfied, because they keep moving, wandering, walking. As such, in this chapter, we also keep moving, gesturing beyond conventional ethnographic writing strategies, searching for a path to collectivise knowledge production by escaping the unidirectional academic text. In attempting to do so, we are aware that we transform ephemeral affective experience into an object, an inscription. For us, this has been part of the journey.

Attempts at an ethnography of walking are not new. To produce this chapter, we experimented with various forms of ethnography, sharing our attempts to transform a walk into other objects, all the while performing together. We are trying to push the representational limits of an ethnography of walking, reflecting on the various inscription modes available to us. In this sense, this chapter is a report on our knowledge engagements with walking practices. This is not a final product or object of our findings; it is a durable manifestation of our individual and collaborative meaning-making.

In our ethnographic process, all of the authors actioned a walk inspired and informed by our first meeting in the aforementioned panel convened by Susanne Österlund-Pötzsch and Dani Schrire at which five walks were described. These walks are often referred to in the main text:

i Matti Tainio presented a study in applied aesthetics. He used running interviews (actually interviewing whilst running) as a method for collecting information about running experiences. His presentation concentrated on the method of running together in order to understand the aesthetic aspects of running.

ii Daniella Seltzer explored the juncture where the social and the spatial meet in the moving body. Her research deals with the walking performance and performativity of previously secular Jewish women who converted to become ultra-Orthodox Jews. In considering the sociality of walking, this presentation also investigated the performance of secular actresses who learn to walk and perform as ultra-orthodox women in films and television shows.

iii Gautam Chakrabarti discussed ritualised walking in an increasingly popular Hindu pilgrimage in North India. This pilgrimage had a revival in the 1980s (with certain popular films promoting it) and involves a substantial amount of singing and chanting while walking. As a cultural revival, this narrativised practice is coterminous with the rise of Hindu Nationalism in Indian politics.

iv Matthew Cheeseman considered ethnography and walking via the methods of creative practice. In his project "Not the path" (2011), he tasked project participants with creating a set of instructions ("a path") to be followed by one of the other participants. Imaginary spaces were thus designed by participants relying on other participants to turn them into geographic spaces. In doing so walkers were asked to retextualise their walks, taking photos and noting impressions, engaging in the ethnographic practices of recording and interpreting in the field.

v Simon Poole described a project of repeatedly walking a route significant to his family and home while interpreting it musically through the method of perambulography via a purposively constructed device that allows the walker to draw on the move.[2] The aim of the research was to draw a connection between home and the physical landscape, and to theoretically develop the notion of "be-longing". The inquiry developed a research practice that could explore folk culture through musical composition; by understanding the landscape through drawing in motion.

Taking these walks and our memories of the panel as inspiration for this chapter, we set out on new walks, physically, affectively, and mentally. We chronicled our experiences, thoughts and interpretations and met digitally to discuss and generate this text. The conversation between and within the following passages sheds new light on our individual efforts but also produces knowledge that speaks about walking as a practice and an experience. Key metaphors emerged, beginning with the idea of memory. This metaphor serendipitously creates points of contact and discursive nodes that allowed us, as writers, to deal with our own associations as we strove to connect to those of others. A closely related metaphor was the concept of home, often in terms of a sense of place, sometimes in the sense of feeling disoriented, sometimes in terms of reconnection. Given the ethnographic intention of our writing, it is perhaps not surprising that physicality and sensuousness proved a third common denominator. Ethnographic registering naturally engaged our senses but the premises of our experiment also gave rise to the sensory experiences of being in and out of control. Finally, a distinct metaphor was variations of rhythm. Sensations of rhythm provided flow and poetry to our walks and writings together, but as the rhythms changed or broke, interruptions and fractures appeared and called for our attention.

Our work aligns with the paradigmatic stance of arts-based practice as research (Bobadilla et al. 2017; Leavy 2009; Sullivan 2005). Because the personal experience of walking is central to our collective composition, our methodology has been influenced by a postmodern orientation towards identity (see Lyotard 1984, 1992). This represents a social and political position that is ever-changing and provisional. It is a standpoint that revels in multiple truths and holds them as all equally valid. For example, Matti's views are different to Dani's but have equitable status, to each other's and any of the other authors. Thus, this research is "Re/search [sic] [that] champions versatility, inter-epistemological acceptance, and diversity of knowledge types, understandings and thus ways of reinterpreting 'impact'" (Poole 2017, 155); it reframes practices such as walking as innovative art-based methods of inquiry into ethnography. As arts-based methods, the conventional values of inquiry are less important, and as such "facts, control, distance, and neutrality" (Bochner and Ellis 2003, 506) have little relevance to us as practitioners (or perambulographers).

If our "twist" could be described as having a purpose or function it would be to undertake research that dissolves the dichotomy of process and product (Benetti and Hiney 2018) or, more specifically, the dichotomy of practice and the presentation of research. The purpose of this is to challenge the dominant popular and elitist cultural modes which have a tendency to pedestalize the final product. We intend to walk a path, when walking might be defined not just as an individual's act but a collective understanding. Methodologically speaking, this understanding also means that collective responsibility is accepted for its success or failure. Moving by foot becomes a knowledge in writing which is more interested in process, contingent learning, community and performance than it is any definitive end, object or understanding of itself as a final product.

This chapter assumes an onto-epistemological standpoint of coherentism, accommodating varying, fluctuating and pluralistic truths. It leans towards auto-ethnography as a sound and proven methodological means of capturing the evocative or transient feelings and thoughts of authors and participants, but troubles any understanding of terms like reliability, validity, and generalisability. Nonetheless, there is enough cogency between autoethnographic methodologies and arts-based practice as research to allow sympathy for these altered contexts (Bobadilla et al. 2017; Grennan 2015). We answer any questions of this work's credibility and reliability by recognising that it is the reader and observer rather than any participant that creates the potential of generalisability. As such, our personal reflections of how we engaged with each-other's walking methodology was cut-up, layered, and juxtaposed, a methodological version of a collage technique. As researchers, it allowed us to unlock, twist, or perhaps untwist conventional patterns of perceiving, thinking, and representing that determine our interactions with our environment.

Our joint ramble thus suggests that ethnographic twists run through the full process of ethnography (from initial ideas through fieldwork to presentation). As such, it strikes us that it is easier and more acceptable to undertake unconventional fieldwork than produce work that is not traditionally presented or published in a conventional format. This chapter was edited in committee with each of its authors performing separate functions within the makeshift team. The editors of this volume then offered feedback to align our text with the "twists" of the collection as a whole. There were further discussions with the publishers in addressing what was possible in terms of design and typography. What follows are six pieces of writing which try to capture the walks of others, meshed together. To keep these individual footsteps alive, we use the paragraph as an organisational principle, segments authored by individuals within our collective and identified by [name]. One could read this chapter via the voices that comprise it, or by ignoring such distinctions and treating the text as a whole. Our ethnographic experiment is thus a multivocal contribution to an ethnography with a twist by different writers on different paths, sometimes intersecting, picking up each other's rhythms when (and if) they walk together.

The resulting text is brought together under a simple artifice: you are about to read the minutes of a society meeting, that of the International Society of the Imaginary Perambulator (ISIP). While this article is evidence of an open and on-going process of knowledge production, a walk-in-progress, it can also be described as the minutes of ISIP.

Matt: To write implies a certain sense of rhythm
Dani: Walking to buy milk with my son after "Walk to Kitty's Stone"
Daniella: Walking the Old City through Ms R
Simon: My walk
Gautam: Walking as a reverie fusing T/time/s
Susanne: NOT THE Easter Sunday PATH
Matti: Walking with atmospheric halos

## The society meets

[Matt] To write implies a certain sense of rhythm, a method, perhaps a way of thinking, too, thoughts follow keystrokes and fingers; to walk is to put one foot after the other, to regulate the step on the landscape, rising and forward, fingers on the keyboard, gripped to the pen, words progressing on the page, matching the heartbeat with uncertain purpose, getting there, to the end of the sentence, putting words down like feet: word after word after word.

[Dani] How can a specific walk be experienced by others, re-told, re-written. In my walk, I try to keep open the idea of a walk transforming into object and retransforming to a bodily performance. Simon's intergenerational walk on the Cheshire ridge inspired me. He engaged walking in two modes: first, recording a succession of the same walk by drawing 36 walks with the use of a perambulograph. Following this, Simon transformed these drawings into a musical score. This way, the spatio-temporal experience of walking was engaged spatially (drawing) and then temporally (as music).

[Daniella] Following Matt's "Not the path" I asked an ultra-Orthodox Jewish woman who lives in the Jewish Quarter of the Old City in Jerusalem to create for me a path through the Old City, one which transmits what it is like for her to live there, taking into account places that affect her, that she frequents regularly and that invite me into her narrative of self. I also asked for a path that would allow me to reflect on what it is like to walk between and through the different Quarters, all this while being visibly read as an Ultra-Orthodox Jewish woman from an outsider's gaze.

[Simon] I had at first anticipated applying another's walking method or thematic approach to a walk that I would take; I presumed it would be largely a methodological discovery, that I would experience a particular way of understanding movement on foot. I use "movement on foot" because what I came to realise was not specifically methodological in nature. It was instead a fracture of memories, discussions and feelings that were overlaid with the unexpected context of "movement on foot" and pain shared by others in the project. In my case, acute arthritis and osteophytes which meant walking more than a mile would mean pain the next day.

[Susanne] I attempted to engage with all of the walks simultaneously, looking for guidance in each of the projects. I decided to do my walk on Easter Sunday and walk to the largest graveyard in Helsinki (about 8km from my home). In this, I wanted to create a reference to the traditional Sunday family walk and the practice of visiting the graves of departed family members during seasonal holidays. Moreover, the route to the graveyard is a familiar one for me and takes me along the shoreline.

[Matti] I think of the movement on my feet and "Not the path" and reflect on how I am not in full control of my walk, which I record, remembering Simon's practice of walking and making notes with his perambulograph. There are connections with walking as a bodily practice as well as hints of scientific-animistic spiritualism. These can be found in my descriptions on walking with atmospheric halos.[3]

## Walking with others means a special time

[Simon] I had been taken by Gautam's talk on pilgrimage and was curious about the religiosity of repetition. I had given some thought to the spiritual nature of "movement by foot" and had considered how Solnit's (2014) and MacFarlane's (2012) work had cogence with pilgrimage. I worried about misappropriation and was all too aware of how a sacralised walk could be trivialised. Nonetheless, pilgrimage presented a model.

[Gautam] In India, every act of self-inscribed walking – especially using a device like Simon's perambulograph – is a reverie fusing the ravages of parallel and conflicting times; the post/colonial, the sacral/secular, the inter/nationalist, the in/tangible are but halos that attempt totalisation. A pilgrimage can be an act of political subversiveness, while secularised public discourses could exude fervent religiosity. Why does a woman walking, with two sacralised vessels of water balanced on a staff, which she carries on her shoulder, be a figure that moves millions?

[Dani] Simon discussed his experience as a Cheshirian whose family has been living on the same ridge for the past 350 years. I ask myself, in which ways can I know Simon's walk? What kind of knowledge is this? I follow Simon's experiment with my own experiment as I tried to re-live the walk elsewhere. I listened to the score a dozen times, engaging it by walking and writing this piece, which tries to convey the ephemeral idea of walking in writing.

[Daniella] I asked Ms. R to design my walk as a means of walking in dialogue with the embodied knowledge I had internalised from previous interviews in which I engaged reflexivity and representations of ultra-Orthodox Jewish women's walking in my previous research. Her first instructions were to dress up wearing modest clothing, which I took to mean ultra-Orthodox dress. I did not attempt to perform specific body gestures I learnt previously. Yet, coming into the Old City and walking through the Muslim Quarter towards the Old City, I walked beyond my usual thoughts, feeling pulled into the imaginary character I never meant to inhabit.

[Susanne] I commenced my walk but discovered that it was impossible for me to hold all the modes in my head at once. However, when I was trying to focus on singular aspects of my walking, I often found myself making connections to other themes. At certain stages of the walk, one or two of the walks resonated more strongly with me in that they illuminated a situation or threw something into contrast.

## Disorientations

[Daniella] I felt disorientated, not knowing the "proper" script of an ultra-Orthodox woman walking in the Muslim Quarter. Whenever I went to the Old City in the past, I wanted to minimize my Israeli body and its privilege, trying not to stick out as a point of respect and to mark my lack of belonging. Here I am, hyper-Jewish. I noticed myself thinking who can I make eye contact with and who can I not? How "should" I appear to feel as I walk down the stairs of the Muslim Quarter? And how am I interpellated by the vendors and tourists walking by? I was treated differently, ignored and no longer perceived as a potential tourist, in sharp contrast to walking in the Jewish Quarter. I felt somewhat like an alien to myself, a tourist with a route, covering the voice-recorder I brought along, pressed to my chest and hidden between papers, embarrassed to be seen talking to myself nonstop. I am not alone, my shadows and reflection walking with me, appearing foreign.

[Dani] An abstract of a talk is not a talk – it lacks a voice and intonation and it is geared towards conveying general information about one's intentions. At its best, it is the difference between an Aarne-Thompson tale type and an actual performance of a tale. An abstract draws contours of an argument, of a narrative, but it cannot sufficiently prepare an audience for the actual performance. When I first met Simon in a restaurant we walked in the sludgy streets of Helsinki. Later, I heard him describe his walk and I filled it with the actual body which I had already walked with. Imagination can replace that which is not known with impressions of actual beings. I have never visited Cheshire, although I drove past once, many years ago. Is the moving image of a walking Simon on green hilly pastures enough? Does that mean I can claim to know his walk to Kitty Stone?

[Simon] My father was diagnosed with terminal cancer four days before I was due to undertake my walk. He was given a couple of months. The next day I ended up on crutches with a sprained ankle, on the same foot that I already have my injury. Coupled with the emotional turmoil of loss, I wanted to resign from the project. In the face of living grief, and what felt like an insurmountable, unforgiving situation I decided to open myself up to a form of spiritual endurance. I would continue my walk. I used my crutches to get to Finland, donned crampons and with ice-spike walking sticks, got on with it. This debilitation brought me somehow closer to Gautam's work, in spite, or because of the obstacles, the walk somehow seemed a pilgrimage. I hoped for some revelation of understanding in undertaking this endeavour.

I had no revelation, no epiphany.

## Reconnecting/a sense of place

[Susanne] The reflected sunlight is creating a glittering avenue on the water. This makes the strongest impression of the walk – the sun glitter becomes a gateway to summers past, to time spent by the water. I am reminded of Simon's project of finding ways to connect home, landscape and identity through walking. This becomes visceral, more anchored in my body, when I reach a section that takes me off the tarmac and gravel roads onto a wood path that leads me over granite bedrock, roots and stones. This is uneven walking, up and down, swaying for a big tree or a boulder. Simon's concept of "be-longing" seems apt, I have an understanding for the landscape that I cannot put into words, but I believe could be expressed in sound, shape, colour – or movement: walking here makes my body feel at home, attuned and relaxed.

[Daniella] My walk started in the Muslim Quarter, passing through the central street, continuing through the Jewish Quarter, and stopping by several nationalist stops commemorating the fallen soldiers during the War of Independence (1948) and the Six Day War (1967). Ms R's instructions connected me not only to the place but also to cultural narratives, writing the self and place into and through one another. The path opened up stories beyond my own, meandering across time, ideas, and history. Re-entering well-trodden, well-known routes invites a different lens, making power structures and the place of the body in space more apparent. Here the presence of the past in the present, between one place and another, and between different bodies as imagined and represented through me, my body.

[Matti] Ever since I saw my first halo, a full ring around the moon, I have looked for these displays. Whenever I'm outside in spring, I search for these halos, rings around the sun, arches or sundogs. The displays are dependent on the occurrence of certain shapes in atmospheric ice crystals. Because of this, they appear only briefly. In Finland, April skies are best. It's usually sunny and it's cold enough for optimum, icy *Cirrostratus* clouds. Most of my outings here are characterised by chasing them. One must be alert.

[Matt] The landscape gives a break. The landscape gives a break from the page. It interjects thoughts into the conversation. The landscape, however managed, is there to interject, to refuse to be ignored, the steps are words – they come – words are like steps, they just come, one after the other, but the landscape, it arrives, it arrives, even in memory interrupting, there, present. It has a form.

[Simon] We were asked if we would like to visit Sibelius Hall, a concert hall and world-renowned acoustic space. It was a couple of miles away and we would have to walk. I was excited. Despite being in a group of people, I elected to listen to music on the way. I am a singer/songwriter, and this is how I know and understand the world. It also allowed me to be with the group but also to remove myself into a personal and private world. This was my world, and I was, to an extent, the arbiter of the experience of it. I thought I was deliberately enhancing the walk and world through which I was travelling: the scenery of Lahti, where we were staying, was to my mind bleak in winter and still had little in the way of vibrancy or colour (see Figure 3.1). Despite its beauty I longed for something else. I listened to *Heartworms* (The Shins 2017), particularly the first song: "Name for you", colourful music in utter contrast to the landscape. The feeling was enervating, perhaps it was the use of birdsong in the tracks – something I use in my compositions – so peculiar to feel the divergence of visual and aural. I saw graffiti of two magpies. In my culture two bring good luck. In my enervated state this seemed to heighten my walking, there was a synchronicity to something beyond, a release from the present.

When we arrived at Sibelius Hall, I lay on the floor, not aware until then of the pain.

44  M. Cheeseman et al.

[Dani] A musical score – just like a walk – is not representational in the same way figurative painting is. Music triggers the imagination as Kendal Walton (1994) notes. Had I listened to *Walking to Kitty Stone* without any prior knowledge, without meeting Simon face-to-face, would I think of it as a score of a walk? Likely not. But I do. I have already acquired some knowledge of the score and I cannot think of it in separation from the act of listening. Can I re-walk a score? This was my original intention. I thought that I could listen to the score in a different setting and see how the knowledge of the piece could be negotiated. At first, I wanted to perform it in the desert, walking the Cheshire ridge in Makhtesh Ramon. The High Negev desert is our family's escape from Jerusalem and every now and then, we go for a weekend there.

## Revelations along the way

[Simon] On a tour of the building we were asked if anyone wished to sing. I shouted "yes please!", walked to the conductor's podium and turned to face the vast space and sang the acapella introduction to a song I wrote called "revelation", followed by the first verse of "sparrows on the roof". These were significant moments,

**FIGURE 3.1** Simon's walk. Photographs by Simon Poole. Copyright: Simon Poole.

precisely because of what the songs mean to me and others. Listeners have connected "revelation" with mortality, while "sparrows on the roof" was partly inspired by my dad's ability to whistle a sparrow's song so perfectly that they reply.

[Daniella] Walking helps us sharpen our senses, opening an opportunity for reflections to transform the ordinary. Following instructions was a release of control, which evolved into a sense of freedom by having someone else decide the route. This was coloured by the need to follow the instructions. Not doing so, or not finding the precise pathways led me to feel as though I wasn't experiencing what Ms R had in mind.

[Matti] Keeping an eye on the sky influences the walks. The sun, the sky and the weather remind me about Matthew's invented walks. Instead of a human designing a walk for me, natural forces make rules for me. Walking with atmospheric halos is a voluntary action, but whenever possible, I like to accept the invitation of the April skies.

[Susanne] As I leap off the path to let an elderly couple pass, I experience self-consciousness, a sense of the aesthetics of movement akin to Matti's description of everyday running practices, not in terms of elegance but in behaving according to an ethic (letting someone pass) and my body negotiating the limited space. This stands in contrast: in general, it is difficult to register the aesthetic/performative aspects of my walking. However, when I enter the graveyard I notice a difference in my gait: I deliberately slow down and think about moving with decorum (reminding me of the women Daniella had interviewed). Nevertheless, I have no real purpose for being in the churchyard, there is no deeper sense of ritual, no grave to lay flowers at. "Walking with Intent" is a phrase used by Marion Bowman (2014) to describe pilgrimage.

[Daniella] Ms R's route invited me to feel the places through her experience, visiting sites important to her:

> At the end of the street turn right onto Jewish Quarter Road. Notice that it gets quieter and calmer as you pass by the shops and enter the Jewish Quarter [...] Go around the corner and walk into the courtyard in front of the Hurva synagogue. Take in the majesty of the building and listen to the sounds of Torah being learned.
> Go out and around the other side and down the steps at the entrance of the Ramban Synagogue that lies beneath the Hurva. Close your eyes and feel the generations of Jews that passed through the door since the 1200s.
> Stop and smell the delicious fragrance of oranges [...] Listen for the sounds of children [...] Listen to the birds and look at the contrast of the leaves of the trees against the sky.

[Dani] Simon connected his score to his environment, seeking community "through this earth we call home", but I never regard the desert as my home, not in the Negev, at least. The polyvocal score of *Walking to Kitty Stone* explores the echoes between generations. There I was, walking in the seemingly lunar landscape of Makhtesh Ramon, a region trodden by the Nabateans two millennia ago, yet leaving no physical impressions, as far as I could tell. It did not feel right; it felt removed from *Walking to Kitty Stone* and counter-productive: despite many attempts to obscure the situatedness of science (Haraway 1988), any scholarship is situated and partial, particularly the experiment I undertook. With this failure to channel walking knowledge from Cheshire to Machtesh Ramon, I decided to take a different path.

*Walking to Kitty Stone* is about be-longing, so I returned home. It was Passover, when Jews retell the walking of the ancient Israelites in the Sinai desert. I returned to my everyday landscape, which as Simon explains in the score (to his daughter?) is full of houses that "aren't part of the environment", except these houses do form *my* environment. Many shops were closed that Saturday and we lacked milk in the fridge. I decided to seize the moment and walk to get some milk with Hillel, my eight-year-old son, who was eager to join me.

## Sensing the path

[Matti] Halo walks follow a pattern: on stepping out, I check the sky for a haze that I know is favourable. If present, I raise my hand to shadow the sun and look. This is the halo-hunter's salute to the sky and it marks the onset of a particular kind of walk. If the result of the first salute is positive, I continue the walk, keeping an eye on the upper atmosphere.

[Matt] To write without a landscape is to do philosophy from the desk. This takes focus, almost meditation. Walking is to apply philosophy, it is to know place. Writing is letting the impressions of knowledge return. To write a people, to write a place. Here a city, there a hill. Technology allows us to communicate at distance with ease. The internet, the postal service. It allows us to write at distance, to connect our thoughts. To tap on computers, to grip the pen, to write about our tools. Writing about walking is writing about our tools.

[Simon] There is singing here. There is sound. There is the sound of the world around. There are other things beyond steps and words. The wind is fresh.

[Daniella] Solnit (2014, 5) writes that "motions of the mind cannot be traced, but those of the feet can". I tried to record my stream of consciousness via audio. This mostly diverted my attention from being in any embodied presence to the act of translating embodied and sensual experiences into words for the recorder. On the one hand this enabled me to remember direct experiences and thoughts as I later began to write the walk, yet during the walk it prompted me to direct such experiences into words, even when there were no "right" words available at a given moment.

I walked imagining I was Ms R, bringing the branch to my nose and hearing the children learning religious texts aloud. Movement through space enables one to tune in and out of the present and travel through senses and memories to different sites and times. Usually I feel like I don't belong in the Jewish Quarter, walking there I felt relief looking like everybody else, noticing my body expand in space, settling into my form, shoulders straightened.

[Dani] We set off, holding hands and walking together in what Hillel never realised and I only gradually became aware of, was another walk to Kitty Stone. As we made our way through the well-trodden streets, they conveyed many family experiences, intimate recollections from the last twenty years of walking around the same neighbourhood that forms part of our city.

How can Jerusalem be anyone's? My wife looks back at seven generations in the city, but I was born in Cape Town, Hillel in Berlin. We regard Jerusalem as our home in a mundane way, but also in the intimate sense that the word "home" conveys. Intercontinental be-longing is still a form of belonging. The last six generations of my own family were born in twelve different towns in three continents, speaking five mother-tongues. Wandering Jews? Probably, but with belongings, walking many paths. There we were, a father and a son walking to get some milk, something I can imagine carried out across these generations in numerous places and occasions. As we walked together, heading for milk to bring home, I finally got a sense of Kitty Stone.

[Daniella] The voice-recorder amplified auditory stimulus from my surroundings, leading this to be both a hyper-embodying and dis-embodying experience at once. I heard the sounds of my body walking, the pressing of my shoes as they made a rhythm on the Jerusalem stone covering the paths, my voice describing what was around, my reactions and small umms and ahhs. The journey was both familiar and strange. As my memory unfolded in parallel to the recording, it was infused with the captured words, my breath, footsteps, sounds of the Old City, all of which triggered visual displays, a Proustian superimposition of two different modes of time.

## Documenting the path

[Daniella] Translating stream-of-consciousness recordings within the creative practice of the walk, played on the seams between absence and presence as I attempted to record thought in order to capture the present, which became absent as soon as it had passed. Walking the route didn't end when I got to the last sentence of Ms R's path, which asked me to touch the Western Wall. It continued as I played the voice recorder and wrote these words. Documenting this walking performance is itself a performance: as Cathy Turner (2000) wrote, "there is an uneasy relationship between performance practice and its analysis". In writing, I noticed myself in many dialogues: with the path, the voice recorder and the social scripts I presumed I should follow as an ultra-Orthodox woman.

[Matt] All of this must be edited together, it must be condensed on the page, this people – landscape – step – these mix of writers, these different rhythms and purposes. Look at these things from the world, from the past, here on the page, experience, live them, walk through them, picture them in your mind's eye, walking step after step in your head on the trail as you keep going, keep going and forget what it was that you were writing about. There may be interjections in the step. There may be interruptions from the landscape, from encounters, from what is discovered on the path. The outside is here and it will intrude, it will break through the page. This perhaps is the greatest thing: that the outside steps over the page, that the outside manifests within, that the writing entertains that which it is not. This is somehow marshalled: other-wise manifested from the self.

[Simon] MacFarlane discusses, in one talk (2012) that the root etymology of the word "path" is shared with the word "learn". Initially, the learning on my walk had been fractured. I had attempted to apply different methods of understanding too forcibly. When I allowed the walk, the path, to reveal itself these fractures became useful filters. The walk became an incredible rendering of the power of context, which shed light on an emotional scenario. The various spectrums of feeling became and were one light, too complex for a simple reflection, but could be filtered with a sensitive and ethical use of our methodological prism.

[Matti] The most frequent halos appear close to the sun, so I squint to avoid the burning glare. I also look for shadows that let me look without getting blinded. When there isn't a shadow I block the sun with my hands. Sometimes, I walk with it behind me, and have to keep turning to see the halos. Stopping is not always possible, so I turn and go on walking backwards. The best halos are photographed.

All this concentration on the sky makes the walk intermittent. There are periods of good walking followed by periods when the purpose seems lost in favour of celestial events. The rhythm of these periods is sporadic, depending on the environmental factors that allow me to look upwards. Otherwise the walking environment is secondary, only worth a glimpse to keep me on route. Because these walks are mostly connected to my daily errands, the environment at the outskirts of the city is familiar and looking at the sky while walking is possible and (reasonably) safe.

A few years ago, I was walking through the centre of Turku when I suddenly saw an impressive display of halos. There was a full ring around the sun, the 22-degree halo, as well as upper tangential arch, sun dogs (parhelia) and my favourite, the parhelic circle. None of these halos are rare but seeing many together is a special event. The full parhelic circle extending as a horizontal ring around the sky makes the display distinct, since it often implies a further possibility of rare halos. Attempting to photograph this display turned my walk into an unusual performance. I crossed the street several times, searching for a vantage point between the high-rise buildings, walking backwards in order to get a better image, with many people passing by in the centre of the city.

[Dani] The old Ottoman train went through the southern parts of Jerusalem. People living next to this abandoned corridor struggled to reuse them. The line was eventually turned into the "Train Track path" which cuts across Palestinian and Jewish neighbourhoods. In this contested city, this one track shared by people of different religions and languages may seem quite striking, a ray of hope. To be sure, divisions cannot be glossed over by a line, but a line it is. Some choose to walk on the former track which has been filled between the sleepers, or on the adjacent narrow lawn, but Hillel – like many children his age – is fascinated by the gaps that still exist on the edge of the old Ottoman track.

## Putting steps into signs

[Matt] Do we choose who we walk with?

Are ethnographers selective?

The words are within you, the words will fall out. There are questions. Provocations, routines, games. Is the path the subject? The purpose? Who else walks it, where are we going together? Is this the structure of the chapter? Six writers, five speakers, language, words, how is it to play out?

To hear a shriek in the air. To sit at one's desk and see the images, almost unbidden, of the walk. To be faithful to the notebook of the imagination.

To set off, into the page, to face the whiteness of the snow, the landscape melting, changing, to imagine the map, the words accompanying in your head, words multiplying and magnifying, spreading out in all directions, language expanding like a cloak over the land/city as you walk. The taste of ethnography in the mind, these words, writers' words, that take their place, that cover it. We need them, as we walk, untethered researchers, free-floating observers, our feet kicking around the page, looking for the footstep of the other, intuiting and overhearing others' words to write with. To walk alongside each other. To invite each other to write our words as we walk, to give them our feet, to let them dictate us.

[Martti] The perambulograph is a special device while my digital camera is not. However, the camera is employed in an unorthodox manner. I point the lens to the sun to capture the halos symmetrically. At times, I block the glaring sun behind an obstacle or raised hand. Both the composition and exposure emphasise the sky, leaving the other parts underexposed. In post-production the image is manipulated to isolate the halos from the background, making these images more peculiar. Sharpening and tweaking the pixels reveal rare halos while the rest of the image becomes distorted beyond recognition. The resulting images are typical for amateur-scientific documentation, where fixed conventions define a successful outcome.

[Simon] The walk I took problematised the idea of ethnographic knowledge in relation to walking and somatic inquiry. Taken alongside the other walks and writings in this chapter, it illuminates our diversity of practices and how this diversity could generate a form of understanding by way of a prismatic core: how our paths crossed.

## To-gather/rhythm

[Dani] We walk to-gether – I walk on the smooth surface and he jumps from one track to the next, balancing himself with each cheerful bounce that lands on the white granular stones in between the tracks. It is a playful walk for him and for me as we get into the mutual rhythm of a walk and talk, the same rhythm that can be heard and experienced in the score: "Pam Pam [clapping]" … Simon's acapella fuses two lines that seem apt: "like the landscape daddy experienced without a … touch of a stone." We finally make it to Kitty Stone, get our milk, taking a different path home.

[Matt] With these companions what is possible? One can walk in a group, one can journey together, friends, pilgrims, sing, think, step after step, word after word, no conflict, no difficulty in the steps, weaving in words with each other's, in pace, in time.

The map becomes a cloak becomes a sense, becomes another landscape, another people, perhaps, or a mirror, a shiny clean mirror, like a shield flashing halos in the sun's face as the walk continues towards our memories of where the horizon might be, every step evoking another's words and every word stepping in the service of the other.

To come home, to reach a destination, end, finish, to draw a line, to come to a full stop? Such an eventually seems unlikely. To reach an end at this point, so far into the project, so close to its beginning, full circle at the end of the page, the right margin and come back again to the left, and finally stop, say "it is over".

## A sense of arrival?

[Matt] How did the group fracture?

[Gautam] Why do I feel unsure of my *locus standi* while meandering lazily through the "revolution"-ravaged streets of the Dark Goddess's own city? Am I looking for the epiphany that eludes Simon ... is there a paradoxical T/truth in Calcutta-Kolkata's ultra-religious hyper-secularity?

[Dani] Did I walk to Kitty Stone? Are Simon's solitary walks under grey skies over green hills similar to my walk accompanied by my son under blue sky in the city of Jerusalem? That is not the question I need to answer. For me the question was always whether I could know a walk. What conditions of knowledge are there in learning these affects? John Wylie's (2005) wonderful account of his walk tries to convey his own experience in ways that are more than representational. Our experiment is different from this, it is not autoethnographic.

Walking experiences differ but all ethnographies are based on an engagement that transforms understandings of cultures. They may leave a physical trace, but ultimately rambles are not about arriving anywhere. I hope that by experimenting with re-experiencing, I have at least reached somewhere.

[Matti] Although images do not document the walk or are by no means connected to the act of rambling after halos, I feel that they capture the essential mood of these April outings when my focus is the sky.

[Susanne] Does this chapter add to (or begin? end?) the Walking Archives – a concept suggested by Dani. Any such archive will have to reflect the jumble of sensations, feelings, associations and thoughts weaving in and out of each other. Only through walking layers upon layers, repetition, a multi-fold of perspectives and methods, finding artistic and creative ways of expressing and interpreting beyond the verbal, paying careful attention to body, performance and identity, looking at the junctions of the body and the landscape as well as the social and the spatial, documenting representations of walking – the list goes on as walking cannot be contained. It is hidden in the everydayness of the activity.

[Daniella] A man invites me to go up to his rooftop and he sees me speaking to a recorder:

"Why do you record your thoughts?"
"For a shared chapter", I said.
"What do you do with the chapter?"
"You think about it", I said.
"So what do you say?"
"The view is amazing", I said.
"No, to your thoughts", he clarifies, "I am not cynical by the way".
"Ah, well, I don't usually record my thoughts as I walk, it's just that I need to write about it", I mumbled as I thought to myself: "Did I expose the mission I am on?"

[Matt] And so the thought comes of not moving, of pretending to move, of writing when one is not walking. For how can one write when one walks? One can talk, one can compose in one's head, into a machine, perhaps, a perambulograph. Writing is the memory of walking. The memory of walking people. Writing is making nonsense of the walk, of interrupting it, of being nature, or positioning words as nature, great words, huge words as corporeal as the Western Wall, as milk or rocks or sun halos, floating onto the path, obscuring it, settling on the path, lending their weight to the page, words ending here, resting in the circular measure of the stop. It seems impossible.

## Postamble: parting ways

A good conclusion is telling the truth – here is where academia and walking part ways. They disconnect in the very act of bringing ethnographic/artistic research to publication. The act of fixing something to the page, which is then sold to publishing markets, implies an end point that considers a host of other considerations that were never part of the twist. Doing so, however, remains worthwhile as it introduces the possibility of our subjunctive walk being read and shared by those that are not us. The metaphor of walking as writing breaks down in publication, but this gives it the possibility of being reborn in other people's minds and, eventually, perhaps, their feet.

## Notes

1 "When walking and writing merge – exploring the potentials and limits of ethnographic writing" at the conference Ethnography with a Twist, University of Jyväskylä, February 2019.
2 The perambulograph is a machine invented by Dr. Simon Poole. It is mounted on a harness and allows the wearer to draw or write on a roll of paper as they walk. Advocates of the machine are known as perambulators.
3 For an explanation of different halos, see "Halos – Contents".

## References

Benetti, A., and A. Hiney. 2018. "Autoethnography as a method for artistic research in music performance: Dissolving the process/product dichotomy". Paper presented at the Institute of Musical Research Study Day, London, April 16.

Bobadilla, N., A. Lefebvre, and P. Mairesse. 2017. "Dysfunction: Ethics, critics, and challenges in art based research dissemination". *Dysfunction Journal* 1 (1): 1–16.

Bochner, A., and C. Ellis. 2003. "An introduction to the arts and narrative research: art as inquiry". *Qualitative Inquiry* 9: 506–514.

Bowman, M. 2014. "*Walking with intent*". Paper presented at Assessing Pilgrimage Studies Today, York, July 5–6.

Grennan, S. 2015. "Arts practice and research: Locating alterity and expertise". *iJADE* 34 (2): 95–105.

"Halos – Contents". Atmospheric Optics. www.atoptics.co.uk/halo/contents.htm (accessed 28 January 2020).

Haraway, D. J. 1988. "Situated knowledges: The science question in feminism and the privilege of partial perspective". *Feminist Studies* 14: 575–599.

Leavy, P. 2009. *Method Meets Art: Arts-Based Research Practice*. New York: Guildford Press.

Lyotard, J-F. 1984. *The Postmodern Condition: A Report on Knowledge*. Translated by G. Bennington and B. Massumi. Minneapolis: University of Minnesota Press.

Lyotard, J-F. 1992. "Answering the question: What is postmodernism?" Translation by R. Durand. Reprint, in *Postmodernism. A Reader*, edited by P. Waugh, 117–125. London and New York: Oxford University Press.

MacFarlane, R. 2012. "Robert MacFarlane on landscape and the human heart – IQ2 Talks". www.youtube.com/watch?v=5q1IK-O5Ypg (accessed 9 April 2018).

Poole, S. 2017. "Re/searching for 'impact'". *Journal of Work Applied Management* 9 (2): 147–158.

Solnit, R. 2014. *Wanderlust*. London: Granta.

Sullivan, G. 2005. "Introduction: Reviewing visual arts research". *Art Practice as Research. Inquiry in the Visual Arts*. Thousand Oaks: Sage.

The Shins. 2017. *Heartworm*. New York: Columbia Records.

Turner, C. 2000. "Framing the site". *Site-Specific: The Quay Thing Documented, Studies in Theatre and Performance*, Supplement 5: 24.

Walton, K. 1994. "Listening with imagination: Is music representational?" *The Journal of Aesthetics and Art Criticism* 52: 47–61.

Wylie, J. 2005. "A single day's walking: Narrating self and landscape on the south west coast path". *Transactions of the Institute of British Geographers* 30 (2): 234–247.

# PART II
# Visuality and multi-modality in ethnography

# 4

# PARTICIPANT-INDUCED ELICITATION IN DIGITAL ENVIRONMENTS

*Riitta Hänninen*

In this chapter, I discuss participant-induced elicitation interview (PIE) in the light of two fieldwork cases focusing on Finnish lifestyle blogging and older adults as ICT users. Collaboration with the people participating in the research has been an essential part of ethnography since the method was first introduced in anthropology in the first half of the 20th century. Thus, in this sense PIE is all about going back to the basics of anthropological fieldwork in contemporary digital environments. Visual orientation is an important element in many ethnographic interview techniques. Nevertheless, I argue that rather than being restricted to photography, this interview method could be further developed in a way that can better take into account the participatory aspects of ethnographic inquiry regardless of the source of elicitation. Drawing on the experiences from my two fieldwork cases, I first introduce PIE as an interview-based research method and then highlight some of the key characteristics of elicitation.

By definition, elicitation refers to a process where something, such as a response, meaning, or answer, is evoked in or drawn out from an interviewee (CD 2019). PIE is based on photo-elicitation (Collier 1957; Harper 2002), where the interviewee is asked to take photographs dealing with the topics of the research (Bignante 2010; Epstein et al. 2006). This type of idea is also included in other visual interview methods, such as autodriving (Heisley and Levy 1991; Ford et al. 2017), reflexive photography (Amerson 2014; Harrington and Lindy 1999), and the photovoice technique (Liebenberg 2018), originally deriving from photonovella (Wang and Burris 1994). Alternatively, the researcher can also use photographs taken by someone else than the interviewee as a starting point for elicitation (Padgett et al. 2013; Chiozzi 1989). Photography has also been employed in other visual methods such as photo interview and photo-diary (Hurworth et al. 2005). All the interview methods or techniques mentioned above share two distinctive characteristics in the context of PIE: they are based on visual material either produced by the interviewee or introduced by the researcher, and they rely on the collaboration between the researcher and the person participating in the research.

The main idea of PIE is that, in addition to photography, there are in fact various other "sources" or points or reference available for elicitation (cf. Harper 2002), including film (Skjælaaen et al. 2018; Gross and Levenson 1995), drawings and artwork (Hogan 2015; Bagnoli 2009), 3D objects in public displays (Du et al. 2018), visually impaired people "watching" or listening to television (Dim et al. 2016), and, as in the two cases examined in this chapter, mobile phones (Symons Downs 2018; Kaufmann 2018) and other digital devices such as tablets, laptops, smart televisions, and even blog posts consisting of both text and visual materials (Hänninen 2018). In this light, I argue that almost anything can serve as a point of reference for PIE just as long as it conveys meaning and relevance to the person participating in the research under the premises of the study in question.

In terms of interviewees taking photographs themselves or just looking at photographs taken by someone else, both of my fieldwork experiences lie between these two approaches. In the case of lifestyle blogging, the photographs included in the blog posts were only part of the source of elicitation as text, too, plays a significant role in blogging. Most importantly, however, the blog posts were originally compiled by the bloggers, not as methodological tools, but for an entirely different purpose separate from the aims of the research. In this sense, the photographs and texts produced by bloggers resemble photo interview and photo-diary rather than the autodriving or photovoice techniques. Furthermore, in the case of older adults' everyday lives and digital technology, PIE was designed to address the actual use of various ICTs by looking into the devices and applications utilized by the interviewees and documenting this use through taking photographs. Thus, I argue that it is more accurate to describe these fields of research in terms of PIE than for example photo-elicitation or other visually oriented research methods.

The central idea of PIE as participant-induced elicitation is based on the active agency of the person collaborating with the researcher. Under the premises of the research, the interviewee creates something subjective and personal that can be further examined and developed together with the researcher (Harper 2002). Alternatively, it is also possible to use something already created by the person participating in the interview, or to come up with something entirely new and relevant in the context of a given fieldwork. While the source or technique utilized in elicitation may vary, it is the focus of the analysis and the idiosyncrasies of the object of research that should determine the method (Hänninen 2012).

Many previous studies in the context of PIE and other related research methods often address some kind of element of power or a question of social inequality. While PIE is well-suited to various kinds of social and cultural phenomena, it is especially useful in research associated with marginal groups or topics that are hidden from or transcend the Western conceptions of reality and thought (Milne and Muir 2019). In this sense, PIE shares an affinity with community-based participatory action research (PAR) in emphasizing the collaborative aspects of elicitation techniques (Liebenberg 2018). PIE can also be useful in digital and virtual contexts as it has the capacity to overcome many of the boundaries associated with for example online and offline environments (Hänninen 2018).

## PIE in the blogosphere – the case of Finnish lifestyle bloggers

My research on the relationship between lifestyle bloggers and their readers took place within the Finnish blogosphere in autumn 2014 (interviewing eight bloggers), autumn 2015 (interviewing three bloggers), and autumn 2017 (interviewing 14 bloggers). The research data was based on extended online observation and a total of 25 interviews, including 23 women and two male bloggers aged between 18 and 50. Because the vast majority of lifestyle bloggers have traditionally been women, the interview data mainly consisted of female bloggers. The main language in the blogs Finnish, although in some instances the bloggers were also using English and Swedish, which is the second official language of Finland. There were also several expatriates among the interviewees, who did not physically live in Finland, but who blogged mainly in Finnish and/or under Finnish blog portals. (See also Hänninen 2018.)

In the case of lifestyle blogging, choosing elicitation (or blog elicitation interview (BEI), as I called it in this context instead of PIE), which is a more general term referring to the participatory aspects of elicitation, was based on necessity. Fairly soon after conducting the first couple of interviews in 2014, I discovered that, while the research data produced through traditional thematic interview was informative enough, there was something missing from it. Although the bloggers themselves did their best to explain their trade to me, the interpretative distance remained too great and "the ontology of the blogosphere", by which I refer to the digital and virtual qualities of blogging, was not truly reflected in the interviews.

I invited the interviewees to choose two to four blog posts that they considered important for themselves as lifestyle bloggers and asked them to contemplate on what these blog posts were all about and why they had chosen these particular posts for our discussion (Hänninen 2018). While the majority of the bloggers were happy to do this, and some of them even emailed me a list of their blog posts of choice so that I could get acquainted with them before our interview session, there were a handful of interviewees who did not find this kind of "pre-assignment" particularly engaging. Some of them did not understand what they were supposed to do, while others could not find the time in their schedules to choose blog posts from their extensive archives. However, in practice this did not pose a big problem, as we could carry out this part of the interview together usually at the beginning of each elicitation interview and work our way from there. In fact, even the majority of bloggers who had chosen their favourite blog posts beforehand found more examples as the interview proceeded and thus added new material to their original lists.

The main problem with using traditional thematic interview in the context of lifestyle blogging, which lies between online and offline environments, seemed to boil down to the multimodality of lifestyle blogging as a social media phenomenon. With the help of traditional thematic interview, it was difficult to grasp all the idiosyncrasies of the online environment through only talking about them without any practical reference to the blogosphere itself. PIE provided here the necessary ethnographic twist to overcome this problem and to carry out the fieldwork using a research method that was better equipped to deal with multimodality. It was also apparent that the fluctuating boundary between the online and offline spheres of social reality needed further methodological support to be better taken into account in the context of lifestyle blogging.

## Older adults using digital technology

The fieldwork focusing on older adults and the role of digital technology in their everyday lives produced 22 elicitation interviews, including one interview conducted with an elderly couple. The data gathering took place in Central Finland in November and December 2018, and the age of the interviewees ranged between 57 and 89. Fourteen of the older adults participating in the research were female and nine were male. In this fieldwork, the purpose of PIE was again to deepen the traditional thematic interview in order to gain a better understanding on older adults' views regarding digital technology in their everyday lives and to see first-hand how they actually used or did not use digital technology on a daily basis.

The older adults were asked to contemplate on their use of digital technology and to come up with two to four examples highlighting their personal relationship with ICTs. The general reception towards this pre-assignment was ambivalent. While approximately half of the participants did choose some examples to cater for the research, it became apparent that the concept of digital technology was fluid among the older adults especially in terms of how they defined themselves as ICT users. Some regarded themselves as experienced and confident with digital technology, while others insisted that they knew almost nothing about it. They were self-conscious about anything to do with digital technology, including the pre-assignment.

In this context, PIE provided an easy and low-maintenance access to the actual use of devices ranging from ordinary mobile phones to smartphones, tablet computers, laptops, and smart televisions, and allowed me and my colleague[1] assisting me with the fieldwork to become familiar with the pros and cons involved with ICTs in practice. Of course, not all the older adults participating in the research had smartphones at their disposal or used all the devices mentioned above. However, this did not pose a problem during the fieldwork as PIE could be adjusted according to the personal preferences of the interviewee.

## Getting into the field – breaking the ice

PIE can lower the threshold to discuss one's daily life and thus enhance the dialogue between the researcher and the person participating in the research by serving as an icebreaker at the beginning of the interview (Kaufmann 2018; Pink et al. 2016; Harper 2002). However, there are multiple reasons why establishing a safe, confidential, and inspiring atmosphere, which can be regarded as the basic elements of a successful interview, can at times prove difficult. For example, the interviewee can be confused about his or her role in the research, or as in Hanna's case in the lifestyle blogging study, the reason was that she felt that she had not been "a very good blogger" as she had not been posting all that much for a while:

I: [...] I just haven't had the time although I would've liked to.
R: That's okay. We can just pick a post at random. Let's take this one from your first year [of blogging].
I: Oh, that one, that's just one of those. There's really nothing to it. [...] I blogged a lot that year, 355 blog posts so nearly every day.
R: Okay, let's take another one. How about this post [a photo challenge]? This looks interesting.
I: That's actually a series of posts that has been circulating around [the blogosphere]. I've been doing it for the past five years. Every month, on the 14th of the month, I take a picture of the same place at the same time and then post it online. It's a kind of collage on how the world has changed between the photos. I've been sending this challenge to other bloggers and that's why it [the blog post] has spread around [the social media]. I now notice that it's my sixth year starting.

The role of PIE as an icebreaker is based on its emphasis on creating trust in the researcher (Hurworth et al. 2005) as well as on the personal and subjective interests of the interviewee. In Hanna's case, discussing the photographs she had taken over the past five years provided the interviewee with a positive point of reference as a lifestyle blogger and made her feel comfortable during the interview. It was also common among both lifestyle bloggers and older adults using digital technology that PIE evoked enthusiasm in the interviewees to show me around in their "digital everyday lives". In the context of lifestyle blogging, this proved to be a very valuable aspect as it opened up a possibility to become familiar with the strong multimodal side of lifestyle blogging and to visit all the other platforms actively managed by the bloggers in social media, ranging from the comment fields of the blogs to Facebook, Instagram, YouTube, and Snapchat. PIE also highlighted the often-blurred line between online and offline worlds in social media (which will be discussed further in the next subchapter) and promoted discussion on, for example, the privacy issues related to the Internet.

Elicitation provides interviewees with an important starting point, or a visual reference (Wiles et al. 2013) while thinking back about their everyday lives (Hänninen 2018; Aroldi and Vittadini 2015). As Bukowski and Buetow (2011;

Padgett et al. 2013) argue, photographs can make the invisible visible by evoking feelings, memories, and thoughts that require verbalization to be accessible to the researcher. Visual stimuli can also enhance sensory awareness and reinforce reflexivity (Harris and Guillemin 2012). Blogs often consist of all the blog posts published by the blogger, which can sometimes stretch back over ten years or more, depending on the blogging history of a given blogger. The first fieldwork also highlights the comparative attributes of PIE by focusing the discussion on the temporal aspects of lifestyle blogging – what blogging used to be in the early years of the trade over ten years ago in comparison with contemporary social media. It also underlines the changes that have occurred in the blogosphere in recent years, such as commercialization, and the ways these transitions have affected bloggers as social media influencers.

Getting the chance to be shown around in a blog thanks to elicitation deepens the understanding provided by thematic interview. At the same time, however, PIE caters to another practical problem evident especially in the case of older adults as ICT users. During our fieldwork, I noticed that it was not always easy for the senior people to grasp what was meant by digital technology in general. This did not mean that they would have had insufficient knowledge regarding ICTs, or that we as researchers would have been interested in ranking the interviewees in terms of their dexterity in digital technology. Instead, some of the senior persons participating in the research were concerned about whether they knew enough to be eligible for the interviews in the first place. The function served by PIE in these kinds of situations was firstly to emphasize the subjective stance of the fieldwork and focus on the ways the interviewees themselves acted as ICT users in their everyday lives. This was possible by looking into the devices and applications the older adults used on a daily basis together with them. Secondly, it was also evident that PIE enhanced the thematic interviews by giving the interviewees a tool to remember and review all the mobile applications at their disposal, as shown in Matilda's, 64, interview account:

R: We've already discussed some of the apps, but I can see that you have the 112 [the Finnish emergency response center] app on your phone as well.
I: Yes, it's the best. I've recommended it to everybody with a smartphone. There have been a couple of times I've had to call an ambulance to our summer cottage. They [the ambulance crew] can see from the application, or one time they all of a sudden asked me, that there was a gate there and whether they could drive straight to the yard. The first time I was just baffled about how they can see everything from it [the 112 app]. I spend a lot of time in the woods by myself [picking wild berries and mushrooms, which is a common outdoor activity in Finland], so if something should happen to me, they would find me [...]
R: [...] I can see that you have the Yle Areena [online platform for the public service media company in Finland] app here as well. [...] Do you watch television on your phone?

I: Yes, sometimes in the summer cottage, but it's so difficult that I've shared the phone's connection to the tablet, because it has a bigger screen.

In the previous citation, there are several examples of the interviewee using digital technology that she had not mentioned before, such as the 112 application I noticed on Matilda's smartphone. We also discussed watching television on the phone and sharing the Internet connection from a phone to a tablet – all new themes and digital skills evoked by PIE through remembering and remembrance (cf. Hurworth 2003). Furthermore, as Collier (1979) has pointed out, a visual source of elicitation produce more detailed information compared to, for example, traditional thematic interview, which is based solely on conversation. These so-called "verbal interviews" can also become unproductive more quickly than interviews based on PIE. The reason for this is that visual points of reference prevent difficulties associated with communication and promote fluency of dialogue between the researcher and the person participating in the study.

Discussing the devices and applications together with the interviewees opened room for fresh insight for both the researcher and the older adults participating in the research. Furthermore, as there was no observation involved in this fieldwork, the elicitation technique was the only comparative medium through which it was possible to reflect on the difference between how the older adults described their use of digital technology and the ways they actually used it. As Hurworth et al. (2005) argue, interview techniques based on elicitation promote multi-method triangulation and thus enhance the validity and reliability of the research.

## The transcendent aspects of PIE

In the context of lifestyle blogging, one of my main research questions focused on understanding the role of lifestyle blogging in the everyday lives of the bloggers. I was interested in finding out what kinds of boundaries existed between online and offline environments and discovered through PIE that, rather than describing the boundaries as such, I should instead focus on the reasons why, in fact, they exist in the contemporary blogosphere. If the online world is as discernible an element of everyday life as Hine (2015) quite accurately points out, why is it important for lifestyle bloggers to maintain a divide between the offline and online environments?

One explanation (Long and Wilhoit 2018; Abidin 2014) emphasizes the significance of privacy and safety issues in the expanding blogosphere. As lifestyle blogging has grown from a personal, diary-like hobby into a multi-million advertising business, the number of readers in contemporary lifestyle blogs, too, have increased (Hänninen 2015). Making one's everyday life less open to scrutiny and drawing a line between online and offline and consequently public and private has become, as Ellen points out in her interview account, an indispensable part of the trade:

> When your children grow older and are no longer babies, you start to think whether you can blog about somebody else's life. [...] My relatives of course want to know how the kids are doing, but I've noticed in other blogs as well that children's faces are not shown in the photos anymore. Instead, the pictures are turning unidentifiable.

In Ellen's interview, it was the blurred faces of her children, that evoked the discussion on the boundaries between public and private. The unidentifiable faces provided a visual anomaly that was irregular enough in comparison with other photographs without the blurring effect to stand out as something worth discussing in the context of the interview. Thus, PIE had the ability to highlight the often-artificial boundaries between the online and offline spheres of everyday life and even transcend them (Hänninen 2018; Harris 2008; Jenkings et al. 2008). In the context of older adults, dealing with the embeddedness of daily ICT use was often associated with previously discussed issues such as remembering and remembrance, but also with "transcending the mundane" or self-evident aspects of digital technology.

Furthermore, in the case of lifestyle blogging, PIE played an important role in supporting the multi-sited aspects of the ethnographic field of research by giving the researcher access to the other social media platforms used by the lifestyle bloggers. Being shown around in the blog of an interviewee held an important temporal aspect to it as it made it possible to dive into the person's blogging archives and become familiar with their blogging history. The method deepened my understanding of lifestyle blogging as a whole through highlighting the integration of social media platforms made use of and developed by bloggers on a daily basis.

In the research on older adults using ICTs, it was important to be able to see first-hand what kinds of devices were used and to flexibly discuss all kinds of applications, platforms, and digital services relevant to the interviewees. Using mobile or smartphones, tablet computers, and laptops as a starting point was easy, because these devices were already "there": in the hand of the senior person answering the front door, on the kitchen table at their home, or ringing in their coat pocket if we met in a café for the interview. Even in cases where the senior person did not find him/herself particularly skilful with ICTs or did not own a smartphone, for example, the devices they did use acted as icebreakers informing me as a researcher about the difficulties, fears, and concerns related to digital technology.

As Harper (2002) points out, it is not necessary to restrict the elicitation-based interview method to professional or academic photography, art photographs, or photographs taken by the person participating in the research. The form of the visual representation is secondary to the relationship between the source of PIE and the cultural and social significance it bestows upon the phenomenon under study (Harper 2001; Chiozzi 1989). Although PIE is predominantly a visual research method, the main focus of the technique lies in the participative collaboration between the researcher and the interviewee. In fact, it can be argued that PIE is capable of transcending the visual by transforming photographs and other similar material into self-reflective discussion and text (Hurworth 2003).

## Creating something new through collaboration

Unlike community-based participatory action research (PAR), which seeks empowerment on a communal level (Liebenberg 2018; Wang and Burris 1997), PIE focuses on individualized interviews by looking at visual objects of shared interest (Padgett et al. 2013; Lapenta 2011; Harper 2002). The main idea of PIE draws on the active agency of the person collaborating with the researcher. Although the source of the elicitation can vary, the participatory aspect of PIE remains the same: something new is created through the collaboration between the researcher and the person participating in the research for the purposes of the study.

PIE is a useful interview technique especially because it resembles the practices of social (and digital) sharing. It allows the interviewer and interviewees to examine and process the phenomena or topic of research together and reach a negotiated interpretation (Hurworth et al. 2005). The interviewee is encouraged to challenge the preconceptions of the interviewer, provide unprecedented perspectives to the discussion, and experiment with different kinds of ideas. In practice, this means that the focus of the method is in the ethnographic research tradition based on "the native's point of view" (Geertz 1973) rather than being driven by *a priori* theory or a concept.

Although PIE involves a very different take on the community empowerment aspect of PAR, PIE, too, can make an impact among the people participating in the research through increasing self-reflection. In the case of the older adults and digital technology, some of the interviewees found out that they could use WhatsApp for other purposes than only communicating with their family members and decided to establish new groups based on their hobbies and other interests. Similarly, one of the lifestyle bloggers picked up the methodological idea of choosing blog posts that have been important to her over the years and wrote a lengthy post about it to her readers. The interviewees were not encouraged or asked to do so, but they wanted to act upon the self-reflexive process initiated by their participation in the research project.

In methodological terms, PIE is often, although not necessarily, accompanied with traditional thematic interview. In this context, the function of PIE is to extend the scope of inquiry and to deepen the understanding regarding the topic of research through collaboration with the interviewee. In the two fieldwork cases discussed in this chapter, the elicitation usually took place at the beginning of the interview, but it can be carried out at any stage of the discussion. The reason for this kind of arrangement was that PIE is well suited for breaking the ice, and it often got the conversation going before I had the opportunity to ask any questions. The traditional list of semi-structured questions characteristic to thematic interview can at first seem opposite to the more visually oriented and collaborative PIE. On the contrary, however, it also serves an important function in the process as it provides the interview with an overall structure by keeping the researcher in check of the things that were initially the focus of the study and the new ideas and perspectives brought into play by the person participating in the research.

PIE has a tendency to produce longer and more detailed interviews in comparison with other types of techniques that are not based on a visual reference (Hurworth et al. 2005; Collier 1979). In the context of lifestyle blogging, the difference between the eight thematic interviews I conducted at the first stages of my fieldwork and PIE was very clear. The things that I found lacking in the thematic interviews were associated especially with the need of a concrete point of reference – both visual and otherwise – to the actual practices involved with lifestyle blogging. The bloggers participating in the research were struggling to find a personal perspective to their trade and the role it played in their everyday lives. Furthermore, as the blogs were left in the background of our discussions, the three-way connection between the researcher, the blogger, and blogging weakened, which led to a sense of "interpretative distance" during the first steps of the fieldwork. Once the missing point of reference was established by making blog posts the basis of the interviews, it became easier for the bloggers to identify themselves with the topic of the research. The need for a collaborative element that would break the ice and help the interviewees to make the topic of the research their own was also evident among the elderly ICT users, who found PIE useful especially as a tool for remembering and remembrance.

## Conclusions

In anthropological terms, the main contribution of PIE to ethnography is that it reintroduces the idea of collaboration into fieldwork by tapping into the participatory aspects of the interview method and using collaboration simultaneously to both broaden and deepen the scope of ethnographic inquiry. In this chapter, I have argued that PIE can, in fact, be based on various other sources of elicitation than only photographs. The main idea of the method is not related to photography as such, but rather the active participation of the interviewee and his or her collaboration with the researcher. Thus, the cultural and social significance of the object that is applied as a starting point of PIE outweigh the form of the source of elicitation, be it visual or otherwise.

Nevertheless, it is clear that PIE is especially suitable to deal with visual sources of elicitation characteristic to social media. In this context, I argue that discussing pictures related to, for example, blog posts can in fact transcend the visual realm of social reality and transform photographs into a textual format. PIE cannot replace traditional visual analysis, but it provides an alternative to it by focusing on the interpretations and meanings evoked by the visual research material. Transcendence is also at play in contexts where PIE, following the daily lives and experiences of the people participating in the research, moves across the often-arbitrary boundaries between the offline and online environments characteristic to both lifestyle blogging and older adults using ICTs.

PIE can serve as an icebreaker in situations where getting into the field has proved difficult through focusing on the personal life of the interviewee. It has the capacity to establish trust in a new situation, where it supports the needs of collaboration. PIE also serves a very specific sensitizing function in interviews. Similarly to the idea of sensitizing concepts (Faulkner 2009), where the researcher introduces in the interview concepts that she has adopted from the persons participating in the research, elicitation creates a common ground between the researcher and the interviewee by emphasizing the significance of the interviewee's everyday life practices as a starting point of discussion. PIE also contributes to remembering things better either by recalling things as opposed to forgetting, or in more comprehensive terms, by evoking memories from the past. In this sense, it can both broaden and deepen the scope of inquiry and open up new perspectives beyond the initial focus of the study.

PIE is an intuitive research method, which makes it approachable to the person participating in the research. In the context of lifestyle blogging, this was reflected especially in the cases where the bloggers were showing me around in their blogs while at the same time discussing the significance of blogging in their everyday lives. Similarly, among the older adults using digital technology, it was not the device, such as a mobile phone or a laptop, in itself that proved important during the course of the interviews, but rather the personal lives of the interviewees opening up through the devices. In this sense, I argue that PIE resembles social and digital sharing, which allows the researcher and the person participating in the research to explore the topic of the research together in dialogue.

## Note

1 I wish to thank research assistant Raija Luostari for her help while organizing and implementing our fieldwork from plan to practice. I also thank adjunct professors Helena Hirvonen, Sakari Taipale, and Mia Tammelin and PhD students Antti Hämäläinen and Joonas Karhinen from the Centre of Excellence in Research on Ageing and Care (CoE AgeCare), Department of Social Sciences and Philosophy, University of Jyväskylä, for their invaluable insight while planning the fieldwork.

## References

Abidin, C. 2014. "Privacy for profit: Commodifying privacy in lifestyle blogging". Selected Papers of Internet Research 15. The 15th Annual Meeting of the Association of Internet Researchers. http://spir.aoir.org/index.php/spir/article/view/918

Amerson, R. 2014. "Reflexive photography: An alternative method for documenting the learning process of cultural competence". *Journal of Transcultural Nursing* 25 (2): 202–210.

Aroldi, P., and N. Vittadini. 2015. "Audiences as socio-technical actors: The 'styles' of social network site users". In *Revitalising Audience Research. Innovation in European Audience Research*, 195–215, edited by F. Zeller, C. Ponte, and B. O'Neill. New York Routledge.

Bagnoli, A. 2009. "Beyond the standard interview: The use of graphic elicitation and arts-based methods". *Qualitative Research* 9 (5): 547–570.

Bignante, E. 2010. "The use of photo-elicitation in field research. Exploring Maasai representations and use of natural resources". *EchoGéo* 11. https://echogeo.revues.org/11622

Bukowski, K., and Buetow, S. 2011. "Making the invisible visible: A photovoice exploration of homeless women's health and lives in Central Auckland". *Social Science & Medicine* (72): 739–746. doi:10.1016/j.socscimed.2010.11.029

CD (Cambridge Dictionary). 2019. "Elicitation". https://dictionary.cambridge.org/dictionary/english/elicit

Chiozzi, P. 1989. "Photography and anthropological research: three case studies". *Visual Sociology* (42): 43–50.

Collier, J. 1957. "Photography in anthropology: A report on two experiments". *American Anthropologist* (59): 843–859.

Collier, J. 1979. "Visual anthropology". In *Images of Information. Still Photography in Social Sciences*, 271–282, edited by J. Wagner. Beverly Hills, California: Sage.

Dim, N. K., C. Silpasuwanchai, S. Sarcar, and X. Ren. 2016. "Designing mid-air TV gestures for blind people using user- and choice-based elicitation approaches". DIS 2016, June 4–8, 2016, Brisbane, Australia. doi:10.1145/2901790.2901834

Du, G., A. Dagbelo, C. Kray, and M. Painho. 2018. "Gestural interaction with 3d objects shown on public displays: An elicitation study". *Interaction Design and Architecture(s) Journal* (38): 184–202.

Epstein, I., B. Stevens, P. McKeever, and S. Baruchel. 2006. "Photo elicitation interview (PEI): Using photos to elicit children's perspectives". *International Journal of Qualitative Methods* 5 (3): 1–11.

Ford, K., L. Bray, T. Water, A. Dickinson, J. Arnott, and B. Carter. 2017. "Auto-driven photo elicitation interviews in research with children: Ethical and practical considerations". *Comprehensive Child and Adolescent Nursing*, 40 (2): 111–125.

Faulkner, R. 2009. "Improvising on sensitizing concepts". In *Ethnographies Revisited: Conceptual Reflections from the Field*, 79–91, edited by A. Puddephatt, W. Shaffir, and S. Kleinknecht. New York: Routledge.

Geertz, C. 1973. *Local Knowledge: Further Essays in Interpretive Anthropology*. New York: Basic Books.

Gross, J., and R. Levenson. 1995. "Emotion elicitation using films". *Cognition and Emotion* 9 (1): 87–108.

Harper, D. 2001. *Changing Works: Visions of a Lost Agriculture*. Chicago: University of Chicago Press.

Harper, D. 2002. "Talking about pictures – a case for photo-elicitation". *Visual Studies* 17 (1): 13–26.

Harrington, C., and I. Lindy. 1999. "The use of reflexive photography in the study of the freshman year experience". *Journal of College Student Retention* 1 (1): 13–22.

Harris, A. 2008. "Young women, late modern politics, and the participatory possibilities of online cultures". *Journal of Youth Studies* 11 (5): 481–495.

Harris, A., and M. Guillemin. 2012. "Developing sensory awareness in qualitative interviewing: A portal into the otherwise unexplored". *Qualitative Health Research* 22 (5): 689–699.

Heisley, D., and S. Levy. 1991. "Autodriving: A photoelicitation technique". *Journal of Consumer Research* (18): 257–272.

Hine, C. 2015. *Ethnography for the Internet Embedded, Embodied and Everyday*. London: Bloomsbury.
Hurworth, R. 2003. "Photo-interviewing for research". *Social Research UPDATE* 40. http://sru.soc.surrey.ac.uk/SRU40.PDF
Hurworth, R., E. Clark, J. Martin, and S. Thomsen. 2005. "The use of photo-interviewing: three examples from health evaluation and research". *Evaluation Journal of Australasia* 4 (1–2): 52–62.
Hogan, S. 2015. "Mothers make art: Using participatory art to explore the transition to motherhood". *Journal of Applied Arts & Health* 6 (1): 23–32.
Hänninen, R. 2018. "On the dark side of lifestyle blogging – the case of negative anonyms". *WiderScreen* 3. http://widerscreen.fi/numerot/2018-3/on-the-dark-side-of-lifestyle-blogging-the-case-of-negative-anonyms/
Hänninen, R. 2015. "'Is this an advertisement or a personal account?' – commercialisation of lifestyle blogs in Finland". *Ethnologia Fennica* (42): 54–69.
Hänninen, R. 2012. *Puuterilumen lumo. Tutkimus lumilautailukulttuurista*. Jyväskylä Studies in Humanities 191. Jyväskylä: University of Jyväskylä.
Jenkings, N., R. Woodward, and T. Winter. 2008. "The emergent production of analysis in photo elicitation: Pictures of military identity". *Forum: Qualitative Social Research* 9 (3). http://nbn-resolving.de/urn:nbn:de:0114-fqs0803309
Kaufmann, K. 2018: "The smartphone as a snapshot of its use: Mobile media elicitation in qualitative interviews". *Mobile Media & Communication* 6 (2): 233–246.
Lapenta, F. 2011. "Some theoretical and methodological views of photo-elicitation". In *Sage Handbook of Visual Research Methods*, 201–213, edited by E. Margolis and L. Pauwells. Thousand Oaks: Sage.
Liebenberg, L. 2018. "Thinking critically about photovoice: Achieving empowerment and social change". *International Journal of Qualitative Methods* (17): 1–9. doi:10.1177/1609406918757631
Long, Z., and E. Wilhoit. 2018. "Disciplined freedom, branded authenticity, and dependable independence: How tensions enact flexibility in lifestyle blogging careers". *Journal of Applied Communication Research* 46 (3): 368–387.
Milne, E-J., and R. Muir. 2019. "Photovoice: A critical introduction". In *The SAGE Handbook of Visual Research Methods*, 282–296, edited by L. Pauwells and D. Mannay. London: Sage.
Padgett, D., B. Smith, K-S. Derejko, B. Henwood, and E. Tiderington. 2013. "A picture is worth …? Photo elicitation interviewing with formerly homeless adults". *Qualitative Health Research* 23 (11): 1435–1444.
Pink, S., H. Horst, J. Postill, and L. Hjorth. 2016. *Digital Ethnography: Principles and Practice*. London: Sage.
Skjælaaen, G., A. Lindseth Bygdås, and A. Landsverk Hagen. 2018. "Visual inquiry: Exploring embodied organizational practices by collaborative film-elicitation". *Journal of Management Inquiry* 1–17. doi:10.1177/1056492618778138
Symons Downs, D. 2019. "Beliefs about using smartphones for health behavior change: An elicitation study with overweight and obese rural women". *Journal of Technology in Behavioral Science* 4 (1): 33–41.
Wang, C., and M. A. Burris. 1994. "Empowerment through photo novella: Portraits of participation". *Health Education Quarterly* 21 (2): 171–186.
Wiles, R., A. Bengry-Howell, G. Crow, and M. Nind. 2013. "But is it innovation?: The development of novel methodological approaches in qualitative research". *Methodological Innovations Online* 8, 18–33.

# 5

# ETHICAL CHALLENGES OF USING VIDEO FOR QUALITATIVE RESEARCH AND ETHNOGRAPHY

State of the art and guidelines

*Marina Everri, Maxi Heitmayer, Paulius Yamin-Slotkus, and Saadi Lahlou*

## Introduction

Visual methods have been essential in ethnography from the start: the iconic ethnographer (or anthropologist) is pictured equipped with cameras and a notebook full of drawings. "Visual" refers to diverse methods of investigations based on the collection, analysis, dissemination of still (photography, drawings, paintings, etc.) or moving images (film, live performance) often associated with audio (e.g. video). But compared to the 16mm B&W camera used in the seminal "Cinéma Vérité" of ethnographer Jean Rouch and sociologist Edgar Morin (Rouch and Morin 1961), which renewed the concept of "documentary", the increased affordability of high-quality equipment and the superior quality of video data compared to other forms of recording brought a "visual turn" (Rose 2014) in many social sciences. Additionally, the rich, visually appealing and seductive nature of video-based data can convey a strong sense of direct experience with the phenomena studied (Pea 1999). Therefore, research relying on visual methods as well as ethnography techniques based on video recordings have steadily increased over the last decade (Gubrium and Harper 2013; Pink et al. 2016). This raises new ethical challenges. Images pose specific ethical issues for research participants because they afford physical recognition of persons, spaces and places, and give the impression of an "objective depiction of reality" (de Laat 2004). Videos can provide confidential information on participants' habits and behaviours. The audio embedded in images puts participants' privacy at risk.

The issue is the following: techniques which aim at depicting or understanding *generic* aspects of behaviour for scientific purposes (where specific identity does not matter) nevertheless document behaviours on specific *identifiable* individuals (therefore making these specific individuals *publicly* accountable for their behaviour). This problem of course applies to many types of data in social science (or medicine), but the visual nature of the data makes anonymization especially challenging. As we discuss below, current guidelines, inspired by medicine, focus on anonymization – which may work for physiology but not for social behaviour – rather than on the actual problem which is the *potential impact of public disclosure of personal behaviour*.

Interestingly, the majority of ethical guidelines do not make specific distinctions between photographs and videos – most regulations apply to both. Therefore, we maintain here the usage of the term "visual" as we discuss the literature on the topic; we will then introduce specifications when referring to ethical issues pertaining to video.

This contribution proposes a comprehensive and consistent point of reference for unified guidelines on the ethical conduct of video-ethnography and qualitative research designs based on video data. The chapter includes four main sections. The first provides a systematic review of current research ethics guidelines to collect visual data with different populations (e.g., adults and children), institutions, and informal settings. The second highlights the main challenges and gaps concerned with a) researcher-researched rapport, b) informed consent, and c) participants' rights (anonymity, confidentiality, data ownership, and release). The third tackles prospective solutions including setting up the research in a way that fosters ethical behaviours by design. It is illustrated with exemplary cases. The fourth provides practical advice for an "ethical twist" towards participants on ethnographic visual research methods.

## Ethnography and visual research ethics guidelines: state of the art

We carried out a systematic analysis of the literature to get a broad overview of ethical issues in relation to visual methods. Three databases (Scopus, Web of Science, Ebsco) were searched independently with the following combination of keywords: video + ethnography + ethic*; visual ethnography + ethic*; video research + ethic*. This provided 54 references, including journal articles, handbooks, and book chapters; four in which ethics was peripheral were deleted. Current regulations and guidelines on visual research were found across different disciplines and institutional boards both in academic and non-academic institutions.

While most ethical issues regarding textual material can be solved using abbreviations, initials, pseudonyms, etc., scientific and institutional boards are still struggling with visual techniques. Very few publications (e.g. Kelly et al. 2013; Wiles et al. 2008) provided a comprehensive account of ethical issues in visual research, for example concerning privacy, researcher-participant rapport, and informed consent. The majority tackled methodological (18 references) and health issues (13 references), the latter comprising research carried out in psychotherapy, clinical psychology, medicine and nursing. Resources on health issues focused on sensitive environments, such as emergency interventions or patients with dementia. Four of them (Schuck and Kearney 2006; Winckler 2014; Derry et al. 2010; Hackling 2013) discussed visual methods and ethical issues in education; six addressed children (Aarsand 2016; Aarsand and Forsberg 2010; Robson 2011; Flewitt 2005; Heath, Hindmarsh, and Luff 2010; Mudaly 2015). In the latter case, they question the role of parents and guardians for informed consent, but do not mention informed assent for children. Lastly, a few papers connected visual ethics to the specific realms of anthropology (four: Eglinton 2013; de Laat 2004; Pope, De Luca, and Tolich 2013; Pink 2011) and sociology (four: Milne, Mitchell, and de Lange 2012; Prosser, Clark, and Wiles 2008; Salmons 2015; Papademas 2004).

The guidelines produced by scientific boards dwell on issues similar to scientific publications. The Association of Internet Researchers (Markham and Buchanan 2012), the American Anthropological Association (2001), the Association of Social Anthropologists of the UK (2011), the British Sociological Society (2017), or the International Visual Sociology Association (Papademas 2009) all provided recommendations on consent and results accessibility, harm and vulnerability, data management, and anonymity and confidentiality with emphasis on aspects consistent with the purposes of their specific scientific community.

Universities and other research institutions, such as the British Economic and Social Research Council (ESRC), often have dedicated research ethics committees. For example, the London School of Economics has a general Research Ethics Policy and Procedures document, a Code of Research Conduct and an Ethics Code (accompanied by an ethics guidance document). Researchers must complete a Research Ethics Review Form, which is the only document explicitly mentioning visual research, linked to potential confidentiality and anonymity issues (London School of Economics and Political Science 2019).

These guidelines conform with the recent EU General Data Protection Regulation (GDPR), put into place to guarantee the *lawful, fair and transparent* collection of personalised data. GDPR does not apply to anonymised data, but it is important to note that while pseudonymisation can be sufficient to anonymise certain types of data, the situation with visual data is more complicated. For example, a video showing a participant commuting to work, even with faces blurred, still shows their home and the work address, which can be identifiers.

In summary, the literature on research ethics seems to converge on general ethics guidelines concerned with participant data protection. Some scientific boards provide regulations on visual research, however without making specific reference to the collection, analysis, treatment and protection of *video data* as well as to the peculiarities of ethnographic research.

## From visual to video-research: critical aspects and literature gaps when using video

We found ample criticism both for research institutions and ethics boards in almost every article we surveyed. The rigidity of formal ethics processes in academic institutions, by narrowly focusing on what regulation will allow (Wiles, Coffey, and Robinson 2010, 21) neglects crucial aspects embedded in qualitative and ethnographic inquiry. These are: the characteristics of *researcher-researched rapport*; procedures for achieving truly *informed consent*; the acknowledgement of *participants' rights*, namely researchers' measures taken to guarantee participants' anonymity, confidentiality, and data ownership and release. Across these aspects, the social and cultural particularities of research contexts play a key role and must be assessed and negotiated beforehand by researchers. These differences might determine, for example, the appropriateness of using video and photography techniques (Kelly et al. 2013), the general understanding that participants have of privacy, consent and data ownership, and what constitutes sensitive activities or images (Cox et al. 2014). For example, while filming breakfast is usually innocuous, documenting sexual practices may not be. Ethical guidelines rarely focus on the actual risk assessment of the disclosure, making it difficult if not impossible to record a football match played by children, while allowing recording of an identifiable adult describing or performing any behaviour as long as an "informed" consent is signed. Overall, we found consensus among social scientists that the "biomedical model", which has served as the basis for ethical guidelines for the social sciences, is deficient when applied to visual research, and ethnographic research more broadly (Atkinson 2009).

## Researcher-researched rapport

There is a power imbalance between researchers and participants, related to status, knowledge, and nature of the relationship in which both parties are engaged (Carroll 2009). During the process of ethnographic data collection, however, the boundaries become "fuzzy" (Gubrium, Hill, and Flicker 2014). Many researchers point out that it becomes difficult to anticipate ethical issues with such a flexible researcher-researched relationship, making reflexive practice an ongoing concern throughout the research process (e.g. Blazek and Hraňová 2012; Cox et al. 2014). Reflexivity must not mean merely going beyond "deploying the method" (Carroll and Mesman 2018, 1151) and reflecting on one's practice as a researcher, but also being continuously aware of, and questioning the prescribed roles of *researcher* and *researched*, and their relationship. In consequence, taking the collected video as depicting a "hard reality" cannot be sufficient for truly reflexive practice; participants' voices must also be included during the interpretation of the data, creating a *third voice*, "which combines the view of the researcher and the researched" (Ruby 1991, 62).

## Informed consent

Pre-formatted checklists distributed by institutional ethics boards, that usually are to be filled out prior to data collection, neither enable researchers to react adequately to issues arising during research, nor do they enable ethics boards to ensure adherence to ethical standards (e.g., Cox et al. 2014; Gubrium, Hill, and Flicker 2014). Rapidly progressing technologies in video-ethnographic research further complicate this issue: "many visual dilemmas emerge in specific contexts and cannot be resolved by appeal to higher principles and codes" (Clark, Prosser, and Wiles 2010, 90).

Achieving truly informed consent with checklists and by handing out paper forms prior to data collection, which is the standard procedure for most academic institutions (e.g. Gubrium, Hill, and Flicker 2014; Lenette et al. 2018), is not possible. In practice, evaluating whether the outcome potentially discloses things detrimental to participants is often difficult to assess before the visual material is presented in the results; at that stage sensible editing can make the material innocuous to individual participants; conversely awkward presentation can make innocuous material harmful.

In practice it is almost impossible to obtain informed consent from everyone that is captured in the video. Consider filming in shopping centres, airports or in the streets. Even providing information about the research project to those entering the video recorded place or space (a common practice in video-research) is often impracticable in natural contexts (Aarsand 2016). Moreover, in most ethnographic investigations, the researcher's level of control can be limited or voluntarily transferred to participants. For instance, the SEBE (Subjective Evidence Based Ethnography) research protocol is based on first-person video recordings; participants carry out the recordings and researchers are not with them in the field, whilst available remotely (Lahlou 2017; Lahlou, Le Bellu, and Boesen-Mariani 2015). Therefore, it is not possible to know in advance the detailed contents of recordings. Furthermore, as participants can review and download their films before handing them to the researcher in SEBE (precisely to make sure they are happy with the content disclosed), they could potentially share this content to third parties. That is true for most investigations where participants collect data themselves, such as story-telling using cameras (Gubrium and Harper 2013), video-tours (Demuth and Fatigante 2012) and self-recording with wearable devices (e.g., Kelly et al. 2013).

### *Participants' rights: anonymity, confidentiality, data ownership and release*

Anonymity and confidentiality are long-established principles in social research practice (Wiles, Coffey, and Robinson 2010). However, visual material makes anonymisation problematic if not impossible (Clark, Prosser, and Wiles 2010). Furthermore, some participants might agree or want to have their personal information disclosed. Asking participants to participate in an ethnographic investigation using visual methods is "equivalent to requesting them to share with the world their insight and perspective" (Schembri and Boyle 2013, 1253).

The release of video materials is a sensitive issue: they might expose participants to stigma, discrimination, and other types of harm (Wiles et al. 2008; Gubrium,

Hill, and Flicker 2014). Particularly important are the considerations around "where, why and by whom" (Gubrium, Hill, and Flicker 2014) are visual materials released. No data is confidential *per se*: we share sensitive data about our health with our doctor, about sexual preferences with our partner, financial details with our banker and so forth (Lahlou 2008). The context of where and to whom the material is published matters. As new technologies allow to easily capture, review, interpret, and share "too much information" (Mok, Cornish, and Tarr 2015), the issues of who controls and stores the data, who is the author or owner, who decides what to share and how have become central in visual research (Schuck and Kearney 2006; Heath, Hindmarsh, and Luff 2010; Cox et al. 2014). Often participants agree to share their videos with the research team but refuse publication of identifiable material beyond that trusted community. New technologies and devices (such as smartphones and digital video) mean that participants can have more control over research materials, but it also means that they may easily view, copy and share them (Mok, Cornish, and Tarr 2015). Additionally, as hinted above, it is difficult for participants to foresee the future implications of the existence of their data and, hence, to give informed consent beforehand (Aarsand 2016; Wiles, Coffey, and Robinson 2010). Failing to appropriately negotiate and acknowledge authorship and ownership of visual data might endanger the integrity of research and the confidence of participants in it (which impacts their insights, contributions, and future willingness to take part – see Cox et al. 2014).

Additionally, in video research there is the assumption that images are objective and can accurately represent "the reality" (de Laat 2004), more than text (Schuck and Kearney 2006). This "myth of film-as-reality" (de Laat 2004, 137) in research has been questioned: images are cultural constructs, and the same videotape can create in viewers different interpretations of the situation (Liegl and Schindler 2013; Rieken and Lahlou 2010).

## Prospective solutions for video ethnography methods

The literature reviewed, beyond caveats and interdictions, provides practical advice for ethical visual research. Among these few it is agreed that "research ethics are contested, dynamic and contextual" (Prosser, Clark, and Wiles 2008, 3). Therefore, besides considering ethical regulations, it is crucial to understand the concrete situations in which ethics regulations are applied. The adoption of reflexive and collaborative approaches can serve this function (see Cox et al. 2014; Gubrium et al. 2014; Liegl and Schindler 2013; Schembri and Boyle 2013; Rose 2014).

### *Researcher-researched rapport: situatedness, reflexivity, and collaboration*

"Because ethics are so embedded in the specific research contexts in which ethnographers work, like decisions about which visual research methods to employ in a project, ethical decisions cannot be concluded until the researcher is actually in the field" (Pink 2011, 11). As a result, a continuous reflexive approach paying attention to what is ethical in the participants, not just in the researchers' culture, is necessary.

Reminding researchers to think about general ethical standards regarding, for instance, privacy, anonymity, and voluntary informed consent is, thus, only *the first step* to truly ethical research. In a second step, contextual judgement and *ongoing consent processes* as outlined by Cicourel (1964) should be accommodated for in standard research ethics procedures (e.g. Carroll and Mesman 2018; Mok et al. 2015). Researchers should plan for, and actively manage and mitigate both the physical and psychological risks that visual research creates for participants (Pope, De Luca, and Tolich 2013; Schembri and Boyle 2013). Mok and colleagues recommend that an ongoing, participatory exchange with the public around the ethicality or acceptability of novel research methods be put into place (Mok, Cornish, and Tarr 2015, 320).

Collaborative approaches include both acquiring a deep knowledge of local contexts and their intrinsic power relations (Liegl and Schindler 2013; Schembri and Boyle 2013), as well as engaging in critical dialogues with participants about potential risks and harm and how to manage them (Cox et al. 2014; Schembri and Boyle 2013). This is particularly relevant when working with vulnerable populations such as children (Mudaly 2015) or exploring illegal activities (Gubrium, Hill, and Flicker 2014).

In our view, the efficacy of video ethnography as a research method depends on establishing a relationship of trust between the participant and the researcher (Lahlou 2006; 2011). It is a necessary condition for participants to disclose their thoughts to the researcher, engage in cooperative observation, and contribute to the interpretation of data (Lahlou, Le Bellu, and Boesen-Mariani 2015). Studies using SEBE,[1] involving different participant cohorts in various settings (e.g. children and families, consumers, office workers, doctors and nurses, drivers, cooks, policemen, nuclear plant operators), consider participants as co-researchers (not "subjects") as they do not only collect the data, but also contribute to data interpretation by commenting on their own video recordings in a face to face interview with the researcher. This Replay Interview (RIW) confronts emic (informants') and etic (researchers') perspectives to find a description that is acceptable to both based on the joint review of the video evidence (Lahlou 2011). This form of democratic collaboration allows participants (of any age, gender, status) to feel empowered, and researchers to test their hypotheses and interpretations *in vivo*. While not all protocols include a phase of confronting the participants with the material and its interpretation, we suggest that discussing the (pre) final version of the visual material to be published, and its interpretation, with at least some of the participants is a major ethical safeguard. These conversations, if done in a pilot, will also inform the researcher on the *actual* ethical issues in that context, and impact the protocol.

## *Informed consent as a negotiation process*

In most cases researchers face the "impossibility of setting a-priori conditions about what participation will involve and what images might be filmed or photographed" (Wills et al. 2016, 481). There is agreement among ethnographers to consider consent as a process that requires negotiations with participants at different stages of the research. This can be done by negotiating consent prior *and* following the video recordings, or by opting for an ongoing consent negotiation to monitor whether the research is continuing to develop within the participants' expectations (Flewitt 2005). This comes with specific consent forms to be handed to participants at different times (video data collection, analysis, presentation, dissemination) (Hackling 2013; Wiles et al. 2008).

With children for whom consent from parents is mandatory, different informed consent models have been proposed. One is a two-stage consent: one for data collection (how data are collected, who collects, constraints on ultimate use) and one for the use (who will have access to which data, how, plans for data publication and destruction). The other is a graduated model providing a menu of uses to accept; for instance, viewing by the research team only, restricted sharing among research teams, presentation at professional meetings, full Web distribution (Derry et al. 2010). Informed consent forms can be restrictive or permissive: both bring advantages and disadvantages. Very permissive forms allow for unrestricted use of the videos but can reduce participants' willingness to participate. Conversely, restrictive forms limiting publication and promoting privacy might favour participants' involvement in the study (Derry et al. 2010; Schuck and Kearney 2006). A compromise which favours sharing appears to be the best solution (Derry et al. 2010, 40).

For children or participants with mental conditions (e.g. dementia), provisional consent can be negotiated with carers *and* participants (Puurveen, Phinney, and Cox 2015, 25), and revisited constantly during the research process (Robson 2011). With adolescents (14–16 years), we used both informed assent forms for adolescents' individual recordings *and* a collective negotiation of informed consent with all family members (parents, adolescents, and siblings or other co-habiting persons) *before the recordings and after* the discussion of findings which happened in a home visit with the whole family (Everri 2017; Everri, 2018).

Researchers should carefully consider the circumstances and adopt a flexible stance to meet participants' needs and settings' conditions (Wiles et al. 2012). For instance, in emergency medical interventions consent for video recording should be sought afterwards given the circumstances: time pressure and patients' and relatives' mental/emotional conditions might alter their capacities (Gelbart, Barfield, and Watkins 2009). In psychotherapy sessions, sensitive content can emerge during the video recording; therefore, an iterative negotiation of consent is preferable (Hutchby, O'Reilly, and Parker 2012).

In addition to obtaining previous consent that specifies the aims of the research, methodological procedures, and data management and dissemination, participants can be encouraged to review, edit, and delete portions of the recordings before the researchers have access to it, as in SEBE (Lahlou, Le Bellu, and Boesen-Mariani 2015). This, together with the collaborative interpretation between participant and researcher, the possibility to withdraw and destroy the data at any time, and the final disclosures about research results, creates in practice several instances of well-informed consent.

Beyond target participants, researchers often need to obtain verbal or written consent by third parties or "*the cast*" (Lahlou 2017): family members, co-habitants, friends, colleagues, and so forth who willingly or not appear in the recorded scene. In this context, *verbal permission* recorded in the video or audio material itself is often an effective solution. In our research projects we asked participants to video record the moment in which permission is sought and given by third parties (Everri 2017; Lahlou 2017). While it is preferable to do that *before* the study commences for reasons discussed in the previous paragraphs, sometimes verbal consent can only be done on the spot – but that does *not* require recording the name of the cast, who can give anonymous (but recorded) consent. This solves a tricky issue: written informed consents need to be linked to the person on the film for blurring, etc., which unfortunately requires visual identification!

While privacy and anonymity of third parties must be protected and no identifying image should be published without their consent (Kelly et al. 2013; Lahlou et al. 2015), this condition must be balanced with reason and risk: in most cases that does not apply to passers-by in public space, where one expects to be seen in public. For instance, the ethical rules of TV industry about filming (e.g. BBC 2019) state that consent is not normally obtained from individuals who are incidentally caught on camera as part of the general scene. However, the right of individuals to ask to stop filming because of a concern of privacy is acknowledged unless it is editorially justified to continue.

In summary, informed consent in video research can be considered as a *collaborative decision-making process* (Banks and Zeitlyn 2015) negotiated among the present parties actively involved in the filming or acting as third parties (when asking consent is reasonably possible). It is an unfolding process and should thus be sought or confirmed at different stages of the research.

## *Acknowledging participants' rights*

There seems to be some consensus in the literature about the need to clearly define and agree with participants the rules and procedures for the ownership and release of materials *before* data collection (Heath, Hindmarsh, and Luff 2010; Schuck and Kearney 2006; Cox et al. 2014; Mok, Cornish, and Tarr 2015; Gubrium, Hill, and Flicker 2014). This includes defining who has rights and access to the data, who can refuse access, for how long and for what purposes the data will be stored, what implications the release of the data might have, how and when it will be anonymised, how copies will be made, and which data will be available to other audiences and how (see Heath et al. 2010). Mok, Cornish, and Tarr (2015) discuss the need to limit the scale and scope of data capture in order to minimize risks and to limit the right of participants to possess and share materials. Schuck and Kearney (2006) recommend constructing multi-media documents and materials to report the research rather than publishing un-critical and un-edited materials. Special care must be taken with digital data that is easy to disseminate. In this vein, there has been an increasing use of *data management plans*.

As an example, management plans for SEBE video recordings (including automated self-recording) include information about a) the nature, type, approximate duration of data that can be collected, with examples; b) it should be specified that participants can forget they are wearing the device and record unwanted or unflattering images with examples provided (e.g., bathroom visits, online banking). Therefore, they should be clearly reminded to switch off the device or delete these scenes and how; c) participants should remove the device or temporarily pause image capture whenever they wish; d) participants should clearly understand that no individual will be identifiable in any research dissemination without their consent, therefore participants will have the opportunity to view (and delete if necessary) their images in privacy. e) Additionally, participants need to know that data concerning illegal activities may not be protected by confidentiality and may be passed to law enforcement depending on the national law and nature of the activity. f) Lastly, participants will not get copies of their images, only a team of specially trained researchers will have access to the image data (Kelly et al. 2013; Lahlou 2011). Nevertheless, in some cases a copy of the data is given to participants as a souvenir, provided they are made aware of the limitations to publication (Everri 2017).

Our research as well as other studies based on wearable devices for video recording everyday life situations (Kelly et al. 2013; Lahlou 2011) transfer part of the control over collection (filming) and management (review and deletion) of data to participants; nevertheless, the researchers must guarantee that ethical guidelines for research are followed still (Aarsand 2016).

Data management plans should provide a set of detailed measures as well as being open to revisions and inclusions of issues that emerge later: such discussions should be accommodated for in the protocol (for example during RIWs in the SEBE protocol). Pilot studies can also serve to test and refine data management plans as well as other aspects that should be included in informed consents (Everri, 2017).

The issue of data ownership can be particularly controversial here. Initially, participants are the owner of the data, who decide to share – by handing the recordings to researchers – their habits, practices, routines, places and spaces. The SEBE protocol empowers participants to exercise their rights of data ownership by allowing them to review and delete their own data, to decide what to share with researchers, and to review researchers' interpretations and comments on the collected material in the replay interview. Taken together, these practices acknowledge participants as the real expert. But once the data have been transferred to the researcher, the ethical responsibility is on the researcher.

## The "ethical twist" for the future of visual ethnography

This chapter examined the ethical challenges faced by ethnographers when dealing with visual data. Interestingly, one of the most often reported challenges is negotiating with academic research ethics committees. Those tend to be risk averse, especially when they are not familiar with a technique. Anecdotes include ethics committee members rejecting video protocols in fear of children using the equipment to record pornographic action, of birthday parties potentially turning into bullying sessions that would be recorded, and so forth. Reality is fortunately less wild than the imagination of some ethics committee members. Experienced ethics committees know that those researchers who made a good risk analysis of their protocol are usually also careful during the research. If necessary, committees should be reminded their role is not just to criticize but also to advise, and discussions should take place. For example, our team's ethical reflections were positively nourished by discussions with the ethics board at the London School of Economics, grounded in a systematic review of potential incidents and risks in 198 films (117.1 of video recording) made with the SEBE protocol. The discussion, despite challenging in the initial phases, proved to be an occasion to allow the LSE research ethics committee to review and update research ethics regulations including aspects related to video research brought to their attention.

Therefore, besides discussions with research ethics committees which is the cornerstone of any research ethics process, we believe the "ethical twist" for visual research is to consider those involved as *participants* in the research rather than subjects of observation, or informers. That "participatory twist" improves the quality of data collected through the trust obtained by transparency and participation. It also helps to solve the complex (and often emergent) issues arising from the disclosure of specific behaviours to other publics, with the informed help of the involved "natives", in the most culturally adapted way.

A *risk analysis* should be conducted; rather than trying to completely avoid risks, which is futile, it is useful to think of how to prevent them, and then what will be done in the rare case something does happen. Risk can often be dealt with by raised awareness, simple precautions, and quick adapted intervention when issues emerge. In automotive driving, active safety (having good brakes, etc.) is considered paramount, still one doesn't brake continuously. We advise the same on research: stay aware all along and be prepared to address emergent issues.

At a more operational level, while we are aware that fellow researchers would like a tick box list to show their ethics committee, we are convinced that each case is specific, and that tick box lists and templates do not foster the participative, reflexive exercise that we believe is necessary. For this reason, we have opted for the provision of a generic (but comprehensive) guide for each researcher to build *their own* ethical guidelines, procedures and cases for their ethics committee (see Table 5.1).

The "solutions" summarized in Table 5.1 have emerged from researchers' experiences, negotiations, mistakes and coping strategies. Bear in mind to adapt guidelines to the local context. Our experience taught us participants are the ones

**TABLE 5.1** Problems and proposed solutions for video research ethics

| Problems/ critical issues | Description | Proposed solutions |
| --- | --- | --- |
| Researcher-researched rapport | Video research methods blur researcher-researched boundaries > Power imbalances > Ethical issues on rapport | Before commencing the study: Apply contextual judgement Practice reflexivity: consider multiple stakeholders' perspectives Consider participants as "research collaborators" Pilot study including some data analysis discussion with participants |
| Informed consent | Collection of video recordings is rarely pre-defined > Emergence of new data from recordings in the field > Ethical issues on dominant "a priori bio-medical" informed consent protocols | Negotiate/renew consent at different stages of the research Involve children and parents in consent negotiations (when children are research participants) Use video-recorded verbal consent from third-parties (cast) |
| Participants' rights | Videos challenge participants' privacy > Provide vivid details > Easy to share > Ethical issues on anonymity, confidentiality, ownership, and release of data | Use data management plans: Details participants' rights and duties Be open to negotiate to reach a balance between participants' protection and usability of the material for scientific scopes Make explicit arrangements in the consent forms |

who know their field best and can both point to potential issues and assess the validity of solutions. Having a transparent discussion with participants on the actual motives of the research, on how it will be used, and addressing candidly the potential problems are the best way forward, for ethical as well as heuristic reasons.

## Note

1 Subjective Evidence-Based Ethnography is a digital ethnography methodology based on first-person perspective video recordings using an eye-level micro-camera mounted on glasses (Lahlou 2006a; Le Bellu et al. 2016; Glăveanu and Lahlou 2012; Lahlou 2010, 2011; Dieckmann et al. 2017; Mutinelli 2017; Jonassen 2016; Zhang 2015; Heptonstall 2015; Gobbo 2015; Evans 2015; Lahlou et al. 2015; Fauquet-Alekhine and Lahlou 2017; Stangeland 2016; Vrabcová 2015; Everri 2017).

## References

Aarsand, P. 2016. "Children's media practices: Challenges and dilemmas for the qualitative researcher". *Journal of Children and Media* 10 (1): 90–97. https://doi.org/10.1080/17482798.2015.1121894

Aarsand, P., and L. Forsberg. 2010. "Producing children's corporeal privacy: Ethnographic video recording as material-discursive practice". *Qualitative Research* 10 (2): 249–268.

American Anthropological Association. 2001. "AAA guidelines for the evaluation of ethnographic visual media". AAA Statement. www.americananthro.org/ConnectWithAAA/Content.aspx?ItemNumber=1941
Association of Social Anthropologists of the UK and the Commonwealth. 2011. "Ethical Guidelines for Good Research Practice". https://doi.org/10.1007/BF00753960
Atkinson, P. 2009. "Ethics and ethnography". Twenty-First Century Society 4 (1): 17–30.
Banks, M., and D. Zeitlyn. 2015. Visual Methods in Social Research. London: Sage.
BBC (British Broadcasting Association). 2019. "Editorial guidelines on privacy". BBC.co.uk. www.bbc.co.uk/editorialguidelines/guidelines/privacy/guidelines
Blazek, M., and P. Hraňová. 2012. "Emerging relationships and diverse motivations and benefits in participatory video with young people". Children's Geographies 10 (2): 151–168. https://doi.org/10.1080/14733285.2012.667917
British Sociological Society. 2017. "Ethics guidelines and collated resources for digital research". www.britsoc.co.uk/media/24309/bsa_statement_of_ethical_practice_annexe.pdf
Carroll, K. 2009. "Outsider, insider, alongsider: Examining reflexivity in hospital-based video research". International Journal of Multiple Research Approaches 3 (3): 246–263.
Carroll, K., and J. Mesman. 2018. "Multiple researcher roles in video-reflexive ethnography". Qualitative Health Research 28 (7): 1145–1156. https://doi.org/10.1177/1049732318759490
Cicourel, A. V. 1964. Method and Measurement in Sociology. Oxford: Free Press of Glencoe.
Clark, A., J. Prosser, and R. Wiles. 2010. "Ethical issues in image-based research". Arts & Health 2 (1): 81–93. https://doi.org/10.1080/17533010903495298
Cox, S., S. Drew, M. Guillemin, C. Howell, D. Warr, and J. Waycott. 2014. "Guidelines for ethical visual research methods". https://artshealthnetwork.ca/ahnc/ethical_visual_research_methods-web.pdf
de Laat, S. 2004. "Picture perfect (?): Ethical considerations in visual representation". Nexus. The Canadian Student Journal of Anthropology 17 (1): Article 5. http://digitalcommons.mcmaster.ca/nexus/vol17/iss1/5/
Demuth, C., and M. Fatigante. 2012. "Comparative qualitative research in cultural psychology: Challenges and potentials". Zeitschrift für Qualitative Forschung 13 (1–2): 13–37.
Derry, S. J., R. D. Pea, B. Barron, R. A. Engle, F. Erickson, R. Goldman, R. Hall, et al. 2010. "Conducting video research in the learning sciences: Guidance on selection, analysis, technology, and ethics". Journal of the Learning Sciences 19 (1): 3–53. https://doi.org/10.1080/10508400903452884
Dieckmann, P., M. Patterson, S. Lahlou, J. Mesman, P. Nyström, and R. Krage. 2017. "Variation and adaptation: Learning from success in patient safety-oriented simulation training". Advances in Simulation 2 (21): 1–14. https://doi.org/10.1186/s41077-017-0054-1
Eglinton, K. A. 2013. "Between the personal and the professional: Ethical challenges when using visual ethnography to understand young people's use of popular visual material culture". Young 21 (3): 253–271. https://doi.org/10.1177/1103308813488793
Evans, S. 2015. "Virtual selves in virtual worlds: Towards the development of a social psychological understanding of the self in contemporary society". PhD diss., London School of Economics, UK.
Everri, M. 2017. "Adolescents, parents, digital media: looking for the pattern that dis/connects". MSCA final research report. https://cordis.europa.eu/project/rcn/195993/factsheet/en
Everri, M. 2018. "La comunicazione familiare nell'era digitale." In Famiglie d'oggi. Quotidianità, dinamiche e processi psicosociali, edited by L. Fruggeri, 151–182. Roma: Carocci.
Fauquet-Alekhine, P. 2016. "Risk assessment for subjective evidence-based ethnography applied in high risk environment". Advances in Research 6 (2): 1–13. https://doi.org/10.9734/AIR/2016/21597

Fauquet-Alekhine, P., and S. Lahlou. 2017. "The Square of PErceived ACtion Model (SPEAC Model) applied in digital ethnography for work activity analysis: Performance and workers' perception". *Current Journal of Applied Science and Technology* 22 (312): 1–13. https://doi.org/10.9734/CJAST/2017/34985

Flewitt, R. 2005. "Conducting research with young children: Some ethical considerations". *Early Child Development and Care* 175 (6): 553–565. https://doi.org/10.1080/03004430500131338

Gelbart, B., C. Barfield, and A. Watkins. 2009. "Ethical and legal considerations in video recording neonatal resuscitations". *Journal of Medical Ethics* 35 (2): 120–124. https://doi.org/10.1136/jme.2008.024612

Glăveanu, V., and S. Lahlou. 2012. "'Through the creator's eyes': Using the subjective camera to study craft creativity". *Creativity Research Journal* 24 (2–3):152–162. https://doi.org/10.1080/10400419.2012.677293

Gobbo, A. 2015. "The making of consumer decisions: Revisiting the notions of evaluation and choice by reconstructing consumer habits through subject evidence based ethnography". PhD diss., London School of Economics, UK.

Gubrium, A. and K. Harper. 2013. *Participatory Visual and Digital Methods*. New York: Routledge.

Gubrium, A., A. L. Hill, and S. Flicker. 2014. "A situated practice of ethics for participatory visual and digital methods in public health research and practice: A focus on digital storytelling". *American Journal of Public Health* 104 (9): 1606–1614. https://doi.org/10.2105/AJPH.2013.301310

Hackling, M. W. 2013. "Challenges of conducting ethical video-based classroom research challenges of conducting ethical video-based classroom research". *ECU Publications Post*, 1–5. http://ro.ecu.edu.au/ecuworkspost2013/839

Heath, C., J. Hindmarsh, and P. Luff. 2010. "Access, ethics and project planning". In *Video in Qualitative Research*, 14–36. London: Sage Publications. https://doi.org/10.4135/9781526435385

Heptonstall, B. 2015. "Cognitive de-biasing strategies in medicine: A subjective evidence-based ethnography approach". MSc diss., London School of Economics, UK.

Hutchby, I., M. O'Reilly, and N. Parker. 2012. "Ethics in praxis: Negotiating the presence and functions of a video camera in family therapy". *Discourse Studies* 14 (6): 675–690. https://doi.org/10.1177/1461445612457487

Jonassen, Z. 2016. "Good practices of replay interviewers: An explorative study of their understanding of the interview setting, attitude, and behaviour". MSc. diss., London School of Economics, UK.

Kelly, P., S. J. Marshall, H. Badland, J. Kerr, M. Oliver, A. R. Doherty, and C. Foster. 2013. "An ethical framework for automated, wearable cameras in health behavior research". *American Journal of Preventive Medicine* 44 (3): 314–319. https://doi.org/10.1016/j.amepre.2012.11.006

Lahlou, S. 2006. "L'activité du point de vue de l'acteur et la question de l'Intersubjectivité : Huit années d'expériences avec des caméras miniaturisées fixées au front des acteurs (Subcam)". *Communications* 80: 209–234.

Lahlou S. 2008. "Identity, social status, privacy and face-keeping in digital society". *Social Science Information* 47 (3): 299–330. https://doi.org/10.1177/0539018408092575.

Lahlou, S. 2010. "Digitization and transmission of human experience". *Social Science Information* 49 (3): 291–327. https://doi.org/10.1177/0539018410372020

Lahlou, S. 2011. "How can we capture the subject's perspective? An evidence-based approach for the social scientist". *Social Science Information* 50 (4): 607–655. https://doi.org/10.1177/0539018411411033

Lahlou, S. 2017. *Installation Theory. The Societal Construction and Regulation of Behaviour*. Cambridge: Cambridge University Press. https://doi.org/10.1017/9781316480922

Lahlou, S., S. Le Bellu, and S. Boesen-Mariani. 2015. "Subjective evidence based ethnography: Method and applications". *Integrative Psychological and Behavioral Science* 49 (2): 16–38. https://doi.org/10.1007/s12124-014-9288-9

Lahlou, S., S. Boesen-Mariani, B. Franks, and I. Guelinckx. 2015. "Increasing water intake of children and parents in the family setting: A randomized, controlled intervention using installation theory". *Annals of Nutrition and Metabolism* 66 (3): 26–30. https://doi.org/10.1159/000381243

Le Bellu, S., S. Lahlou, V. N. Nosulenko, and E. S. Samoylenko. 2016. "Studying activity in manual work: A framework for analysis and training". *Le Travail Humain* 79 (1): 7–28. https://doi.org/10.3917/th.791.0007

Lenette, C., J. R. Botfield, K. Boydell, B. Haire, C. E. Newman, and A. B. Zwi. 2018. "Beyond compliance checking: A situated approach to visual research ethics". *Journal of Bioethical Inquiry* 15 (2): 293–303. https://doi.org/10.1007/s11673-018-9850-0

Liegl, M., and L. Schindler. 2013. "Media assemblages, ethnographic vis-ability and the enactment of video in sociological research". *Distinktion: Scandinavian Journal of Social Theory* 14 (3): 254–270.

London School of Economics and Political Science. 2019. "Research ethics: Guidance on LSE research ethics, code of research conduct, and training". https://info.lse.ac.uk/staff/divisions/research-and-innovation/research/research-ethics/research-ethics

Markham, A., and E. Buchanan. 2012. "AOIR guidelines: Ethical decision making and internet research". www.aoir.org

Milne, E. J., C. Mitchell, and N. de Lange, eds. 2012. *Handbook of Participatory Video*. Lanham, MD: Rowman and Littlefield.

Mok, T. M., F. Cornish, and J. Tarr. 2015. "Too much information: Visual research ethics in the age of wearable cameras". *Integrative Psychological and Behavioral Science* 49 (2): 309–322. https://doi.org/10.1007/s12124-014-9289-8

Mudaly, N. 2015. "The rights of pre-verbal children involved in video-recorded research: An examination of the ethical issues". *International Journal of Children's Rights* 23 (2): 391–404. https://doi.org/10.1163/15718182-02302008

Mutinelli, S. 2017. "The psychology of waste: A subjective evidence-based ethnography for domestic activity". MSc. diss., London School of Economics, UK.

Nash, M., and R. Moore. 2018. "Exploring methodological challenges of using participant-produced digital video diaries in Antarctica". *Sociological Research Online* 23 (3): 589–605. https://doi.org/10.1177/1360780418769677

Papademas, D. 2004. "Editor's introduction: Ethics in visual research". *Visual Studies* 19 (2): 122–126. https://doi.org/10.1080/1472586042000301610

Papademas, D. 2009. "IVSA code of research ethics and guidelines". *Visual Studies* 24 (3): 250–257. https://doi.org/10.1080/14725860903309187

Pea, R. 1999. "New media communication forums for improving education research and practice". In *Issues in Education Research: Problems and Possibilities*, edited by E. C. Lagemann and L. S. Shulman, 336–370. San Francisco: Jossey-Bass.

Phelps, J. M., J. Strype, S. Le Bellu, S. Lahlou, and J. Aandal. 2018. "Experiential learning and simulation-based training in Norwegian police education: Examining body-worn video as a tool to encourage reflection". *Policing (Oxford)* 12 (1): 50–65. https://doi.org/10.1093/police/paw014

Pink, S. 2011. "Planning and practising 'visual methods': Appropriate uses and ethical issues". In *Doing Visual Ethnography*, 40–62. London: Sage Publications. https://doi.org/10.4135/9780857025029.d5

Pink, S. H., H. Postill, J. Hjorth, T. Lewis, and J. Tacchi, 2016. *Digital Ethnography. Principle and Practice.* London: Sage Publications.

Pope, C. C., R. De Luca, and M. Tolich. 2013. "How an exchange of perspectives led to tentative ethical guidelines for visual ethnography". *Ethics and Academic Freedom in Educational Research*: 97–111. https://doi.org/10.4324/9781315872711

Prosser, J., A. Clark, and R. Wiles. 2008. "Working Paper # 10 Visual research ethics at the crossroads". *Crossroads* 44 (November): 1–35.

Puurveen, G., A. Phinney, and S. M. Cox. 2015. "Ethical issues in the use of video observations with people with advanced dementia and their caregivers in nursing home environments". *Visual Methodologies* 3 (2): 16–26.

Rieken, J. C., and S. Lahlou. 2010. *Theories, Protocols and Techniques Used to Elicit and Record the Production of Know-How by Experts.* London: London School of Economics/ISP.

Robson, S. 2011. "Producing and using video data in the early years: Ethical questions and practical consequences in research with young children". *Children and Society* 25 (3): 179–189. https://doi.org/10.1111/j.1099-0860.2009.00267.x

Rose, G. 2014. "On the relation between 'visual research methods' and contemporary visual culture". *Sociological Review* 62: 24–46.

Rouch, J., and E. Morin. 1961. *Chronique d'un Été.* France: Argos Films.

Ruby, J. 1991. *Picturing Culture: Explorations of Film and Anthropology.* Chicago: University of Chicago Press.

Salmons, J. 2015. *Qualitative Online Interviews.* Thousand Oaks, CA: Sage Publications.

Schembri, S., and M. V. Boyle. 2013. "Visual ethnography: Achieving rigorous and authentic interpretations". *Journal of Business Research* 66 (9): 1251–1254. https://doi.org/10.1016/j.jbusres.2012.02.021

Schuck, S, and M. Kearney. 2006. "Using digital video as a research tool: Ethical issues for researchers". *Journal of Educational Multimedia and Hypermedia* 15 (4): 447–463.

Stangeland, H. 2016. "Technology-enhanced learning in operative policing: Expert illustration videos and subjective evidence-based ethnography (SEBE) as learning tools among Norwegian police novices". MSc. diss., London School of Economics, UK.

Vrabcová, T. 2015. "I would never eat that back home. Analysing changes in food habits among Canadian and Chinese students in London: subjective evidence-based ethnography". MSc. diss., London School of Economics, UK.

Wiles, R., A. Coffey, and J. Robinson. 2010. "Anonymisation and visual images: Issues of respect, 'voice' and protection". *International Journal of Social Research Methodology* 15 (1): 41–53.

Wiles, R., A. Coffey, J. Robison, and J. Prosser. 2012. "Ethical regulation and visual methods: Making visual research impossible or developing good practice?" *Sociological Research Online* 17 (1): 1–10.

Wiles, R., J. Prosser, A. Bagnoli, A. Clark, K. Davies, S. A. L. Holland, and E. Renold. 2008. "Visual ethics: Ethical issues in visual research". *ESRC National Centre for Research Methods Review Paper 11.* http://eprints.ncrm.ac.uk/421/

Wills, W. J., A. M. Dickinson, A. Meah, and F. Short. 2016. "Reflections on the use of visual methods in a qualitative study of domestic kitchen practices". *Sociology* 50: 470–485.

Winckler, M. 2014. "The temptation of documentation: Potential and challenges of videographic documentation and interpretation. a case-study from a civic education research project in Germany". *Journal of Social Science Education* 13 (1): 108–117.

Zhang, M. 2015. "How is the decision-making distributed in a complex dynamic system? An explorative study of air management teams in the intensive care unit using subjective evidence-based ethnography". MSc. diss., London School of Economics, UK.

# 6

# DRAWING AND STORYCRAFTING WITH ESTONIAN CHILDREN

Sharing experiences of mobility

*Pihla Maria Siim*

### Studying mobile childhoods in the Estonian–Finnish context

Transnational family studies have stressed the affect that cross-border mobility has on people's family lives, lifestyles, and everyday practices (Bryceson and Vuorela 2002). Individual choices to move are often related to the needs of the family and to family dynamics and are shaped by movement, separation, and reunion. Children are often at the centre of family migration processes: as motivators for migration – to guarantee their wellbeing – or as migrants themselves (Coe et al. 2011, 3–5). In spite of this, the majority of the research on transnational migration has concentrated on adults, the voices of children remaining largely overlooked. Children have rather been treated as non-persons lacking both feelings and agency of their own (Dobson 2009; Punch 2009; Zeitlyn and Mand 2012; Fresnoza-Flot and Nagasaka 2015).

A focus on children within studies of migration and transnational communities is necessary and essential, as children either move across borders or remain where they are under a variety of circumstances, but always affected by the migration of their family members. There are thousands of children involved in migration, encountering changes in their circumstances and environments in the Estonian–Finnish transnational space. However, research into children's experiences of intra-EU migration is only beginning to emerge (Moskal and Tyrrell 2016, 455). Generally, there is a lack of literature focusing on research into mobile children that helps to understand what it is actually like to be a child affected by migration. Children are not only mobile across places but move through the social roles associated with childhood in particular places (Zeitlyn and Mand 2012, 990; Fresnoza-Flot 2018, 15). "Mobile childhood" thus includes not only spatial, but also temporal and contextual mobility (Fresnoza-Flot and Nagasaka 2015).

Lately, migration scholars have started to highlight the children's viewpoints and experiences of mobility – not only stressing their vulnerability but also paying attention to their subjectivity, agency and the uniqueness of their viewpoint. This also calls for methodologies more attentive to the everyday, lived experience of migration (Dobson 2009; Coe et al. 2011; Ní Laoire et al. 2011; Fresnoza-Flot 2018). Since 2013 I have studied Estonian families in which some of the family members live or work in Finland. With the first of the research projects (2012–2014) in which I was involved, the focus was solely on children's experiences of migration, and the data was produced with children.[1] The aim of the project was to focus on the ways children comprehend migration in East and North Europe, and on their descriptions and interpretations of translocal family life (Assmuth et al. 2018).

Since the 1990s, Finland has been the main destination country for migration from Estonia. In the 2000s, emigration from Estonia to the longer-serving EU member states grew, while at the same time the proportion of labour migration increased significantly. Estonians compromise the largest group of foreign citizens in Finland. According to Population Register Estonia, there were 52 400 Estonian citizens living in Finland in July 2019, in addition to which 18 500 people had registered a Finnish contact address. According to one estimate, in 2012 there were about 30 000 people working in Finland but living permanently in Estonia (Statistics Finland 2013). Indeed, Estonia is one of the major countries of origin for commuting workers in Europe: the highest shares of cross-border workers are among Slovakians (5%), Estonians and Hungarians (just over 2% each). Men were clearly dominant (92%) among those who worked abroad but resided in Estonia (European Commission 2019).

Taking into account the number of regular contacts across the border and intensive movement back and forth, it is possible to talk about an Estonian–Finnish transnational space (see Jakobson et al. 2012). In recent years, the volume of emigration has been smaller and return migration has increased. In 2018, Estonia's net migration was positive for the fourth year in a row, and the net migration with Finland was positive for the second year in a row (Statistics Estonia 2019). However, these trends may also change according to the economic and political situation.

Since I started to work with children, I have pondered on whether particular methods should be used. The aim of child-centred methodologies is usually to recognize children as active agents who hold different competencies from adults. However, it should be recognized that childhood is not the same experience for every child, but rather is mediated by the social, cultural and moral norms of each place. Childhood should thus rather be considered a relational experience, one that is influenced by wider social and economic processes, as Zeitlyn and Mand (2012, 990–991) have pointed out.

Keeping this in mind, I started fieldwork with individual and group interviews, interviewing different members of the same family, both children and adults. While interest in narratives has grown in many fields – we can even talk about a narrative turn – narrative research has focused mainly on adult narrative and adult life experience (Karlsson 2013, 1110). I did not have previous experience of interviewing children under 14 years old, and it was challenging to figure out how to formulate the right (open) questions for children. I interviewed children either with their parent(s) or alone. Parents were helpful asking additional questions, but they also intervened unnecessarily, disrupting the interview and the connection with a child (see Siim 2016). During the interviews preschool-age children rarely gave long, detailed answers or reflected on their experiences at length. They seemed rather to live in the moment or look towards the future, and not be very eager to talk in detail about what happened in the past.

These experiences lead me to try other kinds of methods in parallel. In this chapter, I will firstly discuss the drawing sessions and related open discussions with children, and then explore in more detail storycrafting and the kind of stories received using this method. Storycrafting is a method that innovatively combines facts with fiction, offering new insights into the experiences of mobile children through a twist that combines the real and the imaginable. Participants are asked to tell imaginative stories, although as our experience shows at the same time these stories reveal a lot about how participants experience and understand the world around them. In this study, children were asked to tell stories, the main characters of which are children of about the same age, moving between Estonia and Finland.

## Drawing and discussing with children

During the 2013–2014 period I regularly visited children's circles and day-care centres in the Greater Helsinki area. In the course of these visits I observed the everyday routines and play of approximately 40 Estonian children during their kindergarten days, making notes. My main interest was in experiences they had that related to mobility and transnational everyday life. Participant observation took a lot of time, leading to information being gained in small pieces, the importance of which was initially difficult to understand. I went through the field notes I had made but felt there was very little in them that was relevant to what I wanted to study.

To recognize the value and character of what one could call "small stories" a "twist" was needed in order to understand and interpret children's experiences. According to Bamberg and Georgakopoulou, more attention should be paid to so-called conversational narratives, and how people actually use these stories in everyday, mundane situations. They have argued for the "worthiness" of stories that they call small stories, both for literal and metaphorical reasons, that are still on the fringes of narrative research. "Small stories" is an umbrella term capturing a gamut of unpresented narrative activities, such as telling on-going events, future or hypothetical events, and shared events. On a metaphorical level it helps to identify the narrative when the fleeting moments of narrative orientation to the world can be easily missed out (Bamberg and Georgakopoulou 2008).

Keeping in mind that small stories do not have to be long and coherent narratives in order to fulfil their function has helped me to recognize the worthiness of children's short accounts. Their stories might be of a different nature, not resembling the long accounts told by parents during their interviews, but they were still key to the children's world and had intrinsic value. I could now better see the richness and uniqueness of the small details in children's accounts, and started to explore in detail what they noticed and considered worth telling. However, my aim was never to pit the accounts of children and their parents against each other. My attitude was that descriptions that seem to be inaccurate or too fanciful to be "true", in a strict sense, have their own validity and help to understand the child's perspective (Punch 2002, 327).

In qualitative research, it has become more and more usual to use participatory and creative, art-based methods to engage children in order to explore means of communication between children and adults beyond the traditional interview. Creative methods draw on inventive and imaginative processes, and for example storytelling, drama, games, drawing and photography are among the methods often applied (see Veale 2006; Gillies and Robinson 2012; von Benzon 2015). Apart from taking part in daily kindergarten activities, I also decided to organize drawing sessions in small groups with children aged four to seven, asking children (n=16) to make drawings based on certain themes. The first task was to make drawings about visiting Estonia or something they miss from Estonia. The children drew for example buildings located in Estonia (their home or the houses of their relatives, their kindergarten), often also the natural surroundings of these buildings; some drew beaches or the ferry journey across the sea to Estonia.

The task for the second session was to draw something that the children like in Finland, which turned out to be a more difficult assignment. Some children drew their house in Finland, others decided to draw Estonia (for example kindergarten or a beach) instead of Finland. Some drew their dreams, and some asked whether they could draw the globe. Often, when children are drawing, they have a mutual affect and learn from each other (see Thompson 1999). In this drawing session, several of the boys attending ended up drawing similar images, although the related discussions were somewhat different:

> Kevin[2] (7) was the one who delayed drawing longest. He wanted to draw something from his dreams (as did Gerli and Marten), but then noted that he could not draw his dream. He also stated that he could not draw anything from Finland, only from Estonia. Then he asked, whether he could draw the whole globe. "This is Mars. Mars has this kind of hole, doesn't it?" He also asked which was the biggest country, Finland, Estonia or Russia, then answers himself: Estonia. Marten teaches Kevin: Mars has two moons. Kevin says: "the globe is my dream world".
>
> […] Eventually Rainer (7) asked, whether he could draw the globe. "Does it mean you like it everywhere?" "Yes". It was interesting to observe, what countries Rainer put on the map. "Here is Estonia, here is Russia. From here I

have travelled by boat. Up there is Lapland". The continents in his drawing were surprisingly correctly sized and shaped in relation to the sea (and in comparison to the drawings made by other children). Rainer also talked about his father's language skills. "Father knows all the languages. German, Russian, English. He is wise like crazy". (Field diary, Pihla Maria Siim, April 2014)

In the research we used drawings to discover what children consider important in their lives, in order to avoid imposing adult-centred concerns (Punch 2002, 321). When performing task-based methods, such as drawing, the initial interaction is between children and the medium (here paper), and the familiarity with the researcher can be built up over time (ibid., 336). An important part of drawing sessions was also the related discussions. In my study, I would not consider it possible to interpret the drawings outside the narrative context and the explanations given by the children themselves. As Kinnunen (2015) has stated when studying children's spontaneous drawing in a kindergarten context, that drawing is often a kind of dialogue between marks (made on paper) and thoughts. Even more important than the drawings can be to follow and analyse the process of telling and drawing: how children live the drawing, are present in them (Viljamaa 2012, 84–87). This field diary describes a session when Linda draw things she missed about Estonia:

Linda (5 years old) took the assignment quite seriously. She said she missed her grandmother and her dog Timmu. Linda said she now lives on the ground floor, and that in Estonia she had lived on the 3rd floor. She was travelling to Estonia to visit her grandmother the following day. She was carefully drawing her grandmother's house, and she definitely wanted to take her drawing home to surprise her mother. Next to the grandmother's house, she drew a pumpkin, although she said granny does not really grow pumpkins. Her granny lives in the middle of a forest. Next to the house, she also drew an apple tree and asked me to help her to draw Timmu, the dog. So, I agreed and tried to draw a dog according to her instructions. It looked more like a cat. Linda said it didn't matter, since her granny used to have a cat too, but it disappeared into the forest. Linda also included the Estonian flag in the drawing. She said she has four grandmothers. At first she thought she had five, but then she used her fingers to count. I asked whether she also has grandfathers. Yes, she has two. "One of them is really funny", Linda said, "a bit fat, just enough", she added. Grandad calls Linda "Masha" (as in the popular Russian cartoon Masha and the Bear). When Linda's cousin is around, grandpa calls them the two Mashas. (Field diary, Pihla Maria Siim, March 2014)

Adult researchers might be confused about the invitation to draw with the children (see Kinnunen 2015) – how would this affect the material and analysis of it? Children, however, do not usually separate doing, knowing and different types of telling, but move between them rather effortlessly (Viljamaa 2012, 84). These drawing sessions offer the possibility to access embodied and emplaced experiences, which may otherwise be hard to verbalize. In the drawings related to visits to Estonia, there were many references to what children did, experienced and sensed (see Bankovska and Siim 2018). In addition, the drawing sessions created a space for diverse and spontaneous narration, as well as the possibility to negotiate the experiences among children. The drawings and stories of other children served as an inspiration and helped them talk about personal experiences.

## Storycrafting as a method

While planning a new project for 2016–2018, I wanted to continue working with children. In addition to drawing, of which I now had some experience, I was interested in trying storycrafting. The storycrafting method was created by Finnish education scientists in the 1980s to make the interactive relationship between adults and children more equal, and to inspire and encourage children to tell about their own world and thoughts (Riihelä 1991; Karlsson 2013). When applying storycrafting methods, the child is asked to tell a story, the researcher writes it down, word for word, and reads it aloud to the child, after which the child may correct the story until s/he is content with the outcome. I was inspired and sanguine about the new kind of knowledge this method could possibly produce. By giving research subjects the possibility to tell fictional stories, it kind of pushes the limits of ethnographic knowledge, which often is based on observation or transmission of information of (presumably) factual events, either verbally or visually.

My earlier experience had proven that during the drawing sessions it was relatively difficult to manage all the tasks alone: to help children in practical matters, discuss the drawings with them, and make notes about what is taking place and discussed during these gatherings. Children also expected me to be part of the activities in many ways: sharpening pencils, helping them drawing, being around and interested in what they were doing. From the beginning, we – our project team – planned that in the new meetings with children, two researchers would be involved, my colleague, ethnologist Keiu Telve, and I.

We modified the method a bit – i.e. we have worked with small groups, mostly two to four children, and given children a certain broad theme for the story, so that the stories told are to some extent related to mobility, living in Finland, or a transnational way of life. We asked children to make up a story in which the main character, a child of their age, moves to Finland and goes to school there, and to write about the things s/he likes to do. In some groups we asked children to tell stories related to growing up (future of the main character); about friendship; about holidays in Estonia; where the main character's favourite places are in Finland; or about Christmas celebrations.

We organized 27 storycrafting sessions in 2018, all of which took place in the Greater Helsinki area, with in total 66 children from Estonia from nine different schools and kindergartens. In order to organize the gatherings, we contacted Estonian kindergarten teachers as well as the teachers giving Estonian language lessons in different schools in this area. In Finland, children whose native language is not Finnish or Swedish may receive lessons on their mother tongue. In many cases, pupils from different classes and of different ages take part in these lessons. If the teachers were willing to co-operate, and gave us permission to work with the children they taught, the parents were asked to give written consent for their child to participate. The children who had permission were invited to participate in the storycrafting sessions in the library or some other free room, while other pupils attended Estonian language lessons at school or other activities in kindergarten.[3] In the publications, we have agreed to use pseudonyms for all research participants.

The language of the storycrafting sessions was Estonian. If the children did not remember some words in Estonian, they used Finnish instead. The participating kindergarten children were 3 to 6 years old, and the schoolchildren 7 to 14 years old. From the 27 stories written during these sessions, seven were created by preschool children, and 20 by schoolchildren. Some of the stories were created by one child only, but usually several children participated. When the story was finished and we read it aloud to the children, they usually did not suggest any changes, but were rather eager to start drawing a related picture.

During the fieldwork, children received us extremely well both at the kindergartens and schools. The school aged children were particularly active and keen to participate in the storycrafting and drawing sessions. Presumably the sessions resembled their everyday activities and were somewhat similar to children's spontaneous, everyday storytelling situations. We noticed that the children felt more relaxed than they usually do in interview situations when a researcher is asking questions, at which times the children feel stronger pressure to answer relatively quickly and to do so in the "correct" manner. One benefit is also that drawing and storycrafting gives children more time to think: the image and story can be changed and added to, which gives children more control over their form of expression (see Punch 2002). Children were also motivated to participate, since they were aware of our plan to publish a children's book (Siim and Telve 2019). This book, published in November 2019, contains all the 27 stories written down during the storycrafting sessions, complemented with short citations from our field diaries, conversation questions, and drawings made by the children. The book is directed to a wider audience, for example families with children who are considering relocation. The aim is to offer families both inspiration and food for thought, to make them aware of the ways children understand and experience mobility and make it easier to start a discussion with their family members.

## New twists: interplay of factual and fictional

Although the stories created by children are rich in fantasy and created in collaboration with researchers, they essentially draw on children's everyday experiences and observations. The stories combine personal experience and fantasy in a fascinating way, revealing what details children notice, what kinds of discussion and comment they remember, what kinds of situation they consider imaginable and what kinds of emotion they ascribe to children of their age. To start with, we gave the children a broad theme for their stories, as explained above, although what followed was for them to decide. Some of the stories were really fanciful, others seemed to draw more on children's personal experiences. I have chosen these two excerpts from the stories because they show the variation that exists:

"Raili's story"[4]

> Raili is 12 years old and lives in Finland with her mother. She also has a little brother. Their house is black. Their parents have divorced and their father lives in Estonia. Because Raili's mother has two children and a low salary, they live in Finland. (Girls, 10 and 11)

"Adventures of Kaspar and Jasper"

> Kaspar and Jasper lived in Finland. Jasper's mother liked the nature in Finland. Kaspar's mother thought it would be easier for Kaspar to learn in Finland. They moved back to Estonia, since they missed it a lot and there was some kind of explosion in Finland and so they had to fly to Estonia. [...] They still speak Finnish but use it rather rarely, although there are a lot of Finns living in Estonia because of the explosion that took place in Finland. (Boys, 9 and 10)

**FIGURE 6.1** Drawing by a 9-year-old boy, 2018. Copyright: Inequalities in Motion: Transnational Families in Estonia and Finland project.

On the one hand, these stories include a lot of detail, presumably observed by children in their everyday lives, or adopted from adults' discussions they have heard. For example, in many of the stories, the main character has moved to Finland because the parents of the family need to work there in order to earn a better income. Stories also include realistic descriptions of family relations, friendship, school life and bullying, and about everyday materialities (such as food, household equipment, and children's toys). On the other hand, as the second story shows, the stories also include elements of fantasy that the children themselves have made up, or about which they dream. They talked, for example, about an explosion in Finland that forces Finns to move to Estonia; about a private aeroplane which the main character can use freely; the possibility of buying things without money; and about a secret children's hut in the middle of the forest.

When starting with the story, the most difficult task for children was often to name the main character in the story. Sometimes there were also disagreements among children about the course of the events in the stories. For example, in one group all three participating girls were very talkative. I felt that two of them knew each other slightly better, and the third one was kind of left out and her suggestions for the storyline were not readily accepted. On the other hand, this might have been also a question of language: her Estonian language skills were not as good as the others.

In the case of two boys aged 9 and 10, I felt that one of the authors would have preferred a more fanciful story, but the other participating boy did not accept all the ideas he suggested. The same was the case with a story called "Jokker', created by two boys from another school in Helsinki. One of the boys suggested that a bus would pick Jokker up from school, and that there would be "moneybombers"; in addition, there are drunk people and smokers around. However, the other author said he did not want to have these details in the book. The story was written down as follows:

> A boy called Jokker moves from Estonia to Finland. He moves together with his mother and father; they also have two cats and a dog. They put all their stuff into a big "work bus" and take the boat to Finland. Only knives are not allowed. They take clothes, Lego, hunting knives, and also food: coca cola, sweets, spaghetti. They'll travel back and forth and are able to bring more stuff from Estonia. On the boat, Jokker always takes a VIP cabin. If he doesn't, he hangs around, although he doesn't like that too much. He likes to travel with Mega Star [a ship built in 2017, travelling between Tallinn and Helsinki], and if he can't take this ship he doesn't want to travel at all. All of his friends are aboard Mega Star and there is a room of game consoles that is free of charge, rather than for two euros, which is the usual price. On the boat he eats a hamburger and potato chips and says "Goodbye, Estonia!" It's always fun on the boat. Jokker would like the trip to last longer than two hours. In Finland he lives in Kulomäki [a district in Vantaa, in Greater Helsinki]. The first thing he sees in Finland is a golden house, which is his home. There are Nintendos

and similar things in his Finnish home. The Estonian home was better, since Estonia is his homeland and he was able to be free there. In Finland he needs to go to school, but Estonian school is worse actually. Mother comes to pick him up from school. While waiting for her, Jokker plays with his phone. He also checks the answers for his homework on the phone. He also plays football. He likes how in Finland you don't need to pay for electricity or for water. When Jokker grows up he will work as a policeman in Finland, he won't move back to Estonia. However, before his death he will return and he will be buried there. (Two 8-year-old boys)

**FIGURE 6.2** Drawing by an 8-year-old boy, 2018. Copyright: Inequalities in Motion: Transnational Families in Estonia and Finland project.

I'll draw a golden house. On the second floor, there's a bed in one room, a television in another, a third room is a games room. Outside there's a swimming pool. On the first floor there's a living room. Outside there's the bus they moved with. Jokker is swimming in the pool with his cat.

As Zeitlyn and Mand (2012, 997–998) have pointed out, in group interviews one or two dominant members might emerge who direct the conversation, with others tending to follow their more confident and articulate peers. Working with groups of children does offer the possibility to observe peer relations and the shifts in power relations. However, it also ideally inspires "naturalness", i.e. children are usually less shy than when meeting them individually. They can build on each other's statements and discuss a wider range of experiences and opinions than may develop in individual interviews (Eder and Fingerson 2001, 183).

## Emotionally loaded stories

As the previous examples indicate, stories also embody the emotions children may have in relation to translocal everyday life, and to their many homes. Sometimes love of both countries is stressed, as described by two girls aged 9 and 10 in their story:

> Children like to live in Finland. No country is bad for living. Everyone likes their own country, but these children like both their homeland and the country they live in now, that is Finland.

Some of the emotions described in stories are related to the children's new homes. For instance, in two stories, the main character has a golden house in Finland. However, in the story cited above, the Jokker's Estonian home was said to be even better, "since Estonia is his homeland and he was able to be free there". However, Jokker will not move back to Estonia, but rather "before his death he will return and he will be buried there". This is a somewhat surprising ending to a story told by two young boys, although some adults I have interviewed have reported similar dreams, i.e. they would like to return to Estonia after retirement and spend the rest of their lives there.

Stories often refer to a child's longing for Estonia. Usually the main character misses his/her parents, grandparents, or other relatives. Time spent in Estonia is described in warm tones. In a story about Annika, the four 6-year-old girls who wrote the story have her go to Estonian during the summer holidays, where she is allowed to do things that are usually forbidden. "She likes to be in Estonia and her grandmother gives her a lot of sweet things, also cacao. She likes how her grandmother doesn't scold her, since she's a very good girl. Annika may even put hair dye on her head. Grandmother has a puppy and a kitten, Tessa and Bella. Annika is very eager to go already". Animals waiting in Estonia are often mentioned in the stories, as well as relative's gardens. "Grandma has a beautiful, old house, surrounded by an apple tree and grass. They call to grandmother to say they arrived and she comes to the door and hugs the child on the stairs" (four 6-year-old girls).

This feeling of warmth, both in a figurative and a very concrete fashion, is also present in drawings. In this picture, related to the story quoted above, the author has drawn a dog and a cat, and two suns "since it is very warm in Estonia". The number 100 refers to the warmth, to the high temperature during the summer. In front of the house you can also see the Estonian flag, with its blue, black and white bands.

FIGURE 6.3 Drawing by a 6-year-old girl, 2018. Copyright: Inequalities in Motion: Transnational Families in Estonia and Finland project.

Our storytelling sessions have confirmed that fictional storytelling often provides an easier way for the children to talk about their personal experiences, wishes, fears and other emotions. As von Benzon (2015, 338) has put it, telling a story may require less conscious evaluation and decision-making than answering a question. During the storytelling sessions with us the children often reflected at length on their own experiences. Working in groups makes it possible for children to share and negotiate these with each other.

In their stories the children also touched on situations that included emotionally distressful experiences, such as the following story which describes in detail the emotions of the main character when her father moved to Finland. I did not meet this kind of story when interviewing the children: usually they said they did not remember how they felt at the time the family moved to Finland. The same applies to friendship and bullying at school: in the interviews these might be mentioned briefly, although they are usually dismissed.

> When Eva's father moved to Finland, Eva was 6 years old. Her father moved to Finland because he couldn't earn enough in Estonia and couldn't find a job. Eva didn't understand too much at that age, she knew only that she would see her father during the holidays. Eva's father came home approximately every two months. When her father went back to work, she cried a lot. She would have given everything to see her father every day. It was not easy to move to

Finland, since she had friends in Estonia. Some of them were angry with her, and didn't care about her anymore, although some continued to be her friend. (Girl, 12)

## Conclusion

Storycrafting helped us obtain a unique picture of children's translocal everyday lives. In the stories created during the sessions, children vividly described their relationships with other children at school, portrayed the futures of the main characters, and playfully sketched children doing things they are not normally allowed to do. Stories also include plenty of children's observations of everyday life, for example regarding financial matters, gender roles and the working conditions of family members.

In storycrafting sessions, participants are given an opportunity to decide what story they would like to share with others. In our case, the most important advantage the method offered was that it allowed participants the possibility to play with the idea of what could happen to a child like them who moved between Estonia and Finland. As compared to interviews, in storycrafting sessions participants tend to talk more about the emotional side of children's lives, for example what they imagine children dream about and what they fear; the emotions children have in relation to homes left behind and about children's special relationships with their grandparents. One of the stories told to us ends with the sentence "Sometimes in Finland this longing for Estonia comes, but he does not talk about it to others". One aim of the method was to enable children to talk about subjects that they do not usually touch upon. The method allows the possibility to overcome some disadvantages that conventional interviews with children present. It may, for example, be challenging for children to verbalize memories, to find the right words to describe abstract processes; or they may tire quickly during interviews (Zartler 2014), feeling that the themes proposed by adult researcher are not relevant to them. As compared to interview, storycrafting and drawing call for different kinds of co-operation between the participants. The researcher also needs to be ready to take steps in the direction of co-creation. Ideally, storycrafting and drawing sessions help to create a shared space and through this also the conditions for a peaceful encounter that leads to child-oriented storytelling (see Kinnunen 2015).

By intentionally giving room to interplay of the real and the imaginary, storycrafting explores the limits of knowledge achievable through ethnographic methods. However, one should keep in mind that in all ethnographic fieldwork, and in the material it creates, factual and fictional elements are often intertwined, whether the participants are adults or children. In narrative research, the aim of the research is usually not to figure out what exactly happened in people's lives, but rather to concentrate on the interpretations that the research participants have of the incidents, for example how narratives are performed and used in identity projects. For me the most important elements in the stories created during the storycrafting sessions are the emotions, interests, and viewpoints they convey. Children have had the possibility to decide what stories will be written down. For them, fiction contributions can be a way to lend their voice to research, contributions that say something valuable about the perspective of the child and of children. In fact, they might tell the researcher more about children's interests than factual accounts (von Benzon 2015, 338).

Researchers have referred to the dynamic and open nature of children's attempts to understand the world, and their interest in crossing and manipulating borders between different ways of narrating. We still know little about the ways in which children move back and forth between the literal and the nonliteral, the real world and the imaginary (Engel 2006, 208–210). The stories created during the storycrafting sessions give the possibility to glimpse children at play, watch them interweave fact and fiction, highlight children's ideas and their ways of thinking. In addition theses fiction stories and the related discussions may help children to work through their experiences and make sense of the world and their place in it (Nicolopoulou 1997, 208).

Our experiences from the storycrafting sessions indicate that carrying them out might be challenging, but when done the results are rewarding. Data generated using creative methods do not conform to the narrow definitions of reality and truth, but rather open up the ways that people organize and represent their experiences to exploration (Veale 2006). Finally, creative methods such as those described here have been more in use with children – it would be exiting to try this with adults as well.

## Notes

1 Families on the Move: Children's Perspectives on Migration in Europe (2012–2014). I continued to work with children on the Inequalities in Motion: Transnational Families in Estonia and Finland project (2016–2018), both funded by the Kone Foundation, Finland, and lead by Professor Laura Assmuth, University of Eastern Finland. Writing this article was supported by the Estonian Research Council's Performative Negotiations of Belonging in Contemporary Estonia (PUT PSG48) grant (2018–2021, PI Dr Elo-Hanna Seljamaa, University of Tartu).
2 I use pseudonyms when referring to the research subjects. Fieldwork notes and stories created during storycrafting sessions were translated from Finnish and Estonian to English by the author.
3 As experienced by Honkanen et al. (2018, 119) not all parents gave permission for their children to participate in the sessions, even when the child was willing. This shows how children lack the power to make decisions on matters that concern themselves.
4 Initially when we started to organize storycrafting sessions in kindergartens, we did not ask children to give titles to the stories, although we later did so with schoolchildren.

## References

Assmuth, L., M. Hakkarainen, A. Lulle, and P. M. Siim, eds. 2018. *Translocal Childhoods and Family Mobility in East and North Europe*. Cham: Palgrave Macmillan.
Bamberg, M., and A. Georgakopoulou. 2008. "Small stories as a new perspective in narrative and identity analysis". *Text & Talk* 28 (3): 377–396. doi:10.1515/TEXT.2008.018

Bankovska, A., and P. M. Siim. 2018. "And so the journey begins: An embodied approach to children's translocal materialities". In *Translocal Childhoods and Family Mobility in East and North Europe*, edited by L. Assmuth, M. Hakkarainen, A. Lulle, and P. M. Siim, 39–61. Cham: Palgrave Macmillan.

Bryceson, D. F., and U. Vuorela. 2002. "Transnational families in the twenty-first century". In *The Transnational Family. New European Frontiers and Global Networks*, edited by D. Bryceson, and U. Vuorela, 3–29. Oxford: Berg Publishers.

Coe, C., R. R. Reynolds, D. A. Boehm, J. M. Hess, and H. Rae-Espinoza, eds. 2011. *Everyday Ruptures: Children, Youth, and Migration in Global Perspective*. Nashville: Vanderbilt.

Dobson, M. E. 2009. "Unpacking children in migration research". *Children's Geographies* 7 (3): 355–360. doi:10.1080/14733280903024514

Eder, D., and L. Fingerson. 2001. "Interviewing children and adolescents". In *Handbook of Interview Research*, edited by J. F. Gubrium, and J. A. Holstein, 181–202. London: Sage.

Engel, S. 2006. "Narrative analysis of children's experience". In *Researching Children's Experience. Approaches and Methods*, edited by S. Greene, and D. Hogan, 199–216. London: Sage. doi:10.4135/9781849209823.n11

European Commission2019. *Annual Report on Intra-EU Labour Mobility. Final Report December 2018*. European Commission. Luxembourg: Publications Office of the European Union. https://ec.europa.eu/social/BlobServlet?docId=20685&langId=hu

Fresnoza-Flot, A. 2018. "Rethinking children's place(s) in transnational families. Mobile childhoods in Filipino international migration". In *Childhood and Parenting in Transnational Settings*, edited by V. Ducu, M. Nedelcu, and A. Telegdi-Csetri, 11–24. International Perspectives on Migration, vol. 15. Cham: Springer.

Fresnoza-Flot, A., and I. Nagasaka. 2015. "Conceptualising childhoods in transnational families: The 'mobile childhoods' lens". In *Mobile Childhoods in Filipino Transnational Families. Migrant Children with Similar Roots in Different Routes*, edited by I. Nagasaka, and A. Fresnoza-Flot, 23–41. Basingstoke: Palgrave Macmillan.

Gillies, V., and Y. Robinson. 2012. "Developing creative research methods with challenging pupils". *International Journal of Social Research Methodology* 15 (2): 161–173. doi:10.1080/13645579.2012.649407

Honkanen, K., J. Poikolainen, and L. Karlsson. 2018. "Children and young people as co-researchers – Researching subjective well-being in residential area with visual and verbal methods". *Children's Geographies* 16 (2): 184–195. doi:10.1080/14733285.2017.1344769

Jakobson, M-L., P. Järvinen-Alenius, P. Pitkänen, R. Ruutsoo, E. Keski-Hirvelä, and L. Kalev. 2012. "The emergence of Estonian-Finnish transnational space". In *Migration and Transformation. Multi-Level Analysis of Migrant Transnationalism*, edited by P. Pitkänen, A. Içduygu, and D. Sert, 159–205. International Perspectives on Migration, vol. 3. Dordrecht: Springer.

Karlsson, L. 2013. "Storycrafting method – To share, participate, tell and listen in practice and research". *The European Journal of Social and Behavioural Sciences* 6 (3): 1109–1117. doi:10.15405/ejsbs.88

Kinnunen, S. 2015. *How Are You? The Narrative In-Between Spaces in Young Children's Daily Lives*. PhD diss., University of Oulu. http://jultika.oulu.fi/files/isbn9789526210285.pdf.

Moskal, M., and N. Tyrrell. 2016. "Family migration decision-making, step-migration and separation: children's experiences in European migrant worker families". *Children's Geographies* 14 (4): 453–467. doi:10.1080/14733285.2015.1116683

Ní Laoire, C., F. Carpena-Mendez, N. Tyrrell, and A. White. 2011. *Childhood and Migration in Europe. Portraits of Mobility, Identity and Belonging in Contemporary Ireland*. London: Ashgate.

Nicolopoulou, A. 1997. "Children and narratives: Toward an interpretive and sociocultural approach". In *Narrative Development: Six Approaches*, edited by M. Bamberg, 179–215. New Jersey: Lawrence Erlbaum Associates.
Punch, S. 2002. "Research with children: The same or different from research with adults?" *Childhood* 9 (3): 321–341. doi:10.1177/0907568202009003005
Punch, S. 2009. "Moving for a better life: to stay or to go?" In *Key Issues in Childhood and Youth Studies*, edited by D. Kassem, L. Murphy, and E. Taylor, 202–215. London: Routledge.
Riihelä, M. 1991. *Aikakortit. Tie lasten ajatteluun* [Time Cards, the Way to Children's Thinking]. Helsinki: VAPK-kustannus.
Siim, P. M. 2016. "Everyday practices of translocal families: Estonian children and a sense of being-in-place". *Ethnologia Fennica. Finnish Studies in Ethnology* 43: 12–27. https://journal.fi/ethnolfenn/article/view/65632
Siim, P. M., and K. Telve, eds. 2019. *Minu kaks kodumaad. Laste lood elust kahe riigi vahel* [My Two Homelands: Children's Stories of Life Between Two Countries]. Tallinn: Helios.
Statistics Estonia2019. "More births and smaller emigration increased the population figure". 9 May 2019 – news release no 53. www.stat.ee/news-release-2019-053
Statistics Finland2013. "Suomessa työskentelee jo lähes 60 000 vierastyöläistä [Already Almost 60 000 Guest Workers Working in Finland]". www.stat.fi/artikkelit/2013/art_2013-09-23_013.html
Thompson, C. M. 1999. "Peer influences in preschool-kindergarten art classes". *Visual Arts Research* 25 (2): 61–68.
Veale, A. 2006. "Creative methodologies in participatory research with children". In *Researching Children's Experience. Approaches and Methods*, edited by S. Greene, and D. Hogan, 254–272. London: Sage. doi:10.4135/9781849209823.n14
Viljamaa, E. 2012. *Lasten tiedon äärellä. Äidin ja lasten kerronnallisia kohtaamisia kotona* [With Children's Knowledge. Narrative Encounters of a Mother and Children at Home]. Acta Universitatis Ouluensis E 129. Oulu: University of Oulu. http://jultika.oulu.fi/files/isbn9789514299940.pdf
von Benzon, N. 2015. "'I fell out of a tree and broke my neck': Acknowledging fantasy in children's research contributions". *Children's Geographies* 13 (3): 330–342. doi:10.1080/14733285.2013.829662
Zartler, U. 2014. "Photo interviews with children: Relating the visual and the verbal from a participation perspective". *International Journal of Child, Youth, and Family Studies* 5 (4.1): 629–648. doi:10.18357/ijcyfs.zartleru.5412014
Zeitlyn, B., and K. Mand. 2012. "Researching transnational childhoods". *Journal of Ethnic and Migration Studies* 38 (6): 987–1006. doi:10.1080/1369183X.2012.677179

# 7

## SHARPENING THE PENCIL

A visual journey towards the outlines of drawing as an autoethnographical method

*Marika Tervahartiala*

The presented research started as a drawn autoethnography focusing on drawing as a method. Surprisingly, outlining the autoethnographic drawing process revealed it to not only be the drawer's autoethnography but also the drawing processes autoethnography of itself and then, in turn, about the drawer. As I draw, the autoethnography, my processes, the drawing sketches me into being. These mutual acts gave rise to an attempt at a methodological approach where the drawing is an inseparable part of all the stages and iterations of the visual autoethnographic research process. Post-disciplinary as well as post-structuralistic approaches are needed to unveil and enlighten the possibilities of drawing as methodology and theory *as* practice (Irwin and Springgay 2008, 106). The autoethnographic drawing as a methodology is located within the umbrella of autoethnographic methodology that uses the researcher's personal experience as data to describe, analyse and

**FIGURE 7.1** Drawing by Marika Tervahartiala, 2019. Copyright: Marika Tervahartiala

understand cultural experience. This specific visual form of self-narrative places these two autoethnographic selves – the drawer and the drawing – within social as well as visual contexts and discourses.

This chapter aims to explore how autoethnographic drawing can be much more than just another visual method to be explored. It draws out drawing as a research methodology and lets the drawing to be[come] (Varto 2017, 21). Thus, the drawing is the methodology and the subject to be studied. The Drawing is presented as a real boundary bender in/of the line and within the lines: exploring the possibilities of a post-disciplinary methodology, fluently and shamelessly combining visual autoethnography, visual arts, even some scholarly comics and artistic research, while also flexing itself with a hint of art educational and transformative research. Drawing knows itself better than academic writing can describe it, thus the drawing is always more than language and words can (ever) know.

In this chapter, drawing is capitalized when referred to as a character, a "knower" or a mode of knowing that exceeds the researcher's abilities and capacity to know. Consequently, the agency in this chapter is shared. Even as a singular autoethnographer, I am not alone on my research journey, as the Drawing has uncovered itself as an emergent and active agent. It has repeatedly and resiliently withdrawn from being a research object and instead insisted on its full existence as an equal co-researcher in the autoethnographic process. As a general principle explaining my relationship with Drawing, I follow the advice of Carolyn Ellis "to rather show than tell" (2019, oral communication). Telling about the autoethnographic drawing (verb) cannot be anything but incomplete and present partial stories due to drawing's flow-like quality and insistence on stretching and bending subjectivities and boundaries of being and knowing.

A growing number of researchers from various fields have recently become interested in visuals: as material and method, produced and used by scholars. "Visuals" include a variety of graphic-based processes and productions such as drawings, comic art/scholarly comics (Kuttner, Sousanis, and Weaver-Hightower 2017; McCloud 1993, 2006), graphic novels (Sousanis 2015b), visual journaling (Shields 2016), sketchbooks and illustrations. Drawing fits into numerous contradicting and overlapping disciplines and areas of contemporary study (Theron et al. 2011, 19). As a research method, drawing is a true post-disciplinary nomad, finding its home wherever the line is drawn (pun intended): fluently sketching itself among other visual methods for example in anthropology and ethnography (Alfonso et al. 2004; Ingold 2007, 2010, 2011; Pink 2007a; 2007b). One can find it in educational research as a/r/tography (Cahnmann-Taylor and Siegesmund 2008; Irwin and Springgay 2008) as well as in health and social science(s) (Theron et al. 2011). It can be spotted in the research of art to research through art and art-based, arts-informed, even artistic research (Knowles and Cole 2008; Mannay 2016; Mäkelä and O"Riley 2012; Mäkelä and Routarinne 2006; Rose 2001; Varto 2013, 2017; Sullivan 2008; Chenail 2008; Bochner and Ellis 2003; Douglas and Carless 2018; Guillemin 2004; Literat 2013; Sava and Nuutinen 2003; Leavy 2018). This explorative chapter on the methodology and ethics of autoethnographic drawing aims to blur the current [drawn] lines between disciplines as allocating or limiting drawing precisely to a specific academic discourse which only disrupts it.

Drawing that corresponds to autoethnography has the quality of being simultaneously used as a method and a methodology. It could simply be the way to present and illustrate research outcomes, but in this chapter I focus on arguing that autoethnographic drawing can "contribute to new knowledge and offer new ways of imagining and encountering the world" as Duxbury (2009, 97) claims about art in general. Constructing my claims, I rely on previous research as well as my own experiences as a practitioner, as an autoethnographer, a drawer and a combination of both. Tongue in cheek, I propose that, by sharpening my pencil, I contribute to the scholarly conversation exploring the possibility of autoethnographic drawing as a methodology.

## Methods, ontological fluidity and the emergent epistemology of drawing

In autoethnographic drawing, the method and methodology, together with epistemology, are interrelated. And although there may be multiple possibilities for each, if used as an epistemological orientation, each element is deeply intertwined. As a result of this, I aim to elucidate the epistemology and ontology of autoethnographic drawing. By outlining the epistemological standpoint, the framework of possibilities can be identified.

To define drawing, I use the concept of drawing instead of visual journaling, sketching or doodling (e.g. Azevedo and Ramos 2016, 143; Tokolahi 2010, 161; Heath, Chapman, and The Morgan Centre Sketchers 2018). Many visual ethnographers use these terms fluently and interchangeably side by side without asking the question "Who owns the words we use?" (Swanson 2008, 89) or without making significant conceptual, or theoretical distinctions between them. The concept of autoethnographic drawing was chosen for my research because it is more related to intentionality than the words "sketching" or "doodling". At least my sketching tends to be messy to the point that it turns into abstract and unfocused doodling. They both are random try-outs, visual splashes of ongoing processes, sometimes done to spend time or amuse others or myself. With the autoethnographic drawing, as I perceive the method, there is always an aim to end up with a finalized picture to the level of completion that it can also be "understood" by those other than the drawer. However, the practical steps of my drawing process are beside the methodological point.

More broad artistic approaches, such as photography, video and sound, have become popular in ethnographic research in the 21st century. These approaches have been actively developed, and their methodological and ethical challenges widely discussed (Alfonso, Kurti, and Pink 2004; Pink 2007a; 2007b; Mannay 2016; Knowles and Cole 2008; Hughes-Freeland 2004; MacDougall 1997). Among the wide and expanding range of visual methods and forms of representation, drawing has only received little attention in scholarship. Drawing as a[n auto]ethnographical research method and especially as a methodological construction is unexplored and relatively under-theorized with only a few examples to mention (e.g. Theron et al. 2011; Weber 2008; Literat 2013; Azevedo and Ramos 2016). Visual autoethnographies (e.g. Scarles 2010) use other methods/methodologies than drawing, mostly photography and video.

Every academic discipline has its ontological sphere (Varto 2017, 62–64), where research phenomena are to be understood and where their existence is accepted and expected. Usually, besides this sphere, the phenomena become blurry, losing their distinctive characteristics (Varto 2017, 62). I claim that drawing is an emergent method and methodology, an event and an entity, in the epistemology of a constant state of becoming. When utilized, harnessed and respected to the potential of its emergent being as an oddity and a chameleon spirit, it can turn every disciplinary hue to its own, with no harm done to its assigning itself fluently to the post-disciplinary transformation. I see drawing as "a living process for communicating and understanding" (Four Arrows 2008, 6). To me, it is also an ontology, a being.

Due to being an ontology, in the initial stages of researching autoethnographic drawing quite often resembles fumbling with a marker pen in the dark. Especially before the process begins, it is hard to point out what should be [re]searched and even more challenging to identify the tools for this quest (Varto 2017, 23). The actual drawing process[es] brings along the needed light and clarity to the focus. As Swanson (2008, 84) in her arts-based research points out: "A researcher can never be absolutely sure, only guided towards what she believes to be the way ahead". To best describe this, I claim that autoethnographic drawing could be compared to GPS-navigation: unless you move (your marker), you will never find out if you are going in the right direction. Drawing as artistic research seizes scrabbling, scribbling, drifting and walking the track: as these are all elementary in grasping the essential part of the process that is creative and evocative. The autoethnographic drawing process is the operationalization of this epistemological standpoint: by drawing, I begin to be, understand and know.

As is true of all scholarship, locating one's work within a methodological community or communities is crucial (Theron et al. 2011, 21). I trace my study alongside ethnographic, and specifically autoethnographic, methodologies. The analysis of visual imagery and exemplary texts on the interpretation of visual materials are well known. The critical visual methodology (Rose 2001) and visual ethnography are useful methodological perspectives, but they cannot be applied for developing the methodology of autoethnographic drawing. This research gravitates towards and emerges from exploratory, more artistic research methodologies. Thereby I operate within a creative paradigm of artistic research methodologies.

The autoethnographic drawing process is reluctant to be reduced into a research instrument and the continuous drawing process resists being formalized into a set of procedures or prescriptions (Swanson 2008, 89). Shifting from one discipline to another, whether inter-, trans- or post-disciplinary, does not suffocate drawing as much as if drawing is subordinated from a way of knowing (e.g. Bochner and Ellis 2003, 508), communicating and understanding (Four Arrows 2008, 6). Drawing that is diminished to an instrument or a plain procedure loses its unique intuitive and creative potential of [un]knowing, not-knowing and [re]creating the negative capability (Bion 1980, 11).

I argue that the autoethnographic drawing does not accommodate any tool-likeness as a method. Rather, it has a tendency to unfold and uncurl, colour outside and over the lines, to grow and flow into a methodology. The autoethnographic drawing by being simultaneously the researcher and the Drawing generates creative research processes expanding beyond researcher's cognition and logic. Understandably, rendering visual research process in a form of a textual methodological chapter is far from untroublesome (see also Swanson 2008, 85). To explore this, I turn to post-structuralism. Post-structuralism considers the research of the underlying structures itself as a cultural product. Therefore, studying the underlying structures cannot be anything but subjective and subject to prejudices and misinterpretations. In addition, the analysis of drawing itself (the visible) is insufficient to provide understanding about autoethnographic drawing as a dialogical process and product as well as the mutual being of one (researcher) and the other (Drawing).

**FIGURE 7.2** Drawing by Marika Tervahartiala, 2019 Copyright: Marika Tervahartiala

## Drawing the line, drawing as an active agent and autoethnographical authority

Bruner claims our thoughts are associated with and largely constituted by images (1984). The Drawing is at least as much the creator of a drawer than the drawer is the creator of a drawing. Based on Baudrillard (1988, as cited in Weber 2008, 43), Weber claims: "images themselves act as objects and take on lives of their own, with no single object beyond the signifier as primary referent.... An image can thus be 'the thing itself' – the object of inquiry". I argue the autoethnographic drawing to be even more than "the thing itself". The Drawing as an active being is beyond "immutable" (Weber 2008, 43) or "object". Once in existence or partially imagined, its independence or authority cannot be oppressed, but it is a "living information system" (Four Arrows 2008, 2) and an entity. The Drawing is also a non-human "personality" (2008, 6) whose knowledge exceeds what I can articulate, and which I have to recognize and respect.

Drawing a line with a marker pen is not a moment of mark nor creation, but a visible continuation of a Drawing's becoming. We humans can imagine, dream and see images with our eyes (wide) shut (Weber 2008, 41). I see, visualize and imagine and understand before I think and, therefore, the Drawing seems to always to be ahead of me (Weber 2008, 41; Berger 1972). The emergent and processual drawing, its dialogical and multidirectional entities deny the autoethnographer's possibility to claim creator status. Due to the emergent and eventing nature of the autoethnographic drawing, it cannot be researched "as such" – by itself. Therefore, making autoethnographical observations on its effects and influence on me, the drawer, is needed, and the process of doing and generating and sharing the Drawing so that the process can be studied as a whole.

Actors share the experience of the role playing the actor instead of the actor playing the role. Autoethnographic drawing comes close to this well-recognized phenomenon: the Drawing (act) seems to be playing [drawing] me and vice versa. Occasionally, the blank page of the sketchbook becomes a stage-like space due to the performative nature of drawing. In the line-making act, the "becoming" of the Drawing is visible. This becoming continues in following perceptual processes. These further becomings can be understood through multiple orientation points: the drawer, the drawing and the relationship(s) and the reader/viewer [be]come [together] with, within and for the drawing or their theme.

In replacing hierarchies and existing power structures like: "Who was here in the first place? Where did it start and from whom? To whom does it belong?" I turn to post-structuralists like Deleuze and Guattari (1996). Their rhizomes seem to be opposite to hierarchies (Swanson 2008, 84–89; Irwin and Springgay 2008, 106). The dialogical space, the intention(s) of Drawing are always in motion, creating a complexity of multiple dimensions. Autoethnographic drawing is still "a terra incognita" that has not yet revealed in all its complexity "what it has, what it is, what it can do, and how it does it, and why" (Swanson 2008, 90). By engaging, I have asked it to come forth and partially reveal itself (see Swanson 2008, 90) and as an insightful partner, the drawing invites and insists that I do the very same.

In the most subjective or self-serving terms, autoethnographic drawing serves as a tactic to reveal, understand and overcome the researcher's mental boundaries (Azevedo and Ramos 2016, 140). I usually draw "on the spot", for example in conferences, seminars and while reading reference materials. I [re]act by creating a visual commentary and/or giving visible form for my thoughts, associations, even attitudes and [pre-]assumptions. Drawing may twist, comment, observe or interpret ideas as well as the content I have the inner and/or visual dialogue with. I draw to be, to become and to understand. Autoethnographic drawing is instant: there is a sense of being in the zone – a feeling related to the concept of flow (Csikszentmihályi 1990). Making a drawing takes only a couple of minutes, but it creates a specific time-space for materializations of wandering and imaginative thought (Azevedo and Ramos 2016, 141). It also challenges this time-space specificity by questioning its limits and boundaries as it recreates itself unbound to its original time and space context.

## In uncertainty, nurture the trouble(d) and stay with the discomfort

"Stay with the discomfort" is a commonly used piece of advice among autoethnographers (Carolyn Ellis 2019, oral communication). Anything somewhat tricky, hard to handle, unknown and the overall discomfort suggests: "Observe and research more closely!" This autoethnographically significant discomfort might be, for example hard-to-hear subconscious whispers and various signifying ruptures in the normally smooth drawing process. It can be a small notion that I change my mind in the middle of drawing; suddenly, I decide not-to-draw what intuitively came to my mind in the first place. Sometimes I sense shivering or faint doubts: "Is there something that I don't want to draw?" that I am not ready to understand or general alertness.

Azevedo and Ramos (2016, 143) mention "paralysis and hesitation in the act of drawing itself". Since I have been drawing all my life and researching it for a few of years, I no longer get "paralysed": hesitation, doubts and the unwillingness or inability to draw belong to my drawing process as a natural part. As in breathing, the pause between inhaling and exhaling, the gaps, stops and empty spaces are elemental in drawing (as a noun and a verb). For an autoethnographer, it is necessary to recognize that "gaps exist between what can be shown, seen or felt and what can be said" (Bochner and Ellis 2003, 507). These cracks and not-knowing in (a) drawing are to be cherished as these fractures are also spaces for a reader/viewer to unknow and not-to-understand. I claim that drawing leaves more room for impartiality than words; the space between the lines is fertile soil for valuable uncertainty, wonder and curiosity.

The autoethnographic process of drawing usually includes several elements of flow, such us intense and focused concentration on the present moment, merging of action and awareness, and altered experience of time (usually time flies for me), but it also has features quite opposite to the flow. Instead of a loss of reflective self-consciousness, some of the reflective and self-conscious elements are amplified by the Drawing, but not necessarily during drawing. Instead of a sense of personal control or agency over the activity, I experience fulfilment in the shared agency. There is an element of relief about the loss of personal control and, therefore, responsibility. Drawing and I flexibly blend the roles of a servant and a master, the observed and the observer. This is not a controllable knowing and far from getting fixed on the familiar and safe (Swanson 2008, 92).

While in the flow, the experience of the activity appears intrinsically rewarding, but the transformative autoethnographic drawing may as well be discomforting and cause friction. "The pain of letting go and just drawing goes against everything I know", describes Rambo (2007, 536) in her article about sketching as an autoethnographic practice. The feeling of losing oneself, becoming fragmented and fluid, a constant becoming or even the possibility of limitless openness are not always comfortable sensations. Hard as they are, to be appreciated just as dreaming and visions (having elements similar to drawing) are potentially valid sources to knowledge (Four Arrows 2008, 2). It is only by cyclically repeating the mental leap of faith of relying on drawing, that there is a primitive urge to control the process as it lessens but does not ever fully disappear. Experience or expertise of Drawing does not free me from still falling back to my inability to let go of control. Especially drawing in academic contexts repeatedly brings forth the requirement to (verbally) explain and validate the drawing (see also Rambo 2007, 537). It is still unsolved how it would be possible to academically praise the not-knowing and unknowing: "What if I do not know, but maybe the drawing does?"

This concept of "taking a leap of faith" has been troubling and explored by scholars (e.g. Duxbury 2009, 98). Whilst this chapter aims not to reach to the areas of transpersonal psychology or to the states of consciousness beyond the limits of the ego and personality, but it is clear that drawing brings along the transformational and intuitive. The faith in the process is usually based on the previous beneficial experiences of trusting on a creative method, as Clements states:

> Transformative changes of heart – the training of ego to tolerate and support collaboration with liminal and spiritual sources – require a temporary suspension of critical thinking in order to access non-egoic input. Afterwards, the ego steps forward to integrate the new material into the study. (Clements 2011, 132)

A drawing autoethnographer does not need reconciliation for the controversial (or) discords (Swanson 2008, 87), but for the ego, which often too eagerly wants to grasp and control the pen.

The researcher's and Drawing's shared bidirectional autoethnographic "I" [eye/ (ai)] can have an intention to emerge as a storyteller and occasionally even a metalevel comic-character. Eventually, there cannot be any mediator for a drawer's "intention" as autoethnographic drawing is a fluid construction of diverse intentions and fluctuating intentionality. For the research to happen and the knowing to emerge, the drawer and the Drawing, which have a shared intention to emerge, become the lines; a picture to be seen and shared. Drawing is consciousness:

> In fact, consciousness is always about intentionality, directionality, agendas, positions or, if you will, a hypothesis. This comes from the experiential aspect of consciousness. Experience registers in our conscious awareness, the situation both as we undergo it, and as we relate to it. (Swanson 2008, 92)

Autoethnographic drawing accepts conflicting and overlapping readings. While the autoethnographer has to be willing to rely on Drawing, the reader/viewer is asked to give up on searching for the sole and "true" drawer's intentions. If the reader/viewer is able to let go and give up on the quest for sole intended message, possibilities for myriads of interpretative perspectives and, even processes of invention arise. They vary and multiply by every reader and reading and by shifting contexts, they create infinite kaleidoscopic possibilities, displacements and replacements. Thus, giving up becomes drawing out, the visual dialogue between the Drawing and the drawer then becomes a trialogue. The autoethnographical drawing desires to be a tempting invitation for a reader/viewer to a dialogical journey as through this journey the Drawing gain infinite possibilities for more lives.

**FIGURE 7.3** Drawing by Marika Tervahartiala, 2019. Copyright: Marika Tervahartiala

## Linearity and binary classifications: time to draw (fight) back

The path into the drawing is not linear: "creative work does not necessarily follow a linear process, nor adhere to objectivity and logic" (Bardsley 2018, 2). The arts are the symbiotic language of the subconscious, as Duxbury (2009, 97; see also Bardsley 2018) states. In this chapter, linear wordiness occurs in spite of the autoethnographic drawing's authority mainly due to the limitations of academic format. Deconstructing binaries of linear/non-linear, words/visuals, is not easily done, especially when the other autoethnographer, the simultaneous subject and object of the research (i.e. Drawing), is visibly absent from these pages. In addition, the sense of time and perceptions of time in autoethnographic drawing is hard to transmit through words, which are neatly marching in order, line after line, forming chapters, then turning into publications that dominate over visuals. Perceiving time in an autoethnographic drawing *is* engaging with the world in associative and flexible iterations.

Being non-linear and time unbound, autoethnographic drawing lets us into a pluralized epistemology. Drawing is somewhat akin to handwriting as it can be described with concepts related to the language: (visual) vocabulary, syntax and grammar. I prefer not to make distinctions between writing and drawing or between one kind of a drawing to another. Instead of categorizing and labelling, I prefer to blur and displace borders, disrupt dualisms between writing(s) and drawing(s).

The coherent or meaningful coming-together between visual drawings and the written text needs further research as processes of folding and unfolding images and text together are to be explored more closely. There might be times of unison, but the text and drawings are also purposely deconstructing each other. Focus on the fight on the hierarchy between visual and verbal attracts the reader into a deconstructive (reading) process(es), and thus remove the focus from the essential and elements and components of autoethnography (see also Four Arrows 2008, 2). Academic words alone cannot present a solid methodology of drawn autoethnography. Words and language alone or in dominant relation to visuals can create an illusion or a reproduction of a creative visual process, its description and even analysis, but they cannot be[come] it. Therefore, methodological knowing and outcomes will be bursting out [in]between the words and the lines. They are only hinting at the visual possibilities and the limitations of this chosen methodology.

I go along with Swanson's remark about research as an object not necessitating a final closure: in her research poetic enquiry is a process of continuous metaphoring, which also lies in the core of my autoethnographic drawing (Swanson 2008, 89). I claim that words can be drained from meanings more thoroughly than drawings. If a drawing is continuously refilled with meanings created by the viewer and the context, no number of words can drain a drawing of meanings. Barthes (1984, 38–39) considers the text as an anchor for the visual: the text loads the image. Instead of this one-way loading from text to image, a deconstructive approach applies, that text loads and unloads the drawings just as much the drawings (re/un)load the text. An essential element is the reader/viewer is an equal part of these ongoing processes of loading, constructing and deconstructing.

## Drawing and drawings in/of/and Academia

As the saying goes: "Publish or perish", but publishing research relying on visuals can be challenging. Most publications rely on certain format(s) of academic *text*. Whether electronic or books, the publications are designed based on textuality: their layouts are fixed, and the amount, size and quality of the pictures is usually limited to a few small-scale black and white illustrative examples. It is obvious in laying out the pages that the composition of the pictures/text plays a significant role in conveying narrative and autoethnography. The meanings can be constructed as in comics: on, with and by the layout of the page(s) (Sousanis 2015a, 1-3; Eisner 1985; Sousanis 2012; Holmes 2008, 97). The fixed format of an academic paper in itself shares authority unequally between words and visuals. Only occasionally it is possible to modify these formats and give the leading role for visual[s], whether they are research material or otherwise. Any window of an opportunity usually belongs to the field of art and/or artistic research: maybe some new electronic form of publishing research including even video, sound or virtual reality – also commonly subordinated mediums. Based on new methods, methodologies and even forms of data, fundamental resharing of authority and power between words and visuals in the academic publications is needed in the near future. This is even more crucial considering Ellsworth's (2005, 156): argument: "some knowings cannot be conveyed through language". Without autoethnographic drawings as equals to text, academia is losing forms of knowing that escape and slip through the language.

Academic formatting concretely renders the way drawings and words need to go hand in hand into something "nonsensical, illogical, and impossible to read", as Holmes (2008, 97) describes. It kills the Drawing. Like Holmes, I have also been struggling with the academic format, having no access to the visual design of the chapter or its page size and orientation, paper quality, lay-outs, margins, etc. Some of my autoethnographical drawings should be partnered with a particular piece of text, but not necessarily like the usual illustrations right before or after the text. To have their agency, they need their intervined presence, side-by-side, like partner in a dance: the drawings want to twirl around the text freely, flirt with it, and the other way around! The fluctuating relationship(s) and power struggle(s) between word and visuals should be clearly visible for the reader: the drawing(s) overlapping the text or willingly hiding behind it. If the particular drawings do not *just as is their wish to have a dialogue*, the beneficial differences of these mediums and their (opposing) voices and intentions is lost. When the visuals cannot be in the comparative or simultaneous reading and process of exchange with the text, they are diminished into indifferent illustrations. A clear power play, conscious or not, is against our autoethnographic voices. For autoethnographers the game is lost if the format of academic publishing just does not recognize Drawing's crucial ontological needs, especially the need to exist on its own terms. Then autoethnographic drawing is pushed into powerlessness, into margins and in between referential practices.

The aim of the chapter is to describe the challenges faced by the visual autoethnographer using drawing as a method. This study is an example of drawn autoethnography, and what can be known and understood by

**FIGURE 7.4** Drawings by Marika Tervahartiala, 2019, layout by Maria Manner. Copyright: Marika Tervahartiala

autoethnographic drawing. One might even claim an autoethnographic drawing to be an 'anti-method', as theory is not an "abstract system distinct and separate from practice" (Irwin and Springgay 2008, 106). Autoethnographic drawing brings along ontological and epistemological questions concerning also other visual methods and their effectiveness. The potential of this perspective is that contemplating on the advantages and disadvantages of these themes may offer new perspectives to visual ethnographers to evaluate authority, entity and the artfulness of autoethnography.

Contemporary participatory visual methods are widely used in various fields to engage and empower the informants, influenced already by the early work of Paolo Freire (1970). The concept of participatory visuals methods is usually limited to the production stage of research and visual methods seem to be participatory only as long as the research is ongoing. Evoked imagination, producing mental images, or any other form of visual thinking, participating in the dialogue with the visual(s) in a research report is usually not considered "participatory". As a drawing autoethnographer, I set an open question on how visual autoethnographic methods could be used to lure the reader/viewer into participating in the visual knowledge production and processes of exchange even when presenting the 'finished' research.

Drawings are interrupting normalized academic formats and challenging to perceive freshly and differently the formats of scholarly publications. Any "sedimentation of the past research practices seeking 'certainty', 'closure' and 'control'" (Berry and Patti 2015, 265) fails and "These meanings therefore must be allowed to emerge in their own right, in their own 'light', according to their own idiosyncratic perspective and agenda, but also according to their own potentialities and potencies of meaning-making – not constrained by a priori definitions and theories of the meaning phenomenon that would restrict it in a narrow way, by prescribing its nature and reach before it is even investigated." (Swanson 2008, 90).

Although this text is not composed in a manner that dignifies Drawing but as a mere presentation of words, the reader is to evaluate if I have managed to deepen and extend understandings and 'the usual terrain' (Swanson 2008, 87) of visual autoethnography with and about Drawing by drawing.

The Drawing is, and the drawings are, more than willing to be juxtaposed with the text and with the reader. On the contrary they favor being different, uncomfortable, displeasing, troubling, even entertaining! Autoethnographic drawing awakens Drawing and by this accepts uncertainty and uncomfortable in research and rather welcomes getting lost in narration with drawing (Berry and Patti 2015).

If image no longer illustrates the words (Barthes 1984, 25), the freedom to create forms of representation that are in harmony with authentic experience, unique abilities and skills, is highly important. This is a significant and meaningful shift not only to the researcher but also to achieve the full potential of the research for/with the readers (see Four arrows 2008, 4). Transformation in readers (Berry and Patty 2015, 265) may be too ambitious goal to draw out. An achievable aim may be to (re)imagine a more autoethnographic and holistic academic life, an inclusive life built on less restrictive ontologies and epistemologies. In the personal change, the development of insights and knowing would be more curious, explorative and open to trouble, discomfort, unknown and uncertain and as a result become more knowing, 'certain', accepting and limitless.

**FIGURE 7.5** Drawings by Marika Tervahartiala, 2019, layout by Maria Manner. Copyright: Marika Tervahartiala

# References

Azevedo, A., and M. J. Ramos. 2016. "Drawing close – on visual engagements in fieldwork, drawing workshops and the anthropological imagination". *Visual Ethnography* 5 (1): 135–160. doi:10.12835/ve2016.1-0061

Alfonso, A. I., L. Kurti, and S. Pink, eds. 2004. *Working Images: Visual Research and Representation in Ethnography*. London: Routledge.

Anderson, R., and W. Braud. 2011. *Transforming Self and Others Through Research: Transpersonal Research Methods and Skills for the Human Sciences and Humanities*. New York: State University of New York Press.

Anderson, R., and J. Linder. 2019. "Spirituality and emergent research methods". In *Routledge International Handbook of Spirituality and Society*, edited by L. Zsolnai and B. Flanagan, 48–55. New York: Routledge. doi:10.4324/9781315445489

Bardsley, L. J. 2018. "Wholeness as a creative exploration of self". *Survive & Thrive: A Journal for Medical Humanities and Narrative as Medicine* 4 (1): Article 16. https://repository.stcloud state.edu/survive_thrive/vol4/iss1/16

Barthes, R. 1984. *Image Music Text*. London: Fontana Paperbacks.

Berger, J. 1972 [2008]. *Ways of Seeing*. London: Penguin Design Series.

Berry, K., and C. J. Patti. 2015. "Lost in narration: Applying autoethnography". *Journal of Applied Communication Research* 43 (2): 263–268. doi:10.1080/00909882.2015.1019548

Bion, W. R. 1980. *Bion in New York and São Paulo*, edited by F. Bion. Perthshire: Clunie Press.

Bochner, A. P., and C. Ellis. 2003. "An introduction to the arts and narrative research: Art as inquiry". *Qualitative Inquiry* 9 (4): 506–514.

Bruner, E. M., ed. 1984. *Text, Play, and Story: The Construction and Reconstruction of Self and Society*. Washington, DC: The American Ethnological Society. https://doi.org/10.1525/a e.1985.12.2.02a00150

Cahnmann-Taylor, M., and R. Siegesmund, eds. 2008. *Arts-Based Research in Education. Foundations for Practice*. New York: Routledge.

Clements, J. 2011. "Organic inquiry. Research in partnership with spirit". In *Transforming Self and Others Through Research: Transpersonal Research Methods and Skills for the Human Sciences and Humanities*, edited by R. Anderson and W. Braud, 131–159. New York: State University of New York Press.

Chenail, R. J. 2008. "'But is it research?' A review of Patricia Leavy's method meets art: Arts-based research practice". *The Weekly Qualitative Report* 1 (2): 7–12.

Csikszentmihályi, M. 1990. *Flow: The Psychology of Optimal Experience*. New York: Harper & Row.

Deleuze, G., and F. Guattari. 1996. *What Is Philosophy?* Translated by H. Tomlinson and G. Burchell, revised edition. New York: Columbia University Press.

Douglas, K., and D. Carless. 2018. "Engaging with arts-based research: A story in three parts". *Qualitative Research in Psychology* 15 (2–3):156–172. doi:10.1080/14780887.2018.1429843

Duxbury, L. 2009. "If we knew what we were doing". In *SCOPE: Contemporary Research Topics (Art and Design)*, edited by L. Schmidt, A. Bramwell, and A. Kennedy, 1–8. New Zealand: Dunedin.

Eisner, W. 1985. *Comics and Sequential Art*. Tamarac, FL: Poorhouse Press.

Ellis, C., and A. Bochner. 2000. "Autoethnography, personal narrative, reflexivity: Researcher as subject". In *The Handbook of Qualitative Research*, edited by N. Denzin and Y. Lincoln, 733–768. Thousand Oaks, CA: Sage.

Ellsworth, E. 2005. *Places of Learning: Media, Architecture, Pedagogy*. New York: Routledge.

Four Arrows (Wahinkpe Topa), aka D. T. Jacobs, ed. 2008. *The Authentic Dissertation. Alternative Ways of Knowing, Research, and Representation*. London: Routledge.

Freire, P. 1970. *The Pedagogy of the Oppressed*. New York, NY: Herder & Herder.
Guillemin, M. 2004. "Understanding illness: Using drawings as a research method". *Qualitative Health Research* 14 (2): 272–289. doi:10.1177/1049732303260445
Heath, S., L. Chapman, and The Morgan Centre Sketchers. 2018. "Observational sketching as method". *International Journal of Social Research Methodology* 21 (6): 713–728. doi:10.1080/13645579.2018.1484990
Holmes, P. 2008. "A journey to praxis". In *The Authentic Dissertation. Alternative Ways of Knowing, Research, and Representation*, edited by Four Arrows (Wahinkpe Topa), aka D. T. Jacobs, 95–110. London: Routledge.
Hughes-Freeland, F. 2004. "Working images. Epilogue". In *Working Images: Visual Research and Representation in Ethnography*, edited by A. I. Alfonso, L. Kurti, and S. Pink, 201–214. London: Routledge.
Ingold, T. 2007. *Lines. A Brief History*. London: Routledge.
Ingold, T. 2010. "Drawing together: Materials, gestures, lines". In *Experiments in Holism. Theory and Practice in Contemporary Anthropology*, edited by T. Otto and N. Bubandt, 299–313. Oxford: Wiley-Blackwell.
Ingold, T. 2011. *Being Alive: Essays on Movement, Knowledge and Description*. London: Routledge.
Irwin, R. L., and S. Springgay. 2008. "A/r/tgraphy as practice-based research". In *Arts-Based Research in Education. Foundations for Practice*, edited by M. Cahnmann-Taylor and R. Siegesmund, 103–124. New York: Routledge.
Knowles, G. J., and A. L. Cole, eds. 2008. *Handbook of the Arts in Qualitative Research. Perspectives, Methodologies, Examples, and Issues*. Los Angeles: Sage.
Koro-Ljungberg, M., T. Löytönen, and M. Tesar. 2017. "Irruptions. DataHoles". In *Disrupting Data in Qualitative Inquiry. Entanglements with the Post-Critical and Post-Anthropocentric*, edited by M. Koro-Ljungberg, T. Löytönen, and M. Tesar, 225–231. New York NY: Peter Lang Publishing.
Kuttner, P. J., N. Sousanis, and M. B. Weaver-Hightower. 2017. "How to draw comics the scholarly way. Creating comics-based research in the academy". In *Handbook of Arts-Based Research*, edited by P. Leavy, 396–422. New York: The Guilford Publications.
Leavy, P. 2018. *Handbook of Arts-based Research*. New York: The Guilford Press.
Literat, I. 2013. "'A pencil for your thoughts': Participatory drawing as a visual research method with children and youth". *IJQM, International Journal of Qualitative Methods* 12 (1): 84–98.
MacDougall, D. 1997. "The visual in anthropology". In *Rethinking Visual Anthropology*, edited by M. Banks and H. Murphy, 276–296. New Haven: Yale University Press.
Mannay, D. 2016. *Visual, Narrative and Creative Research Methods. Application, Reflection and Ethics*. London: Routledge.
McCloud, S. 1993. *Understanding Comics*. Northampton, MA: Kitchen Sink Press.
McCloud, S. 2006. *Making Comics*. New York, NY: Harper.
Mäkelä, M., and T. O'Riley, eds. 2012. *The Art of Research II. Process, Results and Contribution*. Aalto University Publication Series, Art + Design + Architecture 11. Helsinki: Aalto Arts Books.
Mäkelä, M., and S. Routarinne, eds. 2006. *The Art of Research. Research Practices in Art and Design*. Publication series of the University of Art and Design Helsinki A 73. Helsinki: University of Art and Design Helsinki.
Pink, S., ed. 2007a. *Visual Interventions. Applied Visual Anthropology. Studies in Applied Anthropology*. New York: Berghahn Books.
Pink, S. 2007b. *Doing Visual Ethnography. Images, Media and Representation in Research*, second edition. London: Sage.

Rambo, C. 2007. "Sketching as autoethnographic practice". *Symbolic Interaction* 30 (4): 531–542. doi:10.1525/si.2007.30.4.531

Rose, G. 2001. *Visual methodologies. An Introduction to the Interpretation of Visual Materials.* London: Sage.

Sava, I., and K. Nuutinen. 2003. "At the meeting place of world and picture: Between art and inquiry". *Qualitative Inquiry* 9 (4): 515–534. doi:10.1177/1077800403254218

Scarles, C. 2010. "Where words fail, visuals ignite: Opportunities for visual autoethnography in tourism research". *Annals of Tourism Research* 37 (4): 905–926.

Shields, S. S. 2016. "How I learned to swim: The visual journal as a companion to creative inquiry". *International Journal of Education & the Arts* 17 (8). http://www.ijea.org/v17n8/

Sousanis, N. 2012. "The shape of our thoughts: A meditation on & in comics". *Visual Arts Research* 38 (1): 1–10. doi:10.5406/visuartsrese.38.1.0001

Sousanis, N. 2015a. "Grids and gestures: A comics making exercise". *SANE Journal: Sequential Art Narrative in Education* 2 (1): Article 8. https://digitalcommons.unl.edu/sane/vol2/iss1/8

Sousanis, N. 2015b. *Unflattening.* Cambridge, MA: Harvard University Press.

Sullivan, G. 2008. "Painting as research: Create and critique". In *Handbook of the Arts in Qualitative Research Perspectives, Methodologies, Examples, and Issues*, edited by G. J. Knowles and A. L. Cole, 239–250. Los Angeles: Sage.

Swanson, D. 2008. "Breaking silences" (with J. Moran and E. Honan). In *The Authentic Dissertation. Alternative Ways of Knowing, Research, and Representation*, edited by Four Arrows (Wahinkpe Topa), aka D. T. Jacobs, 83–94. London: Routledge.

Theron, L., and C. Mitchell, A. Smith, and J. Stuart, eds. 2011. *Picturing Research. Drawing as Visual Methodology.* Rotterdam: Sense Publishers.

Tokolahi, E. 2010. "Case study: Development of a drawing-based journal to facilitate reflective inquiry". *Reflective Practice* 11 (2): 157–170. doi:10.1080/14623941003665976

Varto, J. 2013. *Otherwise than Knowing. Ten Meditations on a Theme Inspired by Harri Laakso.* Helsinki: Aalto University.

Varto, J. 2017. *Taiteellinen tutkimus. Mitä se on? Kuka sitä tekee? Miksi?* Helsinki: Aalto University.

Weber, S. 2008. "Visual images in research". In *Handbook of the Arts in Qualitative Research. Perspectives, Methodologies, Examples, and Issues*, edited by G. J. Knowles and A. L. Cole, 41–54. Los Angeles: Sage.

Zsolnai, L., and B. Flanagan, eds. 2019. *The Routledge International Handbook of Spirituality in Society and the Professions.* New York: Routledge.

# PART III
# Ethnography of power dynamics in challenging contexts

# 8
# RETROSPECTIVE ETHNOGRAPHIES

Twisting moments of researching commemorative practices among volunteers after the refugee arrivals to Europe 2015

*Marie Sandberg*

## Introduction

The *Museum without a Home – an Exhibition of Hospitality* was a travelling exhibition curated by Oxfam and Amnesty International Greece in 2016. It exhibited everyday items donated by Greek citizens to refugees arriving during the so-called "long summer of welcome" in 2015. On display, for example, were a jacket donated by Spyros and a backpack donated by Mara. As the accompanying exhibition text explained, Spyros lived near the Greek-Albanian border where many refugees were temporarily hosted in 2015 and while helping out as a volunteer he became acquainted with one of the Syrian refugees, to whom he decided to give his jacket. Further, it is described how Mara, living in Athens, would pass by Victoria Square on a daily basis back in 2015 in order to provide refugee children with pencils, paper and other school supplies; the backpack was among her donations.

Since November 2016, the *Museum without a Home* exhibition has travelled the world. As can be seen from Oxfam's webpage, the exhibition is "dedicated to humanity", the overall mission being to display, "the new historical contribution of hospitality, humanity and solidarity towards migrants and refugees" (Oxfam org. 2018). The concluding statement attached to each exhibition text reads: "A small act of solidarity that deserves a big THANK you". The text confirms the aim of *Museum without a Home* as a celebration of hospitality in which the focus is on the citizen helpers rather than the refugee arrivals (Poehls forthcoming). The exhibition thus configures a clear distinction between the "generous helper" on the one hand and the "needy receiver" on the other.

It goes without saying that the exhibition could have benefited from including the narratives of incoming refugees. However, in this chapter I would like to zoom in on the volunteers and their "good deeds", in particular on how those deeds were recollected among volunteers seeking to provide relief for refugees arriving to

Europe, once the sense of urgency had been diffused or deflected after the brokering of the EU–Turkey deal in 2016.[1]

Scholars of humanitarianism argue that humanitarian acts of "doing good" implies a range of hierarchies and power relations that are not always visible (Fassin 2012). Being able to provide help and assistance assumes a privileged position, which can ultimately victimize the ones in need (Ticktin 2016). In the anthropology of humanitarianism, there is a growing interest in the everyday forms of humanitarianism, such as the loosely organized, informal networks in focus here (Brković 2016). Less attention has so far been devoted to the role of ethnographer(s) in examining what "good deeds" or the doing of "the right thing" entailed for citizens who volunteered in the long summer of welcome in 2015. In order to capture volunteers' motives and self-reflections, further emic exploration is thus still much needed (Cabot 2018; Rozakou 2016). A point of departure for this article, therefore, is that, if volunteer practices are to be understood as actions that do more than offer hospitality or donations – as they are presented in the *Museum without a Home* – careful ethnographic attention needs to be directed towards the ways volunteers themselves reflect on and commemorate events and their involvement in volunteer refugee reception work. This attention requires additional methodological reflection on the role of ethnographers in researching on "doing the right thing" among volunteers.

The chapter[2] will present fieldwork insights from an interdisciplinary research network, *The Helping Hands Research Network,* which explored various ways of doing informal volunteer work in support of refugees coming to Europe, with special emphasis on arrivals to northern European countries in 2015.[3] Between May 2017 and October 2018, the network visited more than 20 initiatives for refugee support in five European cities, Copenhagen, Nijmegen, Glasgow, Hamburg and Flensburg. Those visits were organized through so-called "fieldworkshops", in which network members opened up their ongoing field sites for their colleagues' short-term visits. Since the fieldwork was conducted after the summer of welcome in 2015, many of the volunteers we have had the opportunity to talk with were looking back at their volunteer practices and motives. Taking a lead from Ferreira and Vespeira De Almeida (2017), I apply the term "retrospective ethnography" in order to bring the issue of temporality centre stage when undertaking ethnographic research on specific past events (Ferreira and Vespeira De Almeida 2017, 208). The commemorative practices of the volunteers will, therefore, be at the centre of my interest here. Whereas commemoration usually designates an official marking of a past event on a collective level (cf. Nora 1998), the commemorative practices in focus here are rather the everyday recollection of the 2015 events by the volunteers.

My analysis will take its cue from anthropologist Sharon MacDonald's notion of *past presencing* (2013, 80–82), which enables an interrogation into the various modes whereby the past may be enfolded to the present, not only at institutionalized levels but also in everyday practices like the commemorations of the volunteers. I will focus on different modes of *memory work* enacted by the volunteers in their reflections on the past events. In order to refine our understanding of volunteer practices and to go beyond seeing volunteerism as offering relief through hospitality or material help, the analysis presents three modes of memory work enacted through volunteers' commemorative practices: the *melancholy of volunteering; acting for the future* and *volunteering as heritage-making*. By looking closely at the different modes of memory work among volunteers, I argue that the retrospective ethnographies not only represented the field of study, namely the volunteers' commemorations, but also enabled a collaborative knowledge production, in which divisions of roles between ethnographers and interlocutors became contorted. As I will argue, the ethnographic interventions played a central role in those recollections, altering divisions in ethnographic research between observer and observed, subject and object, recollector and recollected.

According to Noortje Marres et al. (2018), ethnographic research is not only an intervening but also an *inventing* enterprise in the sense that it creates new objects of and sites for research. Taking this point further, building on Gassan Hage (2005), the fieldwork process co-constructed volunteering as a research object that can be studied across Europe's borders (in this case The Netherlands, Germany and Denmark), not in the shape of a multi-sited research endeavour, but as a "single site with its own specificity" (ibid., 466). As I will intend to show, the field-workshops developed a collaborative knowledge production jointly produced between volunteers as well as the hosting and visiting researchers respectively. Ultimately I argue that in order to nurture such inventive knowledge production, retrospective ethnography should therefor include a sensitivity towards the twisting moments, which enhance ethnographically informed knowledge production as a collaborative endeavour.

## Researching welcome initiatives and "good deeds"

In 2015, more than 1.3 million refugees and asylum seekers arrived in Europe (Fladmoe et al. 2016). Western and Northern European countries suddenly experienced an overburdening of their national asylum systems. By contrast, this situation was not new to the Mediterranean countries, which in previous years had been asking for support from their Northern/Western European colleagues to handle the flows of refugees arriving in Europe every year. It was the 2015 influx of refugee arrivals to Europe, however, that later acquired the name "the summer of Welcome" (Karakayali and Kleist 2015). This name came about as a result of the peak in mobilisation of civil engagement, now also among Western and Northern European countries (Della Porta et al. 2018). "Venligboerne/Friendly neighbours" in DK, "A Drop in the Ocean" in Norway along with a range of "Refugees Welcome" initiatives in several European cities are only a few of the many local initiatives that mushroomed at the time. A common trait of many of these welcome initiatives was that they were started outside established aid organisations like the UNHCR, UNICEF and Red Cross, and that social media played a central role in recruiting volunteers (Fladmoe et al. 2016, 33).

In the still burgeoning research field of the anthropology of humanitarianism, a lively discussion about help, helpers and receivers of help has evolved over the past years, a main focus being on established aid organisations. As mentioned, offering assistance initiates a relation of power that places those capable of giving aid above those receiving it. What gives people this role? How clear-cut is it? And when or how does – or *can* – the receiver give something in return? Such questions problematize the concept of reciprocity and exchange as intrinsic elements of gift-giving known from Marcel Mauss' anthropology of relations (1990). The social anthropologist Didier Fassin describes humanitarianism as a prevalent moral economy of Western societies, and one that bears an inherent contradiction. On the one hand, humanitarianism, as seen by the West, involves an ideal of universal equality embracing all of humanity; on the other hand, on the battlefield, humanitarianism accords unequal value to and makes a clear selection between lives worth saving, lives worth risking, lives that have to be sacrificed, and lives that can expect only limited protection (2007, 519). Humanitarianism thus establishes and reflects a hierarchy of humanity.

Research initiatives aiming to study more informal initiatives that welcome refugees like the ones that proliferated in 2015 have likewise been growing recently (Della Porta et al. 2018; Sutter 2017). Yet, these are still very much in their exploratory phase. Little, for instance, is known about the dynamics behind the various kinds of refugee initiatives or about the reasoning, aspirations and justification offered by volunteers. Moreover, there is a particular lack of ethnographically informed studies of informal volunteer initiatives in a European perspective that include the volunteers' retrospective self-reflections. This type of investigation requires careful attention being paid to the role of the ethnographers in the collaborative production of knowledge.

## Collective field-workshops

Even though ethnography would traditionally comprise "some kind of in-depth and fairly small-scale study, often over a lengthy time period" (McDonald 2013, 8), today we see many fieldwork projects conducted over shorter time periods and involving several locales or field sites, as with the fieldwork insights presented here. The aim of conducting fieldwork at several European locales was to explore the possible similarities or convergences in the volunteering practices across European borders. However, as Ghassan Hage argues, lumping together several sites into one field of research does not automatically make the research multi-sited (Hage 2005, 466). So rather than making a point about the many sites we have included in our research, I suggest with Hage that the volunteer practices can be treated as one field site (the volunteer phenomenon) with its own specificity. This requires reflexivity on the selections made and on the motives for highlighting some actors and networks rather than others, and these I will briefly outline in the following.

The research network's focus on Northern European reception was chosen in an attempt to fill a knowledge gap, since much research on volunteerism in light of the 2015 refugee influx to Europe has been conducted in a Mediterranean context. Our field-workshops were not designed to carry out fully-fledged comparisons but rather to bring together experiences from the various volunteer initiatives in order to gain a better understanding of the processes of volunteer mobilisation in a European perspective. We have, therefore, also chosen to emphasize the volunteer work of the less formalized organisations rather than those of the more established humanitarian organizations like the Red Cross.

During the field-workshops we pursued a combination of methodological strategies, including group-based in-depth interviews, walking tours, group discussions and museum visits (see Sandberg and Andersen, forthcoming). In the following section, I will present three examples from The Netherlands (Nijmegen), Denmark (Copenhagen) and Germany (Flensburg) respectively, each representing different ways of recalling events in the aftermath of the 2015 arrival of refugees to Europe, which can be found in our ethnographic material. Crucially, as I would like to show, our presence as ethnographers played a central role in the re-enactments, which highlights memory work not only as an individual endeavour, but a result of collaborative achievement in which ethnographers can take an active part.

## Volunteers' commemorative practices

It was in the wooded outskirts of Nijmegen, close to the border to Germany, at a place called Heumensoord, that one of the larger tented camps in the northern part of Europe was erected in 2015, housing 2900 refugees. In the Netherlands, the intake of refugees rose from 30,000 to nearly 60,000 in 2015.[4] The Heumensoord camp was run by the Central Organisation for Asylum seekers (COA),[5] with its headquarters in The Hague. As far as the Dutch authorities were concerned, the Heumensoord camp was only meant to be for a couple of weeks, however the camp continued to operate from September 2015 until June 2016, a period of 10 months that included the winter season (Aparna et al. forthcoming). This huge clearing in the woods was available for the refugee camp because the place was the temporary home of people affiliated with the military who were participating in the *Vierdaagse* (International Four Days March), which is the world's largest multi-day marching event taking place with Nijmegen as final destination every year (Vierdaagse 2019).

Despite its significant size, the camp made little impact on the daily lives of the 170,000 Nijmegen inhabitants, placed as it was at a (safe) distance from the centre of town. Nevertheless, the thought of having a camp in the woods haunted several locals, such as the volunteer "collective" JustPeople. This initiative was formed in October 2015 as an "independent and informal collective of volunteers who organize and coordinate direct support and activities for and with people who come as refugees to Nijmegen" (JustPeople 2017). As the initiatives' name indicates, the group promotes an ethos of egalitarianism, stating that all are equal as human beings – we are *Just*People. JustPeople started going out to the tent camp in the woods with a coffee urn on a cargo bike, offering coffee and a chat. This venture resulted in several friendships over time and it also initiated further activities such as the establishment of a bicycle workshop in order for the refugees to be able to be more mobile and gain easier access to the town centre.

In December 2017, our Dutch colleagues in the research network organized a workshop in which JustPeople (and the initiative Asylum University, see Aparna 2018) met with us in order to share knowledge. One of the participants was Mahmoud, a Syrian refugee in his 20s. He had lived in the Heumensoord tent camp back in 2015 and then became an activist joining the initiative. When I later spoke with Mahmoud, he told me how he immediately became curious when he saw JustPeople's cargo bike with coffee outside of the Heumensoord camp, especially because the people surrounding it were young people. Mahmoud had a degree in Business Management, yet he deserted from the army in Syria and came to Germany before deciding to apply for asylum in the Netherlands. So he arrived at IND (the Dutch Immigration and Naturalisation Service) in Eindhoven, where every asylum-seeker has to report, and was then transferred to the camp at Heumensoord. When the tent camp was shut down in June 2016, just before the *Vierdaagse*, he managed to get asylum and to rent an apartment in Nijmegen, rather than be transferred elsewhere.

We also met Max, a Dutch student of psychology. In a later conversation during the field-workshop, Max told me about his parents, who would do what he classified as "charity work" through Christian organisations, in which they supported various humanitarian projects in Uganda. In Max' view, this kind of volunteering makes him uncomfortable since in his view it is merely colonial and based on missionary ideologies. So clearly, for Max, engaging in JustPeople is a way of moving away from patronising forms of charity towards more egalitarian relationships between human beings.

## Memory work I – the melancholia of volunteering

During our field visit in 2017, we took a walk of two kilometres together with six members of JustPeople, including Mahmoud and Max, from the Radboud University in Nijmegen centre through the forest to the premises of the former camp, which now stands as a large empty clearing surrounded by old oak trees.

The members of the JustPeople initiative had not been to the place since the camp was closed back in the spring of 2016, so they told us how strange it was "to be back there". Upon arrival, we formed a circle, and the JustPeople members and the Helping Hands scholars involved in this initiative (and hosting the workshop), began to share their stories. The rest of us, the visiting field researchers, formed part of the circle too and took notes, and also asked questions during the process when JustPeople members told us how it had all begun.

Engaging in this circle as a visiting ethnographer was at first a bit of a twisting moment in which our roles as visitors contorted into eyewitnesses of past events recollected. The circle enacted a process of commemoration, an act of memory work, in which past events were recollected by the volunteers and presented to the rest of us. Also, the present state of volunteer activities was evaluated. Since the success of the work of JustPeople, they had difficulty in recruiting new members and keeping their team spirit after 2016 (fieldnotes, December 2017). Mahmoud, who had experience from living inside the tent area, recollected how there was always a sense of movement inside the camp. It was only after 22:00, when the lights were turned off, that the noise of activity decreased. Often the heating system broke down, and this turned the humid interior of the tents freezing cold. Whereas it was clear that no one in the group would wish for any tent camps to be re-erected, a certain atmosphere was created in this circle. Through the sharing of commemorative narratives, the Heumensoord tent camp was re-enacted as an unofficial "locus of memory". However, whereas Pierre Nora (1998) coined this term with particular reference to official commemoration sites or events, this small ceremonial circle evoked an everyday act of memory work shared by volunteers, activist researchers and witnessed by the guest researchers. The memory work involved enacted an interesting composite what was both a *looking* back and also a kind of *longing* back. There was a sense of *Sehnsucht*, or melancholia in the air, which was highlighted when Max explained how he missed the atmosphere of collectivity when looking back at the events in 2015 (fieldnotes, December 2017). This kind of memory work exemplifies a longing for a past fellowship, a community arising from an activity that is no longer there.

Participating in the memory circle at Heumensoord released a kind of memory work which speaks, then, of the *melancholia* of volunteering – a paradoxical longing towards the time when things were exceptional (Sandberg and Andersen, forthcoming). It can be seen as a paradoxical longing because clearly none of the volunteers would wish for the crisis and the erection of tent camps to start all over again.

This particular mix of euphoria or pleasure and melancholy is comparable to MacDonald's point that emotions, "may contribute to processes of remembering and forgetting, of feeling compelled or unable to speak about the past" (2013, 79). This sense of melancholia is not to be conceived of as an individual or inner state of mind, but rather a performative practice (Butler 1997). This first mode of memory work, highlights how volunteering not only has a certain rhythm of being on/off the mission, but also has an aftermath of ambiguity attached to itself, in which volunteers, including those with refugee background like Mahmoud, are coming to terms with – often traumatic – experiences and the joy of making a difference and of being in the right place at the right time.

Since the memories of the events of 2015 were obviously not shared by the visiting ethnographers, it was not a collective but rather a collaborative memory process, enabled through the volunteers' recollections and our follow-up questions. The role of ethnographers in the process of studying retrospective accounts of doing good were thus a kind of midwifery of memory in which recollections of the time when events were taking place were compelled to be spoken about.

## Memory work II – acting for the future

The second mode of memory work I would like to highlight among the volunteers' commemorative practices leads us to another site in the European landscape of informal refugee reception: to the Copenhagen Main Central Station. Fatima is a 23-year-old student in Copenhagen, and one of the coordinators of Hovedbanegårdens frivillige (Volunteers of Copenhagen Central Station), initiated in 2015.[6] Even though the initiative is no longer active, Fatima still works as a volunteer and has also been active in the previously mentioned Danish initiative known as Venligboerne (Friendly Neighbours). In the late summer of 2015 Fatima heard through a friend about what was going on at Copenhagen Central Station, and they decided to drop by. Fatima ended up being at the Central Station every day for eight months. Fatima's grandparents are from Morocco, but both her parents were born in Denmark. To her parents' regret, Fatima stayed away from lectures at the university throughout this time.

Most of the volunteers at Copenhagen Central Station were either students or pensioners, and the group included people aged between 15 and 65. The ranks of volunteers also included people who were themselves asylum-seekers, some working as interpreters for the refugee arrivals. Many refugees got stuck at Copenhagen Central Station when, on 12 November 2015, Sweden introduced temporary passport controls for those crossing the border from Denmark. They could either return to Flensburg in Germany, from where they had arrived at Copenhagen, or try to apply for asylum in Denmark, yet for most of the incoming refugees the country of destination was Sweden (see Sandberg 2018).

Fatima describes how chaotic her first time at Copenhagen Central Station was. Refugees and volunteers were all over the place, surrounded by huge donations of clothes and food. There was a lot of frustration among all present, including the staff from the Danish Railway Company (DSB), who seemed to disapprove of the presence of the volunteers. The volunteers managed to organise the chaos into daily routines and structures surprisingly quickly. Refugees were arriving from Syria, via Turkey, Greece, Macedonia, Serbia, and on from there via Flensburg in Germany to Copenhagen. Every half hour, a new train would arrive from Flensburg with approximately 50 refugees on board. In the first few months, this amounted, according to Fatima's estimate, to 1,500–2,000 people reaching Copenhagen Central Station a day. As we walked through Copenhagen Central Station together, Fatima recalled the events of 2015:

> We had our shifts, and our tasks were mostly to help the refugees arriving to get some rest, perhaps a shower. Later on, we created the "Safety Zone" in collaboration with DSB [The Danish Railway Company]. Often we took care of the children so the parents could relax and get some sleep. (Interview, 9 February 2018)

Creating zones of safety where refugees could withdraw and re-group, as it were, also reconfigured the station from barrier to temporary shelter. To get a shower and a nap (while someone looks after your children) is both a very mundane and pragmatic way of humanizing oneself and a symbolic stepping out of categorical notions of migrants as being part of a (threatening) "migration flow".

When Fatima gave us a tour around Central station now completely void of refugees, it becomes clear that she shares a similar state of melancholia as members of JustPeople in the aftermath of the reception challenge. However, there is a further dimension I wish to highlight here, namely a historical awareness directed towards the future:

> Yes, I miss it. I have had bad experiences and good experiences. So, I won't let it go, because I feel that I have developed as a person through experiencing this. And one day, this refugee crisis will become part of the history books, and when that time comes, I'd like to be able to sit and say, "Gosh, I was part of this". (Interview, 9 February 2018)

In Fatima's recollection of events, she is clearly aware of the aftermath – her actions were made in order to prove that Danish citizens were not all xenophobic and that someone did act as a counterweight to anxiety and to antipathy towards refugees. This memory work is, therefore, clearly oriented towards the future and the way her actions will become part of a new collective memory. Yet, it was only in Fatima's concluding reflections, when we were about to say farewell to each other, I realized that we, the ethnographers accompanying Fatima around the premises of the Central Station, were in fact regarded as "history books". Ultimately this wish was the reason why Fatima wanted to share her story with us. It was in this twisting moment, I got a glimpse of the future life of my own work as fieldworker doing retrospective ethnography, leaving me not only dizzy because the spotlight was suddenly directed towards me and my efforts, but also with a sense of obligation of returning Fatima's wish into reality.

Let us now return one stop, so to speak, to another train station, namely Flensburg Central Station, in Northern Germany. Several of the refugees who came to Copenhagen Central Station came directly from Flensburg. This example serves to illustrate a final and third mode of memory work enacted in volunteer commemorative practices.

## *Memory work III – volunteering as heritage-making*

In Germany, the 2015 refugee arrivals to Europe was tackled in a very different manner than in Denmark and the Netherlands (Sutter 2017). Chancellor Angela Merkel's dictum "Wir schaffen das" [We can do it]", meaning that Germany would be capable of handling the refugee influx, is reflected in this quote from one of the initiators of Refugee Welcome Flensburg, Karin:

> The homepage of Refugee Welcome Flensburg] had already 5,000 likes, because there was a sense that, now it was the time to show the openness of this city, and in general there was this positive atmosphere of "yes, wir schaffen das!" (Interview, 19 January, 2018)

Refugee Welcome Flensburg was established during the late summer of 2015, when around 60,000 people passed through this station, Flensburger Bahnhof. We met Karin in January 2018. She worked 20 hours a week at the Bahnhof, aside from her full-time employment. She recalled the atmosphere almost as a kind of euphoria, and in fact she compares the first days of the refugees arriving with the days after the fall of the Berlin Wall, as we shall see in the next quote:

> When we came down there, there were hundreds of people and donations, piled up in front of the Bahnhof (…) so the message – not only from our side – had gone viral all over Flensburg, and one had the feeling of … comparable to the fall of the GDR wall, because there was this "Yeeess"! And, in fact, it was a bit overwhelming for the people arriving, as they were loaded with presents and clothes, and they just stood there with so many bags of food (laughs). It was kind of crazy! (Interview, 19 January, 2018)

As at Copenhagen Central Station, the chaos was quickly organised into daily routines. Yet, as Karin explains, no one had overall control, "it was all individuals who gathered at the Bahnhof, and everyone would know someone (to contact for further help)". Around 80 volunteers (200 in the beginning) came on a regular basis, which included interpreters speaking Farsi and Arab. In time, the activities became even more organised, the Fire Department ensured safe exits in case of fire, and some localities were offered to Refugee Welcome from Deutsche Bahn.

According to MacDonald (2013), heritagization is a social process in which the past is presented and interpreted. Focus therefore needs to be put on the ways in which these interpretations can travel and make the past keep being present. Memory work as a kind of heritage-making became especially apparent when we visited the premises of the former Refugee Welcome sites at the Bahnhof. It was in a sense like entering a small museum. All the central props and furniture were there from the days when "it was all going on", Karin explains, as we pass through the premises (Interview, 20 January, 2018). Stored in this room are several photo collages put together by the volunteers which captured cheerful moments of smiling people and hugs from "the long summer of welcome". On the wall hangs a framed notice announcing that Refugee Welcome Flensburg were elected People of the Year 2015 by the *Flensburger Tagesblatt* readership. This mode of memory work turns the volunteers' deeds into cultural heritage, which enters a recursive process that continues to make the events of 2015 become present, again and again. And the process continues in this present article.

Visiting Refugee Welcome Flensburg at the Flensburger Bahnhof was like entering a museum, yet of another kind than the Oxfam/Amnesty *Museum without a Home* in which the celebration of hospitality was unidirectional, focusing solely on the giver, and merely glorified the acts of solidarity. As MacDonald argues, different cultural objects have different "memorizing capacities" (2013, 82), which means that they can help establishing links to the past. The memory circle in the woods on the outskirts of Nijmegen, the small tour Fatima gave us at the

Copenhagen Central Station, the photo memory wall at Flensburger Bahnhof all have such capacities of enabling links to a past sociality, which is after all not possible to re-establish.

Exemplified by these three different volunteer initiatives and traceable in several of the other 20 initiatives we have been visiting are the three modes of memory work presented here: memory work as melancholia, as oriented towards the future and as co-creating cultural heritage. Together, they show that the neat distinctions between the "generous helper" on the one hand and the "needy receiver" on the other, which are exposed by the *Museum without a Home* exhibition, turn out to be much more complex when scrutinized in detail. In many senses, the commemorative practices of the volunteers show that they were also needy receivers – as participants of a sociality that was no longer there.

## Ethnographic in(ter)ventions

Yet, another dimension of the volunteers' commemorative practices needs to be addressed: As I have already indicated our presence as researchers studying the 'volunteer phenomenon' at those particular moments had further temporal implications and ultimately released a set of twisting moments in which our role as ethnographers became contorted. An example was when our presence in the memory circle compelled a longing back to the events of 2015. The twisting moments of our ethnographic encounters occurred during the field-workshops at the very moment when remembrance became part of not only an individualized but a collaborative process. This is the moment, Ferriera and Almeida describe as the,

> terrain par excellence of the ethnographer who maps the past, where observation is not merely present, but becomes participant because it arouses, incites and assimilates the process, making it possible to access information that could not be obtained through daily social interactions. (Ferriera and Almeida 2017, 208)

As co-present and participating ethnographers, we contributed to the volunteers' reflections upon their actions and memories, for example when we were guided around Copenhagen and Flensburg Central station by our volunteer interlocutors. But the process also contorted the divisions between observer and observed since the recalling of events and more overall the aim of communicating those recollections to us temporarily changed the spotlight directing it onto our research aims and efforts. The process of retrospective ethnography meant that, in those recollections, relations and roles were contorted, so that as ethnographic researchers we became:

1. *Midwifers* of memory: The memory work of the volunteers was stimulated by our presence and questions (as in the memory circle at Heumensoord).
2. *Documentarists:* Our recording, notes and transcription of the volunteers' experiences of past events would make the volunteers' actions travel – into conference

halls, journal articles, class rooms – and eventually make them "part of history books" (as Fatima was hoping for at the Copenhagen Central Station).

3. *Visitors*: as researchers, we were only short-term visitors, which adds a temporality of ephemerality to our ethnographic understanding. We entered new research terrains, only for a short visit, and this raised the question whether we were pursuing some kind of academic tourism? However, as a museum needs not only curators but also visitors in order to be a museum, I would argue that we were not tourists but *visitors*, in our colleagues' research fields as well as at the 'Museum of Volunteering' at Flensburger Bahnhof.

Returning to Marres et al. (2018), our ethnographic study not only represented but also invented our field of study. By virtue of our ethnographic participation, through our questioning, our taking pictures, our drinking coffee, we enacted volunteering as an object (the volunteer phenomenon) that can be studied across borders, in Nijmegen, Flensburg, Copenhagen.

I have argued that, as ethnographers, we can allow for more complexity than is admitted by Oxfam and Amnesty International at *Museum without a Home*, which encapsulated a specific commemoration celebrating volunteers as hospitable helpers. Unpacking the complexities of refugee volunteering by exploring the volunteers' different modes of memory work can make us more knowledgeable about the volunteer phenomenon in different settings across European borders. Retrospective ethnography, therefore, includes sensitivity towards those twisting moments, when ethnographically informed knowledge production becomes a collaborative intervention.

## Acknowledgements

This paper is an outcome of the Helping Hands Research Network, financed by the Danish Research Council (DFF/6107–00111), led by Marie Sandberg (PI) and Dorte J. Andersen.

## Notes

1 The EU-Turkey statement refers to the agreement made in March 2016 in which Turkey "agreed to accept the rapid return of all migrants not in need of international protection crossing from Turkey into Greece and to take back all irregular migrants intercepted in Turkish waters" in this way closing down the Balkan route for arriving migrants (source: www.consilium.europa.eu/en/press/press-releases/2016/03/18/eu-turkey-statement/, accessed 19 August 2019).
2 The chapter is based on a keynote lecture held at the "Ethnography with a twist" conference Jyväskula February 12–14 2019, organized by EUROHERIT — *Legitimation of European cultural heritage and the dynamics of identity politics in the EU*.
3 The network gathered 12 researchers (ethnologists, anthropologists, human geographers, borders and migration scholars, and political scientists), from six different countries, Denmark, Sweden, Norway, Germany, the Netherlands and Scotland. It was funded by the Danish Research Council for Independent Research 2017–2019 (DFF/

6107–00111), with Marie Sandberg as the PI. http://saxoinstitute.ku.dk/research/resea rch_projects_and_networks/helping-hands-research-network-on-the-everyday-border-workk-of-european-citizens/
4 Of which half of the 60,000 refugees came from Syria. https://refugeesnetherlands. weebly.com/statistics.html# (accessed 28 January 2019).
5 COA is responsible for the reception, supervision and departure (from the reception location) of asylum seekers coming to the Netherlands.
6 Fieldwork on *Refugee Welcome Flensburg* was conducted with Dorte J. Andersen and with research assistant, ethnologist, Line Bygballe Jensen. Fieldwork on *Hovedbanegårdens Frivillige* was conducted in collaboration with research assistant, ethnologist, Line Bygballe Jensen.

## References

Aparna, K. 2018. "Asylum university: Re-situating knowledge-exchange along cross-border positionalities". In *Decolonising the University*, edited by G. K. Bhambra, K. Nisancioglu, and D. Gebrial. London: Pluto Press.

Aparna, K., O. Kande, J. Schapendonk, and O. Kramsch. Forthcoming. "'Europe is no longer Europe': Montaging borderlands of help for a radical politics of place". In the special issue "Europe Trouble Welcome Culture and the Disruption of the European Border Regime", edited by M. Sandberg and D. J. Andersen. *Nordic Journal of Migration Research.*

Brković, Č. 2016. "Scaling humanitarianism: Humanitarian actions in a Bosnian town". *Ethnos, Journal of Anthropology* 81 (1): 99–124. https://doi.org/10.1080/00141844.2014.912246

Butler, J. 1997. *The Psychic Life of Power. Theories in Subjection.* Stanford, CA: Stanford University Press.

Cabot, H. 2018. "The European refugee crisis and humanitarian citizenship in Greece". *Ethnos, Journal of Anthropology* 84 (5): 747–771. https://doi.org/10.1080/00141844.2018.1529693

Della Porta, D., ed. 2018. *Solidarity Mobilizations in the "Refugee Crisis". Contentious Moves.* London: Palgrave Macmillan.

Fassin, D. 2012. *Humanitarian Reason: A Moral History of the Present.* Berkeley: University of California Press.

Ferreira, S., and S. Vespeira De Almeida. 2017. "Retrospective ethnography on 20th century Portugal: Fieldwork encounters and its complicities". *Social Anthropology/Anthropologie Sociale* 25 (2): 206–220. doi:10.1111/1469-8676.12416

Fladmoe, A., S. Sætrang, I. Eimhjellen, K. Steen-Johnsen, and B. Enjolras. 2016. *Nordmenns bidrag i flyktningsituasjonen 2015/2016.* Bergen and Oslo: Senter for forskning på sivilsamfunn og frivillig sektor.

Hage, G. 2005. "A not so multi-sited ethnography of a not so imagined community". *Anthropological Theory* 5 (4): 463–475. https://doi.org/10.1177/1463499605059232

JustPeople. 2017. https://justpeople.nl/about/ (accessed 22 January 2020).

Karakayali S., and O. Kleist. 2015. "Strukturen und Motive der ehrenamtlichen Flücht- lingsarbeit (EFA) in Deutschland". *Berliner Institut für empirische Integrations- und Migrationsforschung.* www.fluechtlingshilfe-htk.de/uploads/infos/49.pdf (accessed 20 April 2019).

Krøijer, S. 2015. "Figurations of the future: On the form and temporality of protests among left radical activists in Europe". In *In the Event: Toward an Anthropology of Generic Moments*, edited by L. Meinert and B. Kapferer, 139–152. Oxford: Berghahn Books.

MacDonald, S. 2013. *Memorylands – Heritage and Identity in Europe Today.* London: Routledge.

Marres, N., M. Guggenheim, and A. Wilki. 2018. *Inventing the Social.* Manchester: Mattering Press.

Mauss, M. 1990. *The Gift: Forms and Reasons for Exchange in Archaic Societies*. London: Routledge.
Nora, P. 1998. *Realms of Memory: Rethinking the French Past*. Chicago: University of Chicago Press.
Oxfam.org. 2018. www.oxfam.org/en/pressroom/reactions/oxfam-amnesty-refugee-and-migrant-solidarity-project-awarded-greece (accessed 22 January 2020).
Poehls, K. Forthcoming. "Exhibiting solidarity work. Or: Temporary displays and their potential to trouble and push museums in their search for representing European mobilities". In the special issue "Europe Trouble Welcome Culture and the Disruption of the European Border Regime", edited by M. Sandberg and D. J. Andersen. *Nordic Journal of Migration Research*.
Rozakou, K. 2016. "Crafting the volunteer. Voluntary associations and the reformation of sociality". *Journal of Modern Greek Studies* 34 (1): 79–102. https://doi.org/10.1353/mgs.2016.0014
Sandberg, M. 2018: "Moving the border. The everyday border work in/of the European border regime". *Jahrbuch für Europäische Ethnologie: Dänemark*, 13: 49–58.
Sandberg, M., and D. J. Andersen. Forthcoming. "Precarious Citizenship and Melancholic Longing: On the Value of Volunteering after the Refugee Arrivals to Europe 2015"."Precarious Citizenship and Melancholic Longing: On the Value of Volunteering after the Refugee Arrivals to Europe 2015". In the special issue "Europe Trouble Welcome Culture and the Disruption of the European Border Regime", edited by M. Sandberg and D. J. Andersen. *Nordic Journal of Migration Research*.
Sutter, O. 2017. "'Wilkommen!' Emotionale Politiken des zivilgesellschaftlichen Engagements für Flüchtende". *Zeitschrift für Volkskunde* 113 (1): 3–23. www.hsozkult.de/journal/id/zeitschriftenausgaben-10420
Ticktin, M. 2016. "Thinking beyond humanitarian borders". In *Social Research: An International Quarterly* 83 (2): 255–271. www.muse.jhu.edu/article/631162
Vierdaagse. 2019. https://en.wikipedia.org/wiki/International_Four_Days_Marches_Nijmegen (accessed 19 August 2019).

## List of interviews cited (all names have been anonymized):

Karin, Coordinator of Refugee Welcome Flensburg, 19 January 2018, Flensburg.
Refugees Welcome Flensburg (group interview at Flensburg Central Station), 20 January 2018, Flensburg.
Fatima, Volunteers at the Copenhagen Central Station, 9 February 2018, Copenhagen.

# 9
# ETHNOGRAPHIC CHALLENGES TO STUDYING THE POOR IN AND FROM THE GLOBAL SOUTH

*Laura Stark*

## Introduction

Contrary to what the UN and World Bank have proclaimed in recent years, global poverty has increased dramatically (Hickel 2016, 7). The United Nations and World Bank measure only how many persons are living under an arbitrarily chosen boundary of 1.9 USD per day, but if the poverty line were raised to the minimum for a normal life expectancy (approx. 4 USD in most countries) then 3.5 billion persons – half the world's population – would be classified as poor (Edward 2006; Hickel 2016, 7). Anthropologists have long studied people in low-income countries typically defined by poverty, but have rarely brought their ethnographic methods to bear on the causes and consequences of poverty *per se* (Ferguson 1997; Booth et al. 1999; Green 2006). The focus of anthropology in the Anglophone literature, for instance, has tended to be rural areas and the study of one ethnic group rather than ethnically diverse urban areas. Topics tend to derive from anthropology's "primitivist reflex" (Kalb 2015, 52) that is, the search for cultural and social aspects with minimal influence from colonialism, market capitalism, globalism, or mass consumption. There has been much less interest in using ethnography to study how poverty affects the people studied through ethnography, including asylum seekers and migrants coming from low-income or materially inadequate conditions. Yet ethnographic research on poverty is sorely needed. The micro-economic research dominating studies on poverty lacks the necessary tools to study socio-cultural power dynamics, and often misrecognizes "on the ground" complexities in the lives of the poorest (Booth et al. 1999; Bevan 2004, 29; Ferguson 2015).

My aim in this chapter is to encourage ethnographers to carve out a space for themselves in research on poverty in the global South by recognizing their strengths in this area, namely sensitive methods in local contexts to answer questions of *why* something happens rather than just *how much can be measured*. Yet qualitative researchers confront very different socioeconomic dynamics in the global South than they do in the global North. They therefore need to be aware of ethical and methodological challenges in studying the poor in the global South. In this chapter I discuss the following challenges: 1) understanding the expectations of persons coming from societies where dependence networks structure socio-economic relations; 2) informed consent among the poor in the global South; 3) personal data among those with meagre identity documentation; and 4) the effects of poverty and stress on participants' memories. These issues call for not merely new methods, but a new overall approach to ethnography that understands how poverty affects the information given by those studied. More broadly, I propose that Northern ethnographers need to rethink familiar ethical and methodological approaches in a "twist" towards a "Southern" approach that encompasses both reflexive recognition of socio-economic differences and the alternative methods of *perceived causation* and *third-person elicitation*. These methods allow the qualitative researcher to avoid asking for personal data and to circumvent the non-verifiability of individual life facts.

The term *ethnography* in this chapter refers to the presence of the researcher in the everyday spaces in which participants live. It also indicates an "open notebook" approach in which interview questions are not predetermined by a research design but instead are adapted to the new information received from participants as the study proceeds. This approach ensures flexibility in asking new questions and the discovery of things not imagined to exist when the research began. When used among the urban poor, the open notebook approach allows researchers to see everyday life and social dynamics in ways they could not have envisioned based on their own non-poverty backgrounds. These moments of discovery serve as clues leading to new and interesting paths of inquiry.

## The setting of my research

As part of an ongoing study of gender and urban poverty carried out between 2010 and 2018, I interviewed a total of 292 persons in two low-income, predominantly Muslim neighbourhoods in Dar es Salaam, a city of 4.36 million inhabitants (National Bureau of Statistics Tanzania 2013). Here, an estimated 50% of the population in informal settlements live on an average income of roughly 1 USD per day, well below the international poverty line of 1.9 USD (Ndezi, 2009). The majority of those I interviewed (roughly 70%) had only a primary education or less. The neighbourhoods I studied fulfilled UN-Habitat's (2010, 14–15) criteria for "slums" as they lacked secure tenure, sufficient living space, sanitation infrastructure, easy access to safe drinking water, and durability of dwelling structures. As a port city that draws migrants from throughout Tanzania, Dar es Salaam is an ethnically heterogeneous but unilingual Kiswahili environment. Although no official census data exists on religious affiliation in Tanzania, Sunni Muslims comprise roughly 75–90% of the residents in the neighbourhoods I studied. Interviews were conducted in Kiswahili with the assistance of female interpreters and female key informants who had first-hand familiarity with the socio-economic circumstances of those interviewed. Key informants and interpreters were found through local non-governmental organizations. All names of interview participants in this chapter have been changed to protect personal anonymity.

I discovered soon after I had begun interviews that I was extremely fortunate in the random choice of my first field site: I had unintentionally begun interviews in a locality that was sympathetic to outsiders for reasons linked to local and national politics. The local authorities there welcomed me immediately, which set the tone for other persons in the neighbourhood. In the neighbourhood just across the road, however, I was not so lucky: a different political situation there meant that the local authorities viewed me with suspicion and demanded a different bureaucratic process in order to grant permission for interviews. Although I conducted some interviews there, I eventually focused fully on the first neighbourhood, which was home to roughly 2,500 persons.

## Skype as an alternative to face-to-face interviews

In 2018, health issues prevented me from traveling to Tanzania, so I decided to conduct my final round of interviews using Skype. Over the last decade, there has been growing attention to alternatives to traditional face-to-face interviews in qualitative research such as Voice over Internet Protocol (VoIP) technologies (Sullivan 2012; Lo Iacono et al. 2016; AlKhateeb 2018). Most existing literature on the use of Skype describes interviews conducted among middle- and higher-income participants. Thanks to the dramatic uptake in usage of mobile phones among low-income persons in the global South, Skype interviews are also possible across vast distances and with chronically poor interview participants.

Through emails with Zakia, a female interpreter with whom I had worked twice before, I explored this possibility. Zakia downloaded the Skype program onto a basic smartphone that I sent her money to buy. She then contacted Neema, a woman in her late 40s who was our key informant in the neighbourhood. Neema agreed to ask residents to participate in interviews as she had done in previous years, and Zakia travelled to the neighbourhood at the agreed time. The strength of our Skype connection was not sufficient for continuous video, but we were able to conduct the interviews using audio.

Whereas in previous field visits I had always begun with a visit to the local government office to obtain their permission, now Zakia went on my behalf to ask the government secretary permission to conduct the interviews via Skype. This permission was granted, and I conducted 20 Skype interviews. Each interview lasted longer than it would have normally taken face-to-face due to the poor quality of the audio and the need to repeat questions and answers. Although challenging (often I had to nearly shout my questions into my laptop to be heard by my interpreter), I obtained important new data for my research. Interviewing without video was surprisingly easy, given that I was already familiar with the flow and rhythm of the interview situation in Swahili. Both Zakia and interview participants were highly accustomed to the use of mobile phones, so this helped to make interviews through mobile-enabled Skype flow smoothly. Zakia also worked hard to ensure comprehension by enunciating clearly, turning to speak directly into her phone when interpreting for me, waiting for me to ask questions, and patiently repeating things.

However, when compared to face-to-face interviews, I noted significant differences. It was frustrating to not observe what was happening in the real-life conversation area, for example, I could not see gestures or facial expressions, and I could not immediately see who had newly arrived to join in the conversation. Skype interviews also exacerbated the ethical dilemma of informed consent. Zakia always told interviewees the purpose of the research and asked for their consent before the Skype call began, but I could not know how the participant had reacted.

One benefit of using Skype for interviewing was that having only two Skype interviews per week rather than face-to-face interviews every day as I had done in the field provided valuable time needed for reflection before the next interview, time that I had rarely enjoyed when in the field. Skype interviews also created a psychological distance between the participant and myself. Many of the stories told by interviewees were distressing, for instance, when HIV sufferers and their relatives told of their suffering, or when sex workers told of the violence and abuse they had endured. Face to face, I had experienced such narratives as important but emotionally exhausting. It was considerably less stressful to listen to them at a distance without a visual connection. What I experienced as sensitive or disturbing topics for discussion, however, were not necessarily what interviewees seemed to experience as oppressive. In particular, experiences of not having relatives to help or support financially seemed emotionally difficult for some persons to talk about.

Skype interviews would *not* have been useful as a means of gathering *initial* data in another country if I had not spent considerable time there already. A relationship of trust with key persons in the neighbourhood as well as with an interpreter were necessary for the success of these interviews. Once relationships of trust with local persons are already established, however, long-distance Skype can create an opportunity to collect additional data if travel is not feasible.

## Dependence networks

I visited fieldsites only during the day and was accompanied by at least one other person as I walked through the neighbourhood: usually my female interpreter or female key informant. I never felt that I was personally in danger, but the fact that I was so easily identifiable as a foreigner by my skin colour meant that I could not live or sleep in the neighbourhoods I studied: I would have been an instant target of theft, since many residents assumed that any white person or *mzungu* was extremely wealthy. Indeed, just by arriving in Tanzania I had shown that I had enough money to fly from another continent, a feat that most residents assumed would always be beyond their means. Everyone assumed that I possessed more money than I would ever need, therefore nearly every meeting with a Tanzanian local became a negotiation in which I was asked for financial assistance: to buy a house for a taxi driver, to help pay for children's school fees, or merely to "help" in the form of giving cash. This quickly became exhausting, for although I understood people's motives for asking, it was difficult to create friendships when people (rightly) perceived that my own economic situation was so different from their own. Later in my fieldwork, my desire to give small amounts of cash to persons in extreme need was frustrated by the fact that I was continually short of cash because the local ATM machines were either empty or difficult to reach from my hotel on the city outskirts.

In cities where all transactions are over-monetarized cash is vital for survival but difficult for the poorest to obtain (de Sardan 1999). People were unable to grow enough food for themselves in an urban neighbourhood, and needed money to pay transportation, rent, medicines, medical bills, and school fees for their children. The end of interviews were often moments when some informants asked for monetary assistance. Some persons told me in repeat interviews that I had promised last time to bring them a gift, although I had no recollection of doing so. At the time, I experienced these situations as uncomfortable, because I did not want to "bribe" my informants with money or gifts, and I did not enjoy being pressured. It was clear to me that everyone needed help desperately, and impression was often overwhelming.

At first, drawing a firm line against giving money was a way to mentally block out the distress and suffering all around me during interview visits. I was also worried about the inflationary effect of monetary help on interview participants. If one resident heard that someone else had received help, they themselves would expect help, and possibly a larger sum of money. For this reason, I gave each participant a tin of powdered chocolate drink (that would have been expensive for them in the shops). A PhD student who conducted interviews separately in the same neighbourhood later told me that participants had complained to her that this chocolate drink was useless for their every needs. One interpreter suggested that sugar (for tea-drinking British style) might make a more useful gift, and so I began to give each participant a two-kilogramme bag of sugar. Yet this did not help those persons who had nothing to eat, no food to give their children, or no way to pay their rent.

Upon reflection, knowing that just a few euros would make a difference in many person's lives, I began making exceptions to my no-money rule for single mothers with no income, persons infected with HIV, and recent migrants to the city sleeping in a relative's house who had no income. I had not yet realized, however, that when interview participants asked for "help" they were actually striving to create a relationship of dependence upon me. What they wanted from me was not simply money, but a relationship that would confer upon them a sense of security as well as the social identity of being the friend of an *mzungu*, a white person imagined to be wealthy.

Once I became more intertwined in a several participants' networks of assistance, I began to reflect further on how these networks were, in fact, structuring nearly all of the socio-economic relations within the neighbourhoods studied. Anthropologist James Ferguson (2013) points out that in much of sub-Saharan Africa relations of dependence have been preferred or prioritized over independence. In Africa, people rather than land have historically been the source of wealth, so the goal has often been to build hierarchical relations in which persons compete for followers. Both patrons and dependents have therefore benefited from "wealth in people" (Ferguson 2013; see also Bledsoe 1980; Iliffe 1987; de Sardan 1999), a term still used by Tanzanians today. Regardless of where one fit in the social hierarchy, dependence conferred social identity: "without networks of dependents you were nobody [...] with them you were a person of consequence" (Ferguson 2013, 226). As the African continent is marginalized within the global network of trade and many unemployed are now locked out of the labour market, what used to be 'kin networks' in the anthropological literature are no longer necessarily robust or numerous social linkages, but often rely on a few persons, whose support has become meagre, irregular, and unreliable (Cleaver 2005). Social networks have shed dependents, and unclaimed persons scramble to find new persons to be dependent upon (Cleaver 2005; Ferguson 2013; 2015).

Advance awareness of participants' socio-economic expectations can ease an ethnographer's entrance into the field and make it easier to draw clear personal boundaries. An awareness that power, income and social relations in the global South are frequently organized through dependence networks also has implications for ethnographers' work with migrants and refugees. As has been widely documented in the migration literature (most notably in work on remittances), dependence networks may motivate or obligate migration, and often continue after an individual or family has migrated. This means that migrants can depend on already existing ethnic, religious and/or kinship networks in the country to which they migrate. They may also be under heavy pressure to send money to kin or friends in the departure country or in refugee camps, which limits the amount they can invest in their own socio-economic integration in the new country (Lindley 2010; Hammond 2011). They may, for instance, find themselves forced to engage in low-paying and exploitative work rather than continuing their education because the risk of losing income is too great when they need to send money regularly (Humphries et al. 2009; Eversole and Johnson 2014). Asylum seekers may also expect to establish long-term relations of dependence with the volunteers and reception centre workers whom they see regularly (World Relief 2017; EURITA 2019).

## Informed consent

Relationships of dependence in the neighbourhood were linked to another methodological and ethical challenge I faced while interviewing: informed consent. To obtain valid free, rational and informed consent from research participants, participants must be accurately informed of the purpose, methods, risks, and benefits of the research, and must understand this information (Campbell 2009). This notion of informed consent, however, rests on Western understandings of the person as an individual. Although I received verbal consent from all participants, the persons whom I interviewed had no way of making "independent" or "free" choices for several reasons. They did not have the educational background taken for granted in Europe or North America that would have allowed them to be able to evaluate their best interests with respect to the interviews I was conducting. Some of my interview participants did not know what a university was, much less what basic research was. Despite my best efforts to explain myself and the purpose of my research, many participants remained convinced that I worked for an NGO, which was for them the most familiar role for a white woman in Dar es Salaam. Many of them were dependent upon social relationships of neighbourliness that revolved around my key informant Neema, who was a respected and trusted middle-aged female member of the community. It is possible that persons she invited to participate in interviews found it difficult to refuse her. Finally, many participants were so desperate financially that they might have been reluctant to refuse the bag of sugar that I gave to everyone who was interviewed.

Overall, there exist very few options for ethnographers to ensure that the people studied participate voluntarily, with no strings attached. Ethnographers can only strive to recognize how Northern assumptions of "free" participation are unsettled by local circumstances, and describe this unsettling for reading and listening audiences. The alternative would be to not study the Southern poor at all. This would mean that those whose voices are already stifled by lack of social power and influence would be further ignored and marginalized by social science.

## Personal data and sparse identity documentation

In Europe, the issue of personal data has come to the fore with the European Union's General Data Protection Regulation 2016/679 (GDPR), which came into effect in 2018. The GDPR strictly regulates data protection and privacy for all individual citizens of the European Union (EU) and the European Economic Area (EEA), as well as the transfer of personal data outside these areas. The term "personal data" within ethnography refers to all potentially identifying markers: personal names, places, exact ages, exact dates, titles or unusual occupations.

Ensuring adherence to this regulation when processing and storing any personal data may demand considerable efforts from ethnographers. When studying life histories or personal case studies, it is difficult to avoid collecting such information. However, answering *why* certain processes or events occur in groups or communities does not necessarily require personal data to be collected, as I discuss further below. Ethnographers taking this approach may choose to collect no personal data at all, and instead record information in the form of fully anonymized conversations and observations (field notes). This means no audio, video or photographic recording, as it is nearly impossible to remove identifying information from these data storage media. Non-identifying information can include gender, approximate age (specifying only 20s, 30s, or 40s, for instance), general education level, and marital status. According to GDPR rules, it is permitted for these *fully anonymized* fieldnotes to be imported from non-EU (third) countries into the EU without further protective measures.

Fully anonymized data has one advantage when studying the chronically poor who may not be literate. Since the principles of data protection do not apply to anonymous information, signed consent forms are not required if no personal data is collected. In my own research I found that in spite of mandatory primary schooling in Tanzania, a surprising number of interview participants reported not having attended school for various reasons and they could not read, much less write. They usually wished to hide this fact from their neighbours, however, and it is possible that many more persons never revealed their lack of literacy. I obtained verbal rather than written consent in order to avoid humiliating these participants, especially since they often came to be interviewed accompanied by neighbours.

Researchers conducting longitudinal studies, however, will need identifying data to keep track of the same participants over time. In this section, I focus on the particular challenges surrounding personal data collection in interviews with the poor in the global South. For instance, most researchers conducting fieldwork assume that they can ask an informant's name, age or other relevant personal data and will receive answers that can be verified – at least in theory – through fact-checking. But this assumption is rooted in the experience of living in the global North, where individuals' lives tend to be highly documented. Northern citizens are constantly reminded by *governmental institutions* (schools, tax offices, registrars), *financial institutions* (banks, credit cards) and *places of employment* that any identity details they tell about themselves should conform to this documented information.

When I began fieldwork, I was unprepared for a system of personal data referencing that differed from my own experience. I began each interview by asking the participant's name, age, educational status, how many children the participant had, and ethnic group affiliation. I assumed that there was only one right answer to each of these questions. I asked about ethnic self-identification because I wanted to demonstrate the ethnically mixed nature of the neighbourhood I studied. Eventually ethnicity and number of children turned out to be the only reliable personal identifiers when I later tried to find someone I had interviewed previously, because names, ages, and educational status could change from interview to interview.

I had failed in the beginning to realize that the names told to me by participants could be of three different types: personal name plus family name, as in Europe; or personal name plus father's personal name. Alternatively, names could consist of a personal name, the father's name, and the grandfather's name. But if the participant was a married woman with children, usually none of these names were used or even known by their neighbours. Instead, neighbours knew adult women by the name of their first child, for example, "Mama Hassan" or "Mama Asha". Whenever I asked my key female informant whether a previously interviewed person was still living in the neighbourhood, she often had no idea who I was talking about, since none of the married female residents knew each other by the combination of names they had told me during the interview.

A particularly perplexing moment came when I began to realize that many interview participants, even young ones, did not know exactly how old they were. Sometimes older informants (over 40) did not know their age or said they were born in a year that did not match the age they had previously told. Sometimes their only way to reckon their year of birth was an important national event that a parent had told them had happened near their year of birth. Additionally, even younger persons occasionally gave different ages in different interviews. Looking at the year of interview and the ages they reported on each occasion, the numbers simply did not add up. Even the key informant I trusted most in the neighbourhood publicly celebrated her 50th birthday in a year which – by my calculations – she was only 48. Likewise, asking about a person's job or business had very little connection to what the person would be doing six months or a year later, since informal jobs and sources of income tended to shift with surprising speed. In an informal economy where every person at the bottom of the social ladder was desperately scrambling for a livelihood, some persons started new businesses the moment they heard a good tip from a neighbour or a relative. Yet many businesses stopped just as quickly. When women had to use their limited micro-business capital for emergencies such as family illnesses, funerals, or children's school fees, they often had to wait until a relative could lend them money to start the business again (Lappi and Stark 2013).

I do not believe that my interview participants were deliberately trying to be confusing. Not all informants were comfortable in talking about their own lives, and indeed with low education levels being common, they may have had little practice in doing so. Still more relevant was the fact was that many persons in this neighbourhood lacked personal documentation against which they could check their recollections: birth certificates had never been issued for them, or had been lost in a flood or fire; those who had never finished school lacked educational certificates; and those who did not own property did not have their names recorded in any local government register. For a fee, local governments issued ID cards, but these were based on what applicants reported about themselves. Moreover, people would not have used such official information in their everyday lives to the extent that persons living in the North do. Most sources of income were informal, and relations and communication were face-to-face or through mobile phones. Most people did not have access to computers, and had no money for newspapers or books.

This led to a realization that the people with whom ethnographers work do not always use systems of institutional Western naming or dates for identifying themselves. Migrants and asylum seekers, for instance, often fail to provide what is considered "reliable" or "legitimate" testimony for asylum officials. In claiming pre-migration persecution, responsibility rests with the asylum seeker to create a believable narrative out of unbelievable events (Shuman and Bohmer 2004, 403). Listeners in the global North tend to judge the "truth" or "falsehood" of personal narratives according to how well-formed they are according to Western conventions (Gergen and Gergen 1988; Shuman and Bohmer 2004). The result can be negative impressions – and negative asylum decisions – based on incomplete evidence and culturally-specific assumptions (Kälin 1986; Jacquement 2009; Fingerroos 2016).

Some migrants and refugees possess some form of official identity documentation by the time they enter a wealthier country. Yet that they would identify with this documentation, and incorporate it into one's own life experience, may not be familiar or natural. A lack of ease with documentation or with the recitation of a "Northern" type of backstory (e.g. organized chronologically around key facts, with the individual at the centre of the narrative) should not be taken as evidence of lying, fraud, or invalid motives. In December 2015, the Director of the Finnish Immigration Service stated publicly that immigration officials can distinguish invented stories from authentic ones: "usually an invented story learned by heart is characterized by many contradictions. There is no easy way to present a ready-made story in a believable way" (Yle Kotimaa 2015). By contrast, research has shown that such "contradictions" can arise because the application and interview process constitute a cultural and linguistic performance that is not familiar to all asylum seekers (e.g. Blommaert 2001; Shuman and Bohmer 2004, 403).

## Memory and stress

I received an additional surprise during fieldwork when several persons I interviewed for the second time (whom I and my key informant remembered well) denied having been earlier interviewed by me or by other Finnish researchers from my department. This was perplexing, since aside from us, no other *mzungu* had visited the neighbourhood for at least a decade, and our arrival in the neighbourhood always aroused residents' interest. While I did not expect them to remember our names or the contents of the prior interview, I had expected that they would have a vague recollection of having been interviewed.

It is possible is that interview participants' memories had been affected by the stress, anxiety and sleeplessness that comes with chronic poverty (Rashid 2018). Recent neuroscience research supports the idea that poverty has adverse effects on memory (Noble et al. 2007; Evans and Schamberg 2009; Duval et al. 2017). Although I did not specifically ask about participants' mental and emotional states, it was evident from the interviews that many residents were living in extreme anxiety over their family's survival because they did not know from where the next day's food was coming. For instance, one Muslim woman told me that it was impossible for her to pray because her mind was occupied with constantly thinking of how to feed herself and her children.

Understanding how stress and long-term suffering affect interview participants' mental states is also vital when interviewing migrants who have experienced poverty and traumatic circumstances. Trauma is defined here as an inescapably stressful event that overwhelms people's coping mechanisms and destroys belief in a stable and predictable world. It can include fear of violence or disempowerment, and may make it more difficult for persons to narrate a coherent or linear story. Instead, when telling of their lives, such persons may select those memories that help them make sense of their present life experiences (Shuman and Bohmer 2004; Phillips 2011).

## Perceived causation and third-person elicitation

Together, these disturbances and surprises during fieldwork with poor residents in the South call for an important "twist" in the way ethnographers view personal information provided by interview participants in the global South. My observations regarding memory, anxiety, and sparse documentation of personal details cast into doubt the reliability of qualitative interviews and large-scale surveys of those who have experienced stressful environments in the global South. If the research goal is to access verifiable, historical facts about individual participants, then it is likely there is no method that would circumvent this problem. Yet if ethnographers aim to understand socio-cultural issues such as poverty and migration, then they need to *envision social reality differently*. Whereas quantitative researchers focus on the question of *how much*, qualitative ethnographers can focus on the question of why social and cultural dynamics are the way they are, with the end goal being not verifiable *fact* but culturally-shared patterns of thought and behaviour. A useful method can be analyzing interview participants' "perceived causation", that is, causal mechanisms and relationships *perceived and deduced* by participants themselves. I define a causal mechanism here as a difficult-to-observe pathway or process by which an effect is produced. By asking participants "why" and listening to their answers, ethnographers can benefit from participants' *subjective* knowledge of how events and circumstances are interconnected. The method of perceived causation circumvents the potential problems of personal data collection discussed above because *it does not need personal data at all*. It utilizes a method of data collection I call "third-person elicitation", in which I asked interview participants to tell what they perceived *other* people in general to do or say, what attitudes and opinions were held more broadly by *other* residents in their neighbourhoods (Stark 2019).

Many of the persons I interviewed had difficulty recounting their own lives in terms of official facts and figures. They were also reluctant to make claims based on their individual experience. Interestingly, however, they were often happy to tell what they had seen their neighbours doing (no names were mentioned), and were often highly articulate when talking about *collective understandings*. Tanzania is a culture that emphasizes decorum, conflict-avoidance and self-restraint (Heald 1995), and for this reason strong expressions of personal opinion are not encouraged. Many participants responded to my questions by giving equal weight to both sides of an issue and describing the different ways that their neighbours or relatives might think about it. For this reason, I began to take a different approach in my interviews, and focused on recurrent patterns of social understanding on topics brought up spontaneously by participants, rather than their individual life histories.

At times, I asked sensitive information about child marriage and premarital sex among Muslim youth, and third-person elicitation thus allowed participants to withhold information regarding their own behaviours that might be socially disapproved and therefore damaging to their personal reputations. Participants were not pressured to tell personal experiences, but they sometimes chose to illustrate a point with an example from their own lives. What I received was information on the socially-negotiated understandings of life in the neighbourhood, information that did not rely on the factuality of personal data provided by interview participants.

In cultures similar to the Tanzanian one in which collective consensus is valued over individual expression, persons may be unaccustomed to constructing narratives or descriptions of their reality that are centred on individual experience. When working with or studying persons from such cultures, third-person elicitation can be a way of gaining background information on the experiences of migrants and asylum seekers in a sensitive and non-intrusive way.

## Conclusions

Researchers using qualitative ethnographic approaches have much to offer the study of inequality and poverty, and should not leave this work to economists. Yet Northern-based methodological frameworks may not suffice when studying the global South. What is needed is a twist towards a Southern-informed approach to studying persons who are living in, or coming from so-called developing countries. Northern researchers coming from middle or upper-class backgrounds have little experience with the effects of poverty on those they study. They cannot assume that in the global South basic human needs are met by governments, that education tends to lead to employment, or that social and economic institutions strive to promote individuals' independence and autonomy. Interview participants from another culture, as well as migrants and asylum seekers, may not be used to describing themselves from an individual-centred perspective, and both poverty and stress can affect the way that people remember facts about their lives. How people understand and remember their life details may also vary considerably in contexts where identity documents are rarely available or difficult for holders to understand or verify. Additionally, researchers may wish to prepare themselves in advance for how they may be viewed by local interview participants and what material benefits participants might hope the researcher will bring. Given challenges in participants' literacy across a broad range of skills (textual, digital, and spatial), it may be preferable to refrain from collecting personal data or written consent, and instead focus on participants' socially-shared subjective understandings of the causal mechanisms in their lives. Since the factuality of data pertaining to individual participants is less of a concern when analyzing such *perceived causation*, the researcher may not need to collect personal data at all, but can instead obtain relevant data by using the methods of *third-person elicitation*, which does not ask for personal experiences but asks interview participants what others in their neighbourhoods do or say.

## References

AlKhateeb, M. 2018. "Using Skype as a qualitative interview medium within the context of Saudi Arabia". *The Qualitative Report* 23 (10): 2253–2260. https://nsuworks.nova.edu/tqr/vol23/iss10/1 (accessed 28 January 2020).

Bevan, P. 2004. "Exploring the structured dynamics of chronic poverty". WeD Working Paper No. 6 (ESRC Research Group on Wellbeing in Developing Countries), UK: University of Bath.

Bledsoe, C. 1980. *Women and Marriage in Kpelle Society*. Stanford: Stanford University Press.
Blommaert, J. 2001. "Investigating narrative inequality: African asylum seekers' stories in Belgium". *Discourse & Society* 12 (4): 413–449. https://doi.org/10.1177/0957926501012004002
Booth, D. M. Leach, and A. Tierney. 1999. "experiencing poverty in Africa: Perspectives from anthropology". www.odi.org/Publications/5025-experiencing-poverty-africa-perspectives-anthropology (accessed 28 January 2020).
Campbell, B. 2009. "Informed consent in developing countries: Myth or reality?" http://pdfs.semanticscholar.org/cee1/38b6fcadf1d577640aceebcc82b755132e4e.pdf?_ga=2.14086193.785219505.1570311116-532853868.1560193164
Cleaver, F. 2005. "The inequality of social capital and the reproduction of chronic poverty". *World Development* 33 (6): 893–906.
de Sardan O. 1999. "A moral economy of corruption in Africa?". The Journal of Modern African Studies 37 (1) :25–52.
Duval, E., S. Garfinkel, J. Swain, G. Evans, E. Blackburn, M. Angstadt, C. Sripada, and I. Liberzon. 2017. "Childhood poverty is associated with altered hippocampal function and visuospatial memory in adulthood". *Developmental Cognitive Neuroscience* 23: 39–44. https://doi.org/10.1016/j.dcn.2016.11.006
Edward, P. 2006. "The ethical poverty line: A moral quantification of absolute poverty". *Third World Quarterly* 37 (2): 377–393. https://doi.org/10.1080/01436590500432739
EURITA (European Resettlement and Integration Technical Assistance Project). 2019. *Mentoring Refugees: A Handbook for Volunteers*. https://ec.europa.eu/migrant-integration/librarydoc/mentoring-refugees-a-handbook-for-volunteers (accessed 28 January 2020).
Evans, G., and M. Schamberg. 2009. "Childhood poverty, chronic stress, and adult working memory". *Proceedings of the National Academy of Sciences* 106 (16): 6545–6549. https://doi.org/10.1073/pnas.0811910106
Eversole, R., and M. Johnson. 2014. "Migrant remittances and household development: An anthropological analysis". *Development Studies Research. An Open Access Journal* 1 (1): 1–15. https://doi.org/10.1080/21665095.2014.903808
Ferguson, J. 1997. "Anthropology and its evil twin: The constitution of a discipline". In *International Development and the Social Sciences: Essays on the History and Politics of Knowledge*, edited by F. Cooper and R. Packard, 150–175. Berkeley: University of California Press.
Ferguson, J. 2013. "Declarations of dependence: Labour, personhood, and welfare in Southern Africa". *Journal of the Royal Anthropological Institute* 19: 223–242. https://doi.org/10.1111/1467-9655.12023
Ferguson, J. 2015. *Give a Man a Fish: Reflections on the New Politics of Distribution* (The Lewis Henry Morgan Lectures). Durham, NC: Duke University Press.
Fingerroos, O. 2016. "The concept of 'family' in Somalis' immigration to Finland: Views from immigration officials and NGOs". *Ethnologia Europaea* 46 (1): 25–39.
Gergen, K., and M. Gergen. 1988. "Narrative and the self as relationship". *Advances in Experimental Social Psychology* 21: 17–56. https://doi.org/10.1016/S0065-2601(08)60223-60223
Green, M. 2006. "Representing poverty and attacking representations: Perspectives on poverty from social anthropology". *The Journal of Development Studies* 42 (7): 1108–1129. https://doi.org/10.1080/00220380600884068
Hammond, L. 2011. "Obliged to give: Remittances and the maintenance of transnational networks between somalis at home and abroad". *Bildhaan: An International Journal of Somali Studies* 10 (11): 125–151. https://digitalcommons.macalester.edu/bildhaan/vol10/iss1/11
Heald, S 1995: "The power of sex: Reflections on the Caldwells' 'African sexuality' thesis". *Africa* 64 (4): 489–505. https://doi.org/10.2307/1161129

Hickel, J. 2016. "The true extent of global poverty and hunger: Questioning the good news narrative of the millennium development goals". *Third World Quarterly* 37 (5): 749–767. https://doi.org/10.1080/01436597.2015.1109439

Humphries, N., R. Brugha and H. McGee. 2009. "Sending money home: A mixed methods study of remittances sent by migrant nurses in Ireland". *Human Resources for Health* 7 (66). doi:10.1186/1478-4491-7-66

Iliffe, J. 1987. *The African Poor: A History*. Cambridge: Cambridge University Press.

Jacquement, M. 2009. Transcribing refugees: The entextualization of asylum seekers' hearings in a transidiomatic environment. *Text & Talk* 29 (5): 525–546.

Kalb, D. 2015. "Classes, labor, social reproduction: towards a non-self limiting anthropology". *Suomen antropologi: Journal of the Finnish Anthropological Society* 40 (2): 50–53.

Kälin, W. 1986. "Troubled communication: Cross-cultural misunderstandings in the asylum-hearing". *The International Migration Review* 20 (2): 230–241. https://doi.org/10.1177/019791838602000206

Lappi, T-R., and L. Stark. 2013. "Neighbourhood vendors and the internal economy of the slum: Informal livelihoods among the chronically poor in Dar es Salaam, Tanzania". In *Rethinking the Urban II*, edited by N. Catak, E. Duyan, and S. Secer, 287–291. CUI '13 Contemporary Urban Issues Conference. Istanbul: DAKAM Publishing. www.academia.edu/35123844/Lappi_and_Stark_2013.pdf (accessed 28 January 2020).

Lindley, A. 2010. *The Early Morning Phonecall: Somali Refugees' Remittances*. New York and London: Berghahn.

Lo Iacono, V., P. Symonds, and D. Brown. 2016. "Skype as a tool for qualitative research interviews". *Sociological Research Online* 21 (2): 1–15. www.socresonline.org.uk/21/2/12.html (accessed 28 January 2020).

Lucci, P., T. Bhatkal, and A. Khan. 2018. "Are we underestimating urban poverty?" *World Development* 103: 297–310. www.odi.org/sites/odi.org.uk/files/resource-documents/are_we_underestimating_urban_poverty_final_web.pdf (accessed 28 January 2020).

National Bureau of Statistics Tanzania. 2013. *2012 Population and Housing Census. Population Distribution by Administrative Areas*. Dar es Salaam: Ministry of Finance.

Ndezi, T. 2009. "The Limit of community initiatives in addressing resettlement in Kurasini ward, Tanzania". *Environment and Urbanization* 21 (1): 77–88. https://doi.org/10.1177/0956247809103005

Noble, K. G., B. D. McCandliss, M. J. Farah. 2007. "Socioeconomic gradients predict individual differences in neurocognitive abilities". *Developmental Science* 10 (4): 464–480. https://doi.org/10.1111/j.1467-7687.2007.00600.x

Phillips, D. 2011. "Wounded memory of Hazara refugees from Afghanistan: Remembering and forgetting persecution". *History Australia* 8 (2): 177–198. https://doi.org/10.1080/14490854.2011.11668379

Rao, V. 2002. "Experiments in 'participatory econometrics': Improving the connection between economic analysis and the real world". *Economic and Political Weekly* 37 (20): 1887–1898. www.jstor.org/stable/4412126

Rashid, S. F. 2018. "The invisible reality of '*Chinta Rog*' (a life of chronic worry): The illness of poverty in Dhaka's urban slum settlements". In *Routledge Handbook on the Politics of Global Health*, edited by R. Parker and J. García, 393–400. New York: Routledge.

Shuman, A., and C. Bohmer. 2004. "Representing trauma: Political asylum narrative". *Journal of American Folklore* 117 (466): 394–414. doi:10.1353/jaf.2004.0100

Stark, L. 2017. "Etnologisia näkökulmia köyhyyden tutkimiseen urbaanissa Tansaniassa". In *Yhteiskuntaetnologia*, edited by O. Fingerroos, M. Lundgren, S. Lillbroända-Annala, and N. Koskihaara, 147–182. Helsinki: Finnish Literature Society.

Stark, L. 2019. "Motives and agency in forced marriage among the urban poor in Tanzania". *Ethnos: Journal of Anthropology*. https://doi.org/10.1080/00141844.2018.1559214
Sullivan, J. 2012. "Skype: An appropriate method of data collection for qualitative interviews?" *The Hilltop Review* 6 (1): 54–60. http://scholarworks.wmich.edu/hilltopreview/vol6/iss1/10 (accessed 28 January 2020).
UN-Habitat. 2010 (Revised and updated version of 2003 report). *The Challenge of Slums*. London and Sterling, VA: Earthscan Publications Ltd.
World Relief. 2017. "Boundaries prevent burnout". https://worldreliefdurham.org/establishing-boundaries-and-avoiding-burnout (accessed 28 January 2020).
Yle Kotimaa. 2015. "Keksityt kertomukset ovat erikoisalaamme: Turvapaikanhakijoille kaupataan mukaan nyyhkytarinoita". Last updated 5 December 2015. https://yle.fi/uutiset/keksityt_kertomukset_ovat_erikoisalaamme__turvapaikanhakijoille_kaupataan_mukaan_nyyhkytarinoita/8501625 (accessed 28 January 2020).

# 10

# ELITE INTERVIEWING

## The effects of power in interactions. The experiences of a northern woman

*Lotta Lounasmeri*

– Are you a social scientist?
– I believe I am.
– And a PhD?
– Yes.
– And you don't know this law?

Who is the interviewer here or, rather, the interrogator?

Throughout my research career, the subject of power has intrigued me: the exercise of power in social settings, whether in written media texts, speeches, images or public and private interactions. As a female academic and a professional in my own field, I wanted to investigate and explain how power works in our societies, but I found myself in the midst of situations defined by these very power relations: here I was, doing a research interview and getting myself utterly questioned and undermined. Finding myself in a defensive position, being left feeling inferior and most of all – fearful and shamed. Wondering why this was, and finding that I, as a woman, had certain experiences of being in this professional world and relating to male interviewees. In my most recent project on political decision making on energy issues, the subject of power hierarchies and my emotions it brought to the surface became the most obvious. I started having discussions about this with my Norwegian colleague who had done extensive interview research in the Nordic countries. It became clear I was not alone in my experiences; it seemed that these encounters with holders of power in society were challenging to start with, but there was an additional aspect to us being women. These discussions led to an exercise in critical reflexivity with a feminist touch, which I address in this chapter: a critical examination of the negotiation of power relations from a gender perspective.

## Introduction

In this chapter, I wish to shed light on the question of how power differences are expressed in interviews between academics and societal elites and how gender plays a role in these situations. This approach requires that I step into unknown territory, viewing my own experiences and emotions as legitimate parts of the research conducted. The traditional social science approach of political science and media and communication studies does not favour or emphasise reflecting on personal experiences. Even though this stress on objectivity demands that we maintain our distance and a degree of abstraction and steer away from the personal, the genre of science – not only anthropology or related disciplines – clearly could benefit from being expanded towards emotional understanding and intuition. Anthropologists such as George Devereux (1967) and Sandra Harding (1987) believed that if researchers acknowledge their subjectivity, they and their work would gain greater objectivity. Researchers' conclusions are necessarily influenced by their personal beliefs, values and behaviour, so it is imperative to assess them as part of the evidence in research.

Mainstream social scientists representing the fields of political science and media studies typically proceed from a general level or a systemic framework and apply its presumed laws to specific local environments and individual cases. In contrast, the anthropological approach starts with the specific, the local and the here and now. In the best case, the anthropological approach can combine a more general political and economic framework with a detailed cultural analysis. The starting point of anthropology is empirical field experience. The general thinking holds that for research to be valid and reliable, other researchers should be able to replicate it in identical conditions and get the same results. But in the human sciences this is an awkward premise. As Ruth Behar (1996) has observed, anthropologists' conversations and interactions in the field can never be reproduced exactly because like all encounters between people, they are unique. Proof of anthropologists' journey of exploration comes in the form of an ethnography whose value lies in what others can learn from a meaningful, identifiable account. As the old story of a group of blind people feeling an elephant tells us, their descriptions of the animal they have never come across will differ from each other, but all versions are equally true and accurate.

Emotions have been a subject of interest to philosophers and anthropologists for centuries, and a discussion on the relevance of emotions to politics has already persisted for decades (Ahmed 2014, 2–19). As Sara Ahmed (2014, 9) has stated, many researchers have argued that emotions should not be seen as merely psychological states but also as social and cultural practices. Such claims have several implications. My emotion is not only mine, but something collective, that is born out of the community. It has a history; it comes to the surface in this very moment but is linked to past collective experiences. I might spend much time contemplating what it is that actually evokes the emotions that I felt during the interviews, that I interpret as connected to fear: shame, guilt, frustration, vulnerability, humiliation and anxiety, as well as anger. In the end, this question is difficult to answer, and it might suffice to understand that these feelings stem from the oppression experienced by women by men – intensified by their powerful positions – a history that exists in the collective, also in the Nordic countries.

Examining the powerful in society is not an easy task, but it is important if we are to understand how they affect how any community takes shape and follows a certain path. Recent decades have seen increased interest in elite interviewing and growth in the literature on the dilemmas of interviewing elites within the social sciences (Djerf-Pierre 2005). This literature identifies common barriers to information and gives researchers practical advice on how to circumvent or lower these barriers (Figenschou 2010, 964). At the heart of elite interviewing, as my personal example shows, are questions of power and power imbalances. The negotiation of status and power is relevant to all research relationships, and to enhance the quality of research interviews, an open, systematic approach to these challenges is necessary (Figenschou 2010, 974).

The body of data on which I draw was collected in three research projects conducted in 2011, 2013–2014 and 2017–2018. For these projects, I interviewed retired Finnish chief editors and media executives (all male), public relations and public affairs consultants (mostly male) and decision makers in the energy sector (mostly male but also female). The last group included senior officials in the political and civil administrative sectors as well as energy companies. Most interviews took place in the interviewees' offices, but as most participants in the first group were retired, the interviews were conducted in their homes or public places. As a researcher, I was on culturally familiar ground in terms of nationality. Moreover, Finland, one of the Nordic countries, is characterised by high gender equality and low hierarchies, allowing easier access to those in powerful positions. However, different kinds of power hierarchies still come into play in our interview interactions: hierarchies between different fields of society, between societal positions and, as I came to experience, between genders.

## Theoretical background to a story of challenging encounters

Amid the current revival of the debate on elites' positions and relationships with other segments of societies, reflections on the role of elites in knowledge production and research are both necessary and relevant. To give a definition, I see elites as ruling groups who hold strategic and central positions in society that enable them to regularly influence significant societal decisions (Dogan and Higley 1998; Etzioni-Halevy 1993). Elites possess considerable power due to their positions in social, political and economic networks, and they have the potential to exercise this power to control and define interview situations. One must also acknowledge the layers of elites; some occupy top positions, and others belong to so-called sub-elite groups, to borrow Eva Etzioni-Halevy's (1993) term. With the recognition that membership in elite groups is not equally distributed among men and women, one important aspect of this discussion becomes the large gender differences within and between elite groups (Hjellbrekke and Korsnes 2016), which have implications for the power relations in interview situations (Odendahl and Shaw 2001). I take this point as my feminist lens through which I try to interpret my personal experiences as an interviewer. In describing my elite encounters, I wish to reveal something subtle but deep: What happens when a female researcher in a softer field of science meets with the hardcore male engineer or high-up politician? How can this encountering help to understand how power plays out in their everyday work?

I discuss this issue from a feminist, intersectionalist position which permits choosing various methods according to the discipline involved (Reinharz 1992, 240–243) As Reinharz has explained, feminism strives to represent human diversity and initiate social change, including in the researcher as a person. Feminism can enhance the understanding of one's own participation in socially constructed realities, both personally and politically. I also draw on insights from indigenous methodologies and writings that have highlighted the embodiment of the research process and question the ontologies of scientific practices (Kovach 2009; Smith 2012).

Interviewing, as a research method, constitutes an interaction between the researcher and the informant. By itself, interviewing is not necessarily defined as an ethnographic method; it is a qualitative method used across the social and human sciences and in medicine, psychology and other disciplines. However, interviewing top decision-makers poses a special challenge for ethnography as the power relationship between the interviewer and the interviewee is the reverse of that in interviews with ordinary people. Knowledge is created in the constructive process between the interviewer and the interviewee, and power is always an aspect of the process. Social scientists face well-known challenges when doing research that uses elite interviews as a data gathering method (Figenschou 2010; Kvale and Brinkmann 2009). Nevertheless, textbooks on interviewing methods regularly state that the power imbalance between the interviewer and the interviewee demands ethical awareness in the researcher, who frequently has the power to define the situation. Social anthropology faces similar questions related to power and the power imbalance between the researcher and the subjects of research, which are contrary to my context: the researcher appears superior to those on whom she wishes to turn her inquisitive gaze, as, for instance, in Behar's (1996) comments on her early work on Spanish peasants.

When the interviewees are members of society's elites, however, the imbalance of power likely favours them, which raises particular questions concerning interview interactions and knowledge production. When aspiring to understand and somehow engage with the powerful in society, the researcher either is easily refused access or meets with a penetrating gaze from the research subjects. Typically, elite informants carefully protect their interests and may attempt to manipulate interviews. The power imbalance can also be observed in limited time availability, questions of anonymity and secrecy and less obvious factors such as unwillingness to shed light on the material the researcher seeks and behaving in patronising and aggressive ways in interviews.

In essence, I see power as a relationship and a contingent condition arising in every moment. Taking a Foucauldian approach, structures and positions offer individuals possibilities to exercise power, but it is visible in the action they take how they use that potential. Power always comes to life in social practices. Individuals also possess different kinds of potential power. Here, one can also refer to Pierre Bourdieu's (1998) idea of fields and Robert Putnam's (2000) notion of social capital. Conti and O'Neil (2007, 68) argued that power is not an intrinsic property of individuals but, rather, flows from the complex relationships among individuals, organisations and institutions. Manuel Castells (2009) discussed the variants of network power and networked power. Paying close attention to the dynamics of power can help us see more clearly what the potential limits and possibilities of power are – for both parties of an interaction.

Drawing on feminist methodological approaches, Conti and O'Neill (2007, 67) have stated that "the power dynamic between the researcher and elite informant[s] not only shapes the interview process but defines how knowledge is created". Feminist researchers have introduced the idea of the micropolitics of research, meaning that the researcher should carefully reflect on all stages of the research process to understand their roles and those of the informants in the production of new knowledge. The researcher should do as thorough and transparent an examination as possible, and this reflection can be seen as a central point in the documentation and dissemination of research (Bhavnani 1991; 1994).

Practicing critical but compassionate reflexivity helps the researcher understand herself and others. In the case of these interview studies dealing with societal power, the interview situations and the research process both evoked a whole host of emotions in me as the researcher. It is hard to remain cool and detached when the research purpose is to uncover powerful people's motives, ideals and values when they are dealing with important societal matters. In fact, in this case, doing so would have been impossible: the interviews initially filled me with a sense of dread and fear so intense that there was absolutely no point in trying to project the role of a disinterested, professional researcher, at least in my own eyes. I came to realise how important it is that the researcher engages with the emotional material that arises during involvement and interactions with the research subjects. Devereux (1967) captured this point, stating that what happens with the observer must be made known to understand the nature of what is being observed. The observer and the object of observation both influence the outcome.

## Negotiating the power balance

Describing my own experience of what happened in the interviews involves explaining how I draw from these encounters. In introducing my data, I draw on the transcribed interview texts, the field notes I wrote about the interviews and my recollections of the specific situations I describe. Going back in time to those situations certainly presents a challenge, but when faced with intense emotional experiences, the body and the mind remember. This account, of course, is subjective and changing as time passes. In analysing the interviews, I paid special attention to the contextual elements such as pauses, interruptions and the interviewees' comments related to the interview setting itself. Moreover, I address what the interviewees disclosed about the research subject itself and how they did so – whether they explicitly drew lines on what they would disclose or stuck to the official story, among other actions.

The tangible background characteristics of the interviewee and the interviewer are important dimensions of the interview dynamics (Kahn and Cannell 1957). These characteristics include elements such as cultural and ethnic backgrounds, age, gender, education and institutional and professional positions. These elements constitute the subjectivities and social locations of both parties. At the same time, one must acknowledge that the resources of power can differ and change, as can the balance of power between the interviewer and the interviewee. More intangible elements such as charisma and psychological and physical conditions have relevance. The researcher's task is to try to understand and reflect on these elements as thoroughly as possible (Haraway 1988; Bhavnani 1994; Conti and O'Neil 2007, 66).

At the time of these interviews, I was in my late thirties and early forties and a Finnish postdoctoral researcher conducting externally funded projects. Having a PhD was a prerequisite to conduct meaningful interviews, and interestingly, my funding source was also a relevant factor. Securing interviews was most difficult for the energy policy project, but my funding from the Academy of Finland gave me credibility and persuaded especially the public actors who, at least in theory, had a different responsibility towards scientific research.

Interviewing people of the same cultural and ethnic background is easy in a way as both parties have tacit and shared knowledge on a range of subjects and use their mother tongue to discuss issues. A downside is the risk of taking things for granted. Accordingly, as a Finnish person, I found it rather uncomplicated to approach the interviews with other Finns as social situations. The aspects that played more significant roles, instead, were differences in institutional and professional positions in society, along with age and gender.

Academia constitutes a field of power in its own right, and the informants might see the potential influence of research. In Finland, despite the public debate on the position and relevance of universities, elites in society still hold academia in high respect, this being the old tradition. Tine Figenschou (2010, 974) noted that in her research, she could be perceived as having power to influence the public image of her research subjects. Similarly, I have experienced that looking into critical, strategic and taboo subjects aroused the informants' interest in varied ways. They either wished to avoid scrutiny, if possible, or to have their say and defend their case to influence how the issue was interpreted. Still others wished to act as whistle blowers, revealing certain grievances or abuses in society (usually after they had already exited certain circles of power). That said, most of the interviewees still strove to exert firm control over the interactions.

Another matter is the professional fields represented by the interviewers and the interviewees. Social scientists and humanities researchers might find it especially challenging to find a common language when the interviewees have different competences such as technical, engineering and natural sciences backgrounds. This following excerpt gives an example of the situations I encountered when the interviewees and I had markedly different fields of expertise:

- You are a social scientist right?
- Yes, I am, and a media researcher. That is one term to use.
- So do you have any idea of how many different subjects there are in the Finnish legal system where an administrative decision has to be taken to the parliament?
- No, this is not the kind of thing I research.
- Okay you don't have an idea, but it doesn't matter, as the answer is easy, there is only one, and it is that decision-in-principle. How well do you know the history of these matters [nuclear decision making]?
- I know [them] to a certain degree, yes.
- You know what happened in the beginning of the nineties? [Starts explaining …]
- What really interests me is your own point of view, if you could tell me, to start with, about your own career and how you have come to this …

In many interviews with the male respondents who were experts in different fields, I had to answer questions about my knowledge of the subject in question and make efforts to steer the interviews towards the issues in which I was interested. This situation aroused a certain amount of frustration of which I was conscious during the interviews, and I had to concentrate on keeping my focus and staying calm. This issue did not come up with the female interviewees, even those who were engineers. Instead, they sometimes expressed interested in hearing about my field of expertise:

- I understand the nature of this research, and, is it correct that you are writing an article-based [book], or is it a …?

This issue was less significant when conducting interviews with media professionals. Issues related to the role of journalism in society came up with the older-generation chief editors, while issues of the role of political communication arose with the consultants. However, I saw these as substantial questions about values and, as such, interesting research results. The consultants were mostly male, and many were close to my age or even younger. We shared similar expertise, so they showed much more understanding and appreciation of my work. The political consultants' field was new in Finland, so it was important for them to appear legitimate and "look good".

In some situations, the interviewees sought for confirmation if they had understood my questions right:

- Was this what you asked about? [After a long answer]
- Yes, it was. So can you think of why it is that people don't trust each other anymore? If it was different before.
- I don't know if this is the right answer, but I would somehow think that it is because ...

Interview dynamics involve mutual interactions: showing appreciation can result in receiving it. In many cases, the balance of power is unequal, but it can also lead the interviewees to see the researcher as not an equal and perhaps not worthy of respect, time and information. Researchers studying elites have described how the interviewees' sense of authority often shape the interviews (Fitz and Halpin 1994; Hirsch 1995; Odendahl and Shaw 2001). How does this authority manifest in interviews? In what ways can the interviewee try to control the situation? It is often challenging for the interviewer to stay conscious of when and how this happens. The power imbalance does not necessarily become an obstacle if the interviewee is willing to share and disclose information, but more challenges arise if the interviewee strongly attempts to conceal issues and divert, manipulate and belittle the interviewer.

In my experience, the interviewees either were not willing to share or were cautiously trying to figure out how much to share. The research topics in question might have been difficult and ones the interviewees did not easily discuss; the topics also often involved confidential and strategically important information. The topics might have related to embarrassing details, and the interviewees might have been concerned for their reputation, other consequences, or simply for losing face. In a rather collegial experience, a consultant interviewee was willing to share an embarrassing story but wanted to make sure it would not leak:

- I could tell one example, but I don't want it to become very public – of a social media blunder ...
- This is completely confidential. I will not cite you by name anywhere.
- Otherwise you can, but this example that I will tell, I don't want it to get out.

One might also interpret this interviewee as a person who knew exactly what to and what not to disclose. In another example, a consultant wished to make sure that not even his occupation would be shared:

- It's kind of like.... I will speak more directly with you when I know this [his background] will not come out. Because then, if the rules are different, I will, of course, regulate my speech accordingly.... If someone can identify me, then that will have an effect [on how I speak].

In the interviews, I experienced efforts to control the situation that were either overt and obvious or quite subtle and polite. In some cases, the informants wanted to open up, most probably for their own reasons and interests. The ways in which the informants chose to interact in these situations derived from not only their professional positions but also their individual personalities. These subtler nuances might have become more visible in the familiar cultural context. My interviewees used subtle gestures and openings such as body language (closing up or taking a very assertive pose), inserting delays and obstacles into initial contacts, establishing how much time was available, demanding confidentiality and asking questions about the research and the researcher. Some tactics clearly were targeted at confirming what I knew, asking about what I knew, hinting that maybe I did not, and trying to find out my motivations and personal opinions. I was also often interrupted to provide answers while the questions were still being posed. Sometimes the interviewees attempted to define what was relevant to the research:

- How would you place [your paper]? If we think of the time when you started in the 1970s, what kind of a paper was it in the Finnish newspaper world?
- -well I don't know if that bears much relevance here, what is relevant concerning your research is that I was chosen [for this position] to change the paper's stance towards the Soviet Union...
- How would you define this concept of self-censorship?
- Well, there is no one definition that exists –
- Correct, there is not, but how do you understand it?

Establishing trust was consistently, if not always, easier with the female interviewees, perhaps because a certain kind of sisterly bonding occurred, if only on a professional level. The women would always bond as equals, with very few exceptions when they refused to do the interviews altogether. The female interviewees might have behaved strategically, but they did not try to question my professionalism and capabilities as the interviewer.

With the male interviewees, the interaction and the balance of trust was negotiated differently. In fact, the male interviewees had more difficulty relating on only a professional level. They unconsciously adopted various roles: the older interviewees sometimes acted as father figures, younger ones would come out as charmers, and some would take a role as educators. In certain cases, the latter role was performed in oppressive and aggressive manners, as discussed. However, the quality of the interactions did not affect the research process in straightforward ways. The male interviewees might have talked more and end up telling more – willingly or unwillingly – than their female counterparts. Moreover, the male interviewees' reactions demonstrated which questions raised the most emotions. For me as a researcher on societal power, the interview situations themselves yielded much material on the subject.

In the most difficult experiences, the interviewees, invariably male, acted defensively. Showing myself as a person rather than merely a cool professional might have led some interviewees to resort to aggressive, fear-driven behaviour. Such behaviour left me feeling intimidated and even fearful. I tried to stay calm and observe the interviewees while acknowledging that I had to use all my concentration to be able to ask the next relevant question. In one interview, I witnessed a consultant bossing around his employees as if to demonstrate his superiority. In another case, a chief editor demanded a detailed account of the interview but did not understand that he would only receive a transcribed text I would later use to analyse the discussion. I, as a researcher, naturally would not subject the analysis to interference from the interviewee. To be fair, once the research was completed, the interviewee did admit that qualitative research was an unfamiliar field to him.

## Reflections and conclusions

I see that in my experiences, the issue of gender became intertwined with my societal and professional positions, and these latter characteristics carried much more weight for the male than the female interviewees. Had I been older and a professor, I might have encountered less questioning. Odendahl and Shaw (2001, 311) have emphasised that gender is an issue in many interview situations, and female interviewers of elite subjects invariably appear more aware of the positive and negative influences their gender may have on the interview process. I was certainly aware, and must admit to the weirdest thing I have expressed in an academic text: maybe my overtly feminine physical appearance played a part here, too. Personal characteristics are important too, and feeling not so confident from the start certainly bore relevance. The less I knew the field I was looking into, the less certainty I felt. Perhaps fear is contagious – catching on from either side of the table?

A particular dilemma arises when the interviewer needs to distinguish when the informants are using an official discourse or institutional language and when they are lying. When a story has a strong, official version and a significantly different, unofficial version, the informants must invest much energy into putting up a show or a façade to convince the interviewer. These efforts can be detected as nervousness, arrogance and the behaviour of closing up and refusing to say much. The interviewees might be uncertain of their position, might feel afraid for some reason or might have a need to show their power and position. Uncertainty might be caused by fears of admitting to making mistakes, not knowing or understanding everything and not trusting the interviewer to be benevolent or take the interviewees' side in matters. The interviewees might be afraid that their motives will be misinterpreted or, worse, their motives that cannot stand the light of day will become apparent. Such situations arose with some of my male interviewees, possibly because I attempted to make personal contact with them.

When experiencing power imbalances and their various consequences in interview situations, how should researchers respond and act? Several researchers have problematized or confessed to practicing types of manipulation themselves (Conti and O'Neil 2007; Figenschou 2010). Conti and O'Neil (2007, 79) feel that the authority relationship in the interview must be strategically managed. Earlier research, though, has found little need to protect elites from the researcher's power in the practice of studying elites (Cookson 1994, 129; Hertz and Imber 1995). For example, Beth L. Leech (2002, 665) has recommended that the researcher pretend to be agreeable and intellectually dim to avoid the risk of causing the respondents to feel threatened. Figenschou (2010, 973) observed that by ignoring patronising behaviour, she may have encouraged her informants' perceptions that she was naïve and inexperienced, leading them to open up more. Catherine Welch et al. (2002, 625) suggested that the researcher encourage the informants' openness by steering a course between the roles of therapist and spy, stressing academic neutrality while showing empathy towards the interviewees.

My own experience tells me that confronting informants who behave patronisingly might not be a good strategy. In any case, the fear I felt on many occasions led me to feel vulnerable, and not especially prone to assertiveness, so I chose to maintain neutral and restrained. I believe that the researcher, as an ethical actor, should attempt to establish mutual respect. Instead of confrontation, it is better to maintain one's own dignity and give space for others' behaviour, so it can also become visible to them. The researcher can aim to create mutual trust by displaying her competence, work ethic and personality through being open, acting professionally and trying to connect on a human level. This comes back to vulnerability – showing one's authentic self. Showing myself meant that I did not try to overtly challenge my respondents but let them speak, and I gently steered the topic towards my interests. This approach might have resulted in obtaining more information, but in some cases, it might have had the opposite effect: the informants did not think I was worth sharing information with as they could not know whether I understood it or whether I was "worth it". Some interviews left me feeling humiliated and wondering how difficult it was to connect across that power gap. These feelings occasionally led me to question my professionalism and competence. Ultimately, my position allowed me to not take the actions of the powerful for granted. Maybe my role became one of a spying therapist.

It takes courage for the researcher to actually put herself on the line and to be a person, not just a representative of academia. Giving full, even heartfelt attention to the interviewees always makes a difference. Everyone needs to be heard, and the interviewer can provide that space where others can talk as much as they want. Often, if not always, this space making makes it possible to rise above liturgical speech and overt control and manipulation of situations. The interviewees also often want to talk about their work and what is important to them.

From my part, in the end, there was no other option but to surrender: to be vulnerable, to take the risk that the interviewees would think that I was stupid or disingenuous and wonder what the purpose of the interview was. However, as Behar (1996) wrote, communicating in vulnerable ways creates a good chance that others will also do so and abandon their cool professionalism. Perhaps most importantly, this has the potential to transform self and others, making them more conscious and thereby more willing to make efforts to build bridges between the familiar and the strange or unknown – the self and others (see Chang 2008, 52). Authentic communication can also entail healing wounds and liberating oneself to become self-empowered (Foster, McAllister and O'Brien 2005). Through these interactions, both parties share something and there is an opportunity to be affected in some way – moved, touched, changed even? Provided that fear does not take over.

## Acknowledgements

I wish to present my heartfelt thanks to my colleague, professor Eli Skogerbo, for her invaluable support in writing this article.

## References

Ahmed, S. 2014 [2004]. *The Cultural Politics of Emotion*. 2nd edn. Edinburgh: Edinburgh University Press.
Behar, R. 1996. *The Vulnerable Observer*. Boston: Beacon Press.
Bhavnani, K-K. 1991. *Talking Politics: A Psychological Framing for Views from Youth in Britain*. Cambridge: Cambridge University Press.
Bhavnani, K-K. 1994. "Tracing the contours: Feminist research and feminist objectivity". In *The Dynamics of "Race" and Gender: Some Feminist Interventions*, edited by H. Afshar and M. Maynard, 26–40. London: Taylor & Francis.
Bourdieu, P. 1998. *Practical Reason. On the Theory of Action*. California: Stanford University Press.
Castells, M. 2009. *Communication Power*. Oxford: Oxford University Press.
Chang H. 2008. *Autoethnography as Method*. California: Left Coast Press.
Conti, J. A., and M. O'Neil. 2007. "Studying power: Qualitative methods and the global elite". *Qualitative Research* 7 (1): 63–82.
Cookson, P. 1994. "*The Power Discourse: Elite Narratives and Educational Policy Formation*". In *Researching the Powerful in Education*, edited by G. Walford, 116–130. London: UCL Press.
Devereux, G. 1967. *From Anxiety to Method in the Behavioral Sciences*. New York: Humanities Press.
Djerf-Pierre, M. 2005. "Lonely at the top: Gendered media elites in Sweden". *Journalism* 6 (3): 265–290.
Dogan M, and J. Higley. 1998. "Elites, crises, and regimes in comparative analysis". In *Elites, Crises and the Origins of Regimes*, edited by M. Dogan and J. Higley. Oxford: Rowman & Littlefield.
Etzioni-Halevy, E. 1993. *The Elite Connection. Problems and Potential of Western Democracy*. Cambridge: Polity Press.
Figenschou, T. 2010. "Young, female, Western researcher vs. senior, male, Al Jazeera officials: Critical reflections on accessing and interviewing media elites in authoritarian societies". *Media, Culture & Society* 32 (6): 961–978. https://doi.org/10.1177/0163443710379667
Fitz J., and D. Halpin. 1994. "Ministers and mandarins: Educational research in elite settings". In *Researching the Powerful in Education*, edited by G. Walford, 32–50. London: UCL Press.
Foster, K., M. McAllister and L. O'Brien. 2005. "Coming to autoethnography: A mental health nurse's experience". *International Journal of Qualitative Methods* 4 (4): 1–15.

Haraway, D. J. 1988. "Situated knowledges: The science question in feminism and the privilege of partial perspective". In *Feminism and Science*, edited by E. F. Keller and H. E. Longino, 249–263. Oxford: Oxford University Press.

Harding, S. G. 1987. *Feminism and Methodology. Social Science Issues*. Bloomington: Indiana University Press.

Hertz, R., and J. B. Imber. 1995. *Studying Elites Using Qualitative Methods*. Thousand Oaks: Sage.

Hirsch, P. M. 1995. "Tales from the field: Learning from researchers' accounts". In *Studying Elites Using Qualitative Methods*, edited by R. Hertz and J. B. Imber, 72–80. Thousand Oaks: Sage.

Hjellbrekke, J., and K. Olav. 2016. "Women in the field of power". *Sociologica* (2): 1–28.

Kahn, R. L., and C. F. Cannell. 1957. *The Dynamics of Interviewing*. New York: John Wiley & Sons.

Kovach, M. 2009. *Indigenous Methodologies: Characteristics, Conversations, and Contexts*. Toronto: University of Toronto Press.

Kvale, S., and S. Brinkmann. 2009. *Interviews. Learning the Craft of Qualitative Research Interviewing*. 2nd edn. Los Angeles: Sage.

Leech, B. L. 2002. "Asking questions: Techniques for semistructured interviews". *PS: Political Science & Politics* 35 (4): 665–668.

Odendahl, T., and A. M. Shaw 2001. "Interviewing elites". In *Handbook of Interview Research: Context and Method*, edited by J. F. Gudbrium and J. A. Holstein, 299–316. Thousand Oaks: Sage.

Putnam, R. D. 2000. "Bowling alone: America's declining social capital". In *Culture and Politics*, edited by L. Crothers and C. Lockhart, 223–234. New York: Palgrave Macmillan.

Reinharz, S. 1992. *Feminist Methods in Social Research*. New York: Oxford University Press.

Smith, L. T. 2012. *Decolonizing Methodologies: Research and Indigenous Peoples*. London: Zed Book. Kindle.

Star, S. L. 1979. "*Strategic* heresy as scientific method: Feminism and the psychology of consciousness". Paper presented at the American Association for Advancement of Science.

Welch, C., R. Marschan-Piekkari, H. Penttinen, and M. Tahvanainen, M. 2002. "Corporate elites as informants in qualitative international business research". *International Business Review* 11 (5): 611–662.

# PART IV
# Embodied and affective ethnography

# 11

# MEMORY NARRATIONS AS A SOURCE FOR HISTORICAL ETHNOGRAPHY AND THE SENSORIAL-AFFECTIVE EXPERIENCE OF MIGRATION

*Marija Dalbello and Catherine McGowan*

## Introduction

Ellis Island in the Port of New York, an immigrant station during the Great Migration from Europe to America at the start of the twentieth century, has been the main symbol of a shared migration experience of European Americans for nearly half a century, signifying and sentimentalizing the grit of immigrant life, and shaping the image of America as "a nation of immigrants", a phrase originating from the title of John F. Kennedy's book published in 1964. That particular structure of feeling has been at the centre of the popular politics of memory that discursively constructed transatlantic migration in public culture. We engaged that discourse empirically by developing an approach for "aggregative" reading across a corpus of interviews from the Ellis Island Oral History (EIOH) collection and in two case studies. We focused on the sensorial-affective dimensions of migration, meaning those that represented the physiological, sensing, or synesthetic imagining of migration in the vernacular narratives of the EIOH collection. Oral history storytelling involves sensorial interpretation of experience in which individuals rely on kinaesthetic, visual, sonic, or olfactory representation of particularly "magical moments" that become devices for resolving complex timeframes of migration or an emotion.

Our test corpus consisted of the Central and Southern European oral history interviews documenting the perspectives of the participants in that historical migration. These pre-elicited oral history interviews document and mediate a historical sensorium of the Great Migration, so far an untapped archive for understanding the sensorial and affective dimensions of migration of particular groups and individuals. Studying migration from the point of view of senses and sensory experiences or material culture, as exemplified in the studies of ethnic food, is not unknown in migration scholarship. Studying an entire historical migration sensorium using a vast body of oral histories is a new and ground-breaking twist in ethnographic research. We define historical ethnography as a tool for historical explanation drawing from the traces of the past, while considering how the relationship between the past and these traces is mediated through oral histories as documents and how the description of experience in the first person reflexively engages the historian-ethnographer's position. In our overall interpretive approach, we draw on and combine the methodological imperatives of history (documentation) and ethnography (reflexivity). We reflect on the methodology for reading life histories combining a macro- (across the corpus) with micro-analytic approaches (of case studies) in order to demonstrate their complementarity and value in historical ethnography.

## Reading across a corpus of interviews

### Ellis Island oral histories: general remarks

The Ellis Island Oral History (EIOH) collection contains 1,893 oral histories by immigrants and some United States government agency employees. The analysis draws interviews from Austria-Hungary, Croatia, and Italy. These Central and South European cases belong to a particular historical sensorium of migration from areas of Europe that are comparable and contemporaneous with the highest emigration and immigration cohort of the Great Migration. Creating the corpus for analysis required web scraping and manual verification and inventory of downloaded files. We extracted demographic information in that subset of the EIOH archive using metadata from each record as well as analysis of transcripts, and sound recordings. The most complete interviews in the archive had audio files with transcripts, passenger information files, ship images, and extracts from ship manifests. We created a summary table that recorded completeness of files in our corpus.

**TABLE 11.1** Summary of the record completeness and file inventory for the corpus

| Country | Records | Type of recording | | | | | |
| --- | --- | --- | --- | --- | --- | --- | --- |
| | | Audio* | Transcript** | Audio Only | Transcript Only | Audio and Transcript*** | No Audio or Transcript |
| Austria-Hungary | 18 | 11 | 11 | 1 | 1 | 10 | 6 |
| Croatia | 11 | 2 | 0 | 2 | 0 | 0 | 9 |
| Italy | 263 | 166 | 187 | 23 | 44 | 143 | 53 |
| Total | 292 | 179 | 198 | 26 | 45 | 153 | 68 |

NOTES: One passenger from Croatia group and six passengers from Italy are listed twice in the Ellis Island Oral History Project because they were listed both under their maiden and married names for the same interview.
* Audio only as well as audio and transcripts of these interviews are available.
** Transcript only as well as audio and transcripts of the interviews are available.
*** Audio recording is available and there is a transcript of the interviews.

The transcripts allowed for the identification of additional dimensions that were also recorded in spreadsheets including *Other Modes of Travel; Passenger Record;* presence of *Audio Filename; Transcript Filename;* as well as *Interview Date 1; Interview Date 2;* whether it was a *Joint Interview; Interview Partner* and the *Immigration Date; Immigration Age; Birthdate;* whether the migrant made *Multiple Trips* and if so, *Trip Date 1, Trip Date 2, Trip Date 3; Special Notes* recorded supplemental information. The features of the cases included in our analysis are presented in Appendix 11.1.

Because oral histories represent a wide-ranging archive of migration, the reconstruction of a historical sensorium of the Great Migration required further "semantic" reduction in order to understand the EIOH archive in terms of migration periods represented and to identify cases corresponding to a particular "generational cohort" and "migration sensorium". The generational cohort was identified by age at which they immigrated and time of emigration/immigration as well as the age when they recorded their life histories. The migration experiences of children and adults may be remembered differently because they belong to a particular historical ecology that defined their sensorium. The elders' memories "from a child's perspective" will result in narrated experiences that reveal "minor details and things in their physical environment that adults do not pay attention to" and retrospective reminiscence of childhood experience that results in a mixture between children's and adults' perspectives, the former re-interpreted "within the framework of later and present experiences and knowledge" (Koskinen-Koivisto and Seitsonen 2019, 25). Understanding the demographic composition of those interviewed addressed the methodological questions of "whose sensorium" is represented in the archive and pre-elicited interviews as useful historical evidence. In this corpus, the memories of youth and childhood "are recounted through an adult filter" (Laakkonen 2011, 304). While the materialized narrated memories carry the experience of multiple sites of memory (Kuusisto-Arponen and Savolainen 2016, 60–61), the individual experiences are "engrained in the body" as "bodily remembering" (Povrzanović Frykman 2016, 82, 84).

## *Migration cohorts and generations in the migration sensorium*

The cohorts in the migration waves were inferred from the dates of immigration embedded in the transcript files and the metadata. Two-thirds of the interviews or 198 out of 292 had that information. The recorded immigration experience shown in Table 11.2 ranges from 1894 to 1964, with majority of the cases situated in the first quarter of the twentieth century.

Most of the interviewees immigrated as children and young adults (Table 11.3), which was relevant for the formation of the migrants' transnational experience and to understand the sensorium within their life histories. Many of them were accompanying larger family groups and were the only surviving members to recollect the migration sensorium. And, most of them were women.

**TABLE 11.2** Dates of immigration (N=198)

| Country | Immigration dates | | | | | | | | |
|---|---|---|---|---|---|---|---|---|---|
| | Before 1914 | 1914–1918 | 1919 | 1920 | 1921–1923 | 1924–1930 | 1931–1938 | 1939–1945 | After 1945 | Without Date |
| Austria-Hungary* | 11 | 0 | 0 | 0 | 0 | 1 | 0 | 0 | 0 | 6 |
| Croatia** | 2 | 0 | 0 | 0 | 0 | 0 | 0 | 0 | 0 | 9 |
| Italy*** | 48 | 21 | 11 | 34 | 39 | 28 | 14 | 2 | 9 | 57 |

NOTES: This table is based on 198 interviews out of 292. One-third (or 93) of the interviews do not have any information about the immigration date. One passenger from Croatia and six passengers from Italy are listed twice in the Ellis Island Oral History Project to represent maiden and married names.
*In Austria-Hungary group, Joseph and Louise Voboril were interviewed together and were counted as one immigrant experience.
**In Croatia group, the passenger duplication immigration date is in the 1913 range (one interview is counted twice).
***In Italy group, the passenger duplication immigration dates are: in 1913, 1914, 1915, and 1917 (once in each year, i.e. four times), and in 1919 (twice).

**TABLE 11.3** Age at time of immigration as reported in the interviews

| Country | Age at immigration | | | | | | |
|---|---|---|---|---|---|---|---|
| | > 2 | 2–4 | 5–9 | 10–15 | 16–19 | 20 < | Unknown |
| Austria-Hungary | 0 | 0 | 4 | 4 | 2 | 1 | 7 |
| Croatia | 0 | 0 | 2 | 0 | 0 | 0 | 9 |
| Italy | 2 | 18 | 67 | 56 | 35 | 26 | 59 |
| Total | 2 | 18 | 73 | 60 | 37 | 27 | 75 |

NOTES: When the immigration date is given, age could be inferred from the interviews and the metadata accompanying each record. One passenger from Croatia and six passengers from Italy have been listed twice in the Ellis Island Oral History Project to represent maiden and married names.

The sensoria represented within their recorded interviews are life spanning rather than migration event-focused, which is important from the methodological perspective. This is due to how interviews were designed – to elicit and privilege certain types of memories (Varricchio 2011).

## *Selecting the cases for analysis*

The life histories situated participants by age, story, generation, and the particular migration wave. The dates of recording, ranging from 1970s until 1990s, were defining this archive as well as the age, cognitive abilities of the interviewees, and the life span they reflected when interviews were collected. At the time of writing, there is little likelihood that any of the project participants is still living.

The Austria-Hungary interviews were collected in the earliest period of the project – in the 1970s and 1980s – when most of the participants were 70 to 90 years old, based on their birth dates, which ranged from 1881 to 1907. Half of them immigrated at the age of ten (five of 11 cases) and two individuals were 19 and 30 years old. The generational structure of Italy interviews points to immigration dates from 1894 to 1929 (based on 166 interviews with transcripts out of 263), also interviewed in their late 80s and 90s. (For a third of the Italian records missing information about the age at the time of immigration, some inferences could be made from the immigration date.) Their age at the time of migration was under 16; birth dates between 1888 and 1910. Given that most of Italian oral histories were collected in the early to mid-1990s, with sporadic inclusion of interviews from the 1970s and 1980s, they show a similar distribution in time of migration, age, and demographic features relevant for this analysis. The only case from the Croatia group was interviewed when she was 88 years old; she immigrated in 1913 at the age of six. We focused on 73 cases from the Italy corpus with 1919 as cut off immigration date. Italy, Austria-Hungary and Croatia groups were situated in the migration wave occurring before and during World War I that affected all of these geographical areas. The participants in the oral history interviews were positioned along a comparable generational cohort of the same migration wave and the migration experiences of Central and South Europeans. The analysis encompassed 84 interviews: Austria-Hungary (10); Croatia (1); Italy (73).

## Coding the sensorium of the Great Migration

The coding of entities and sensory events and statements that fall within the phenomenological experiences through the senses (seeing, taste, touch, temperature, smell, and sound) and the complex multisensory-affective themes ("the sensorium" of a historical experience) were coded in the audio and text files using an open source PDF reader *Skim*, developed as the tool for this project and Avid Pro Tools for marking timestamps and extract coded segments. The resulting sensorial modalities shown in Table 11.4 include descriptions and incidence shared across the cases.

*Visual* sense or sight includes descriptive instances or imagined scenes prompting visual representation by the interviewers who were focusing on scenes of arrival. Several immigrants commented on the absence of now emblematic city skyline and scarcity of tall buildings or the sight of the lights running the length of the bridges or waiting to see the expected sight of the Statue of Liberty (as if spoken about or seen in a picture). One immigrant described the scene of separation; others would describe the homes they left, in visual imagery – for example, as made of stone or wood logs. *Sound*, while rarely mentioned, is tied to singing or voices of people and shouting, sound of horns, specific musical instruments, music, or musicians. The cheering and shouting on arrival to the Port of New York is noted in some interviews. The descriptions of the urban environment and its sounds are limited. (Some of the interviewees continued to travel to their new homes beyond the confines of the city and their experience of the city was fleeting.) *Touch* includes instances of a stranger teaching the immigrant how to wash her hands and fingernails in a manner that evokes the sense of touch; other codes mention kissing or embrace; or, the feeling of objects (such as the velvet couch in the second-class cabin). The synesthetic memories of *taste* included a complex multi-sensory experience of food – when remembering its preparation and reflecting on what was ordinary and common or what was novel. They reflected on what they ate on board of the ships and on the memories of new foods once they arrived to America or remembered foods in nostalgic terms. The subthemes within memories of food on the ships included bread, which they had made and brought with them or bread provided on board. The familiarity of rye or other dark-grain bread would be contrasted with white bread. In other examples, they would remember wine-making, the butchering of meat according to traditional methods, or picking their own fruits from the garden contrasted with store-bought fruits. The memories of new foods associated with the arrival to America included bananas, which were noted a few times as a new and exotic food. One passenger was particularly fascinated by soda and another amazed by the cheapness of apple pie at Ellis Island. Mary Thome shares about being able to "taste and smell the good gingerbread squares." *Smell* occurs in the context of food memories.

The National Park Service (NPS) interviewers worked with pre-existing templates aimed at the elicitation of particular memories of the steerage experience, Ellis Island inspections, and experiences at school. The incidence of shared

**TABLE 11.4** Modalities with codes and descriptions

| Modalities | Descriptions | Coding of interviews (1894–1919) (N=84 interviews) | | | | | |
| --- | --- | --- | --- | --- | --- | --- | --- |
| | | Austria-Hungary (N=10)[a] | | Croatia (N=1) | | Italy (N=73) | |
| | | Incidence of Sensorial Modality | Number of Interviews | Incidence of Sensorial Modality | Number of Interviews | Incidence of Sensorial Modality | Number of Interviews |
| Food, eating, cooking | (1) food from the home country (2) food on board of ship (3) new foods they ate once they arrived to America Subthemes: white bread on the ship; dark/rye bread of the home country, bananas and soda as new foods | 45 | 10* | 0 | 0 | 279 | 66 |
| Touch | kissing, embracing being touched by a "stranger" or be taught how to wash their hands and fingernails | 15 | 6 | 1 | 1 | 10 | 10 |
| Sight / visuality (powerful and evocative imagery) | family members or home in the old country (seeing grandfather for the last time; old home made of "stone" or "logs") | 15 | 6 | 4 | 1 | 138 | 54 |

(*Continued*)

**TABLE 11.4** (*Cont.*)

| Modalities | Descriptions | Coding of interviews (1894–1919) (N=84 interviews) | | | | | |
|---|---|---|---|---|---|---|---|
| | | Austria-Hungary (N=10)* | | Croatia (N=1) | | Italy (N=73) | |
| | | Incidence of Sensorial Modality | Number of Interviews | Incidence of Sensorial Modality | Number of Interviews | Incidence of Sensorial Modality | Number of Interviews |
| Sound | sound of instruments, singing, musicians, horns people shouting | 8 | 5 | 2 | 1 | 41 | 27 |
| Bullying / Belittling | from not understanding English or not being able to speak English language in school | 5 | 4 | 0 | 0 | 50 | 30 |

NOTES: One passenger in Croatia group and six passengers in Italy group are listed twice in the Ellis Island Oral History Project (with records for both their maiden and married names). The sensorial incidences were not counted twice in those cases. The incidence of sensorial modalities is recorded as many times as it appeared in the interviews but not all of those interviewed used representations that we coded as sensorial.

*Two passengers (Joseph and Louise Voboril) from Austria-Hungary group were interviewed together in the same audio recording and they "talked over each other" and finished each other's thoughts in the course of the interview.

sensory themes across this corpus and the high frequency of "food" or the presence of "bullying" theme may have resulted from leading, consistent, and deliberate questions posed by the interviewers, such as "were you called greenhorn" or "And what was it like being, you know, not having the language and going to school" or "Well, how was school different in New York compared with the school you'd been in Italy?" These questions were assuming difficulty of assimilation due to language barriers or seeking a story of bullying. Mario Varricchio discusses the ideological impact of this interview guide and its role in constructing the archive to support the celebratory discourse of America as a nation of immigrants (2011). The interviewers' interventions often created confusion or forced breakdowns in the oral histories. For example, the Statue of Liberty was the leading sighting image that the interviewers insisted on: "What did you feel when you first saw the Statue of Liberty?" In some instances, the interviewees themselves closed that discussion by offering a negative response. Other respondents resisted in different ways. Their tactical evasions, including meaningful digressions, are discussed in the micro reading sections in this chapter. The invitation at the close of the interview, typically in the form of questions such as how do you feel about the decision to come to the US or looking back on your life, what are you most proud of – versions of the interview question, "Are you happy you came to America?" (Varricchio 2011, 28) elicited free-association and storytelling. The questions offered space for reflection outside of the interview protocol and often situated the narrations within interviewees' affective-sensorial context.

In the emerging migration sensorium that was shared, there is a high incidence of food and touch memories, and the powerful, evocative imagery that they recalled and described visually. Touch memories often follow a handful of themes such as clothing, straw beds, itching from bedbugs on the boat, waking to the feeling of urine falling on them from the child in the bunk above, physical touch during the Ellis Island inspection process. Next, two themes are presented in depth: visual sense (sight) modality, which has a high incidence across the corpus, and a complex affective-sensory theme of "bullying". Both of these themes are tied to the structuring of the interview questions, the effect critiqued by Mario Varricchio (2011) but nevertheless represent the dominant dimensions of the sensorium based on the "aggregative" reading of the corpus. The micro-readings address complementary acoustemological dimensions.

## Modalities of the migration sensorium: aggegative analysis and interpretation

### *Visual sense (sight) modality*

The incidences of looking, seeing and visual metaphors mentioned in the interviews are exemplified by Rozia Frankel's statement that Ellis Island and the New York City bridges look "like a string of pearls with the lights on". Anna Vislocky describes the Statue of liberty looming "like a monster". Mary Thome recalls scenes in the inspection station, when immigrants adjusted their appearance to look healthier and elude or trick the "scopic regime" of medical inspections that aimed to control how they would appear or be seen (Jay 1994, 149; Rose 2016, 3). Stephen Houbrick associates the (colourful) plumed hats of the gendarmes harassing his mother and the dark clothes of the immigrants:

> Everybody wore black clothes, black shawls and the men had the fedoras on. All dark clothes, I don't know why they wore dark clothes in Europe like that but that's what we come over with. It was the cheapest maybe.

In the interview by Andrew Lichanec, his departure is visually constructed: "looking through the window and I saw my grandfather standing under a tree until I got out of sight". This is a bridging afterimage that he claims has been one that "stood in my memory all the time". Yet, the point of observation fluctuates – from Lichanec seeing his grandfather "through the window" to seeing himself from his grandfather's vantage point, "until I got out of sight". The conflicting point of production of the image represents seeing the past as an act of distancing. This is an organizing representation of his migration experience. Lichanec further recalls the event entirely in visual terms "today, at my age, I don't know why, but I could draw a picture of that man standing there, the way he was looking". This particular life history is organized in imagistic moments.

Vincent Cioffari, who immigrated in 1917 as an 11-year old, recalls a series of visual events with haptic or sound dimensions – an earthquake and iron bar reinforcements in the houses of his home town, the arrival of the first car to the town, a water fountain in the town centre and the boat carrying immigrants dodging a German torpedo on its transatlantic crossing. He describes seeing rainwater collected for washing in terms of "music" of raindrops falling on the metal pots. While the mere frequency of the sensory modalities may not be particularly insightful for analysis of differences among the senses in this corpus or to generalize migrant experience, the frequency of particular sensorial representations in individuals' ontologies point to meaningful patterns. The "interconnected and interrelated" (Pink 2012, 5) nature of sensory modalities requires the analysis to be focused on shared patterns as well as their presence in the context of individual interviews.

## *Bullying*

Disorientation surfaces in the affective-sensory theme of bullying. The immigrants who included this experience in their life histories remembered the cruelty and negative affects. The five incidences across four interviews in the Austria-Hungary corpus respond to the interviewers' elicitations, such as "how did you learn English, did the kids at school help you?" or "did you ever hear the expression, 'greenhorn'?" and, "did kids make fun of you?" Being humiliated or ridiculed were reported by Andrew Lichanec together with strategies he used for overcoming that difference: "Oh yes, the kids always pick on you, you know, and make you a little uncomfortable, but after a while it, you're with them and it kind of would, you know, wear off". Mary Thome captures her own ambivalence:

> Eventually, oh, I looked so funny, too. I had different kind of clothes. I had old country clothes on, stockings with circles around them, long dress down to my ankle, and I had to wear all the, those were the only clothes I had for an awfully long time ... And, of course, the kids made fun of me because I was dressed so funny and I didn't know what was going on.

Mary Vokaty fought back: "They made fun of all the foreigners. When they came here they called us greenhorns. And, but somehow, maybe the grownups, I don't now how they took it, but I didn't". Rozia Frankel, whose entire life history prior to arrival to America was a chain of upheavals, reflects on the "unfortunate experience in school [being] the cruelty of the American children" but remembers another child, a friendly neighbor (an ally) who helped and "guided me back from school". The neighbourhood and the school provided the boundaries and surfaces for reflecting the sensory-affective experiences of these individuals. These children negotiated their own social order where they "domesticate the new spaces" in the urban territory, independently of the order of adults (Koskinen-Koivisto and Seitsonen 2019, 25). Their narratives emphasize social re-positioning linked to achieving the mastery of English and the strategies and agency that children had to demonstrate in their everyday lives in the shared experience of migration.

These incidents are multi-sensory performances of memory. The instants mediated through sense descriptions in the constructions in the oral interviews are analogous to the "madeleine". For Marcel Proust, the construction of smell is the launching point for an inscription of memory in this instance of "Proustian" writing (Danius 2002). The imagistic moments and ocular-centric representations in the vernacular memories of the EIOH collection, similarly, are representations created through cultural repertoire drawn from an individual's sensorial affordances. The individuals' recollections emerge in relation to a shared sentiment or "structure of feeling" (Williams and Orrom, 1954) that surfaces in "aggregative" reading using a macro-approach and analyzing the corpus as well as through idiosyncratic individual performances that exemplify subjective sensory strategies and ontologies (dimensions of the "real") that organize their migration narrative.

## Micro-readings of individual experiences

Two micro-readings of oral histories presented next will show how the analysis can be rooted in particular senses and how narrative choices and expressions rely on particular visual, kinaesthetic, sonic, or olfactory language representation as a surface for a shared experiential world of self and others (MacDougall 1998, 53). Storytelling draws on particular sensorial interpretations and intents preserved in the "magical moments" that summarize experiences in the life stories of these migrants.

## Microreading I (acoustemology): the case of Rozia Frankel

Rozia Frankel, a Jewish immigrant from a historical province of Galicia in Austria-Hungary, remembered the exact moment when her mother decided to emigrate, which relies on a sonic sensorium. The mother is the emigrating link that structures her own migration story and the main protagonist of the magical instant at the centre of Rozia Frankel's migration experience,

> Then we stayed there for a year and then someone came from the United States to visit, a couple of people that she knew, *and they were talking English and mother was very much impressed with it* [emphasis added]. And she left me with some family in Stryj, and the boys were taken care of through court, and she migrated to the United States in 1910 or 1911, I don't remember exactly, and I remained, but by 1913 my grandfather felt that I ought to be with my mother.

This acoustemological event is staged as a "turning point" in Frankel's migration story and gives it a fairy-tale character. There is an arbitrary and intuitive dimension to this particular event that makes it epiphanic and destinatory. Frankel's account is performed as a kinship narrative (Van Vleet 2008). Otherwise factual and well-remembered, her departure story has a nested structure in which migration involves a complex family history and exemplifies the condition of women migrants for whom America enables social restructuring. In this family legend, one overcomes social exclusion of widowhood (the mother who emigrates) and of becoming orphaned (her immigrant daughter). They can have a new life as migrants even if the story does not support re-establishment of a family home when their picaresque lives become relocated. Positioned within a migration narrative is the critique of the social order in the country of origin. The death of Rozia Frankel's father, disinheritance of her widowed mother due to religious laws in Austria-Hungary that invalidated their marriage in a synagogue, and dispersal of siblings to various relatives are central to this narrative. The act of emigration may be seen as a ritual that enables transformation (Van Gennep 1909). The epistemological goals and affects of this memory narration are organized through a sonic event, situated within a historical sensorium, and supported by sensorial language. The imagistic events that involve "an exploration of sonic sensibilities, specifically of ways in which sound is central to making sense, to knowing, to experiential truth" and suggesting that "experience of place is grounded in an acoustic dimension" (Feld and Basso 1996, 97) are also revealed in another case.

## Microreading II (acoustemology): the case of Marie Kovac (Di Bella)

Marie Kovac (married Di Bella) came to America in 1913 from Rijeka, Croatia when she was six years old, adopted by her aunt after her mother's death. She was 88 years old at the time of the interview that was conducted in 1995 by NPS's Janet Levine.

The interviewer's reliance on the interview guide systematically obstructed Marie in creating a coherent story from within her own associative links and she fends off numerous, often misleading questions by the NPS interviewer, who operated on the multiple assumptions about the immigrant's class and experience of passage. Nevertheless, Marie Di Bella (Kovac) courteously acknowledges at the conclusion of the interview, "you brought everything forth with your questions" as she apologized for her supposed lack of performance: "I am sorry I cannot contribute the right way, you mean, remembering". In response to interviewer's question implying that she would have a sensational first impression of America on arrival ("What did you think about America?") she responds, reasonably: "How can a child think of it, I have not seen it yet, how could I think of it?" The question about her arrival to Ellis Island and what it meant to her, Marie Di Bella (Kovac) answers,

MARIE: I should remember, I do remember, but what I am trying to say is I do not remember any particular details, you know, it was evening and then of course we did not leave until morning and *that was exciting, America, you know, the word alone, New York* [emphasis added] ... well there is not much to tell about, I can tell nothing I can recount

INTERVIEWER: Do you have any impressions about Ellis Island coming here?

MARIE: I forgot ... we were together my aunt my cousin and I, and this is very nice, decent, the people were pleasant in ... *Ellis Island is a big word to Europeans, it used to be, you know, in Europe many years ago when they reached there they know that they are safe, in New York* [emphasis added].

Probed on the experiences of childhood, a recurrent motif in her interview refers to music from the street in her family home in Rijeka, described as "off the main street six-room apartment, nice ... with a built in fireplace in the kitchen to cook on [that] kept you warm in the winter" and "a large wall, very pleasant wall and we played outdoors all the time". She added, "everyone went to the window to hear music; in Europe there is a lot of that". She returned two times to her hometown in 1973, after she was widowed, and again remembers acoustically,

[W]hen I made it my business to get the courage to do it alone, I went to Europe and I went to the spots that I remember with pleasure, you know, the parks, where in the evening we would hear music playing in Dalmacija, oh this I wanted to replenish my memories with the same.

The narrator repeats and comes back in semi-indulgent semi-awareness to the recurring, metonymic, and involuntary surfacing of the themes. Against the fragility of her age, Marie Di Bella (Kovac)'s disposition and mood recalled in the repetition of the word "pleasant" is supported by sensory markers: a velvet couch that she remembers from the second-class cabin that was shared with her aunt and cousin, the monumental staircases they ascended at dinner time, and a penny with an

"Indian" figure that someone gave her on the boat. Often she would recall "pleasant" to avoid interviewers' assumptions, such as in this exchange,

MARIE: Ivernia was the ship [she spells the name] – the passage was very pleasant, it was very pleasant, we had a beautiful dining room, a beautiful staircase going to the dining room a lot of servers? It was very nice.
INTERVIEWER: [notes that she must not have been traveling steerage]
MARIE: No, no, I was with my aunt and cousin ... so that was a bedroom with two beds, one higher than the other; my aunt had a lower one and my cousin who was younger, she was there ... and I was tucked in on a velvet couch on the other wall, you know, so it was cozy.

The recurring sentiment word "pleasant" is attached to the journey, the passage through Ellis Island she could not remember, the train journey to Cleveland, growing up in the United States, and growing old.

She does insist on the relevance of songs she heard in her native Rijeka in Croatia, sung in the parks and referring to a gentile, urban culture of Austria-Hungary, which she searched for on her return visits, without success. At the end of the interview, she remembers a tune and starts singing: "*Samo reci mi da te ljubim ja, to nije istina – naranana*" and then continues "*Ružice brala, dragom je dala – la ra la la la*". Then she cries slightly, overtaken by the emotion of her sudden memory and abandoned in its sound. She immediately translates (actually, mis-translates) the words in English as if to explain her lapse to the interviewer: "Picking flowers and giving [them] to my lover". The sound of her voice singing the song comes to life as if from another register–as alive and different in the way she pronounced "Dalmacija" in fluent Croatian without any trace of an English accent, as if she bracketed her memory or as if this facility burst through in her narrative. That word is oddly different as is the song when contrasted to the spotless English of her interview. She shifts to another linguistic register. The place of her childhood, that de-Americanized onomastic, is an ontological intervention that melds temporalities. Just as Marie was about to elaborate on this memory, the NPS interviewer cut her off, then switched off the tape. One may guess that the NPS interviewer was emotionally alienated by these expressions or could not understand their relevance in Marie's migration story and how she represented time with this real-time performance of sound. The oral history interview is a representation of Marie Di Bella (Kovac)'s sensorium. The song that she is trying to remember throughout the interview stood out as a main event of that interview together with the velvet couch she recalled in the second-class cabin of the immigrant ship. The understanding of the senses is shared – by the researcher and in the voice of that "distant" participant. Her memory demonstrates how corporeal and sensory knowing is constructed and "relating ways of knowing to specific sensory modalities" and that the "sensory categories [that] are used by people in the ethnographer's own culture or to elucidate the sensorium of people in other cultures, [are] an exercise that might involve forms of comparison" (Pink 2012, 6–7). Marija Dalbello and Catherine McGowan could recognize and construct these experiences through their own distinct experiences and sensibilities. This interview only exists in audio and thus demonstrates how an auditory record can produce a sense of intimacy, with sounds and silences, and repetitions, distinct from a transcript.

## Conclusions

The aggregative or macro- and micro-readings delineated the sensorium of migration mediated in the EIOH archive. We focused on a subset of interviews from Central and Southern Europe in order to emphasize the potential for historical ethnography using pre-elicited oral history archives. We recognized that oral history interviews were constructed texts and a medium that revealed the cultural politics of archives as exemplified by the interviewing techniques of the NPS staff. Although we recognized the ethical pitfalls of a project that relies on particular ideologies of migration thus inscribed in the archive, we also recognized that aggregative analysis could contextualize sensorial events across the corpus and provide access to a shared experience of migration and the shared structure of feeling of a historical sensorium. The systematically collected memory narrations recorded with a number of individuals have inherent potential for comparative analysis. This research has shown the potential of working with an existing corpus of pre-elicited oral histories that can be transferred to a range of community archives documenting the voices "from below" and genocide archives. We also reacted to particular life histories in a personal way that has both influenced the coding and the interpretation of individual interviews.

This project has shown that research of how sensoria are constructed is both a phenomenological and epistemological project involving sensory knowing and intertwined sensoria – of the participants and the researchers who coded and interpreted this corpus, each activating specific sensory modalities. Reading the cases through the affective-sensory lens of poignant moments that stand out in each individual narration, structuring these first-hand accounts of life narrations, is a subjective, affective, and sensory project. We claim the subjectivity of our analysis and we relied on our responses to interpret them. The historical ethnography in the archives is also an exercise of poetic interpretation by which subjective readings uncover first-person points of view and immigrants' perspectives, assuming the intentionality and directed attention of a conscious self in the context of a subject interpreting her life (Dalbello 2019). The aggregative analysis used a sensory-affective approach across the corpus. The micro-analysis has shown that the apparent serendipity of moments follows the classic phenomenological approach in which bursts of meaning reveal the sharpening of attention of the self towards objects through epiphanic instants (Kearney 2008, 38).

Outlining the sensorium of the Great Migration from Europe to America from an oral history archive shows that the analysis is steeped in affect-driven response that provides a position for the cultural analysis of migration. The critical standpoints for the political analysis of culture and the sentiments around the migration experience of the past and in the current formations of citizenship rely on the ability to address such construction and politics of the archives.

# References

Dalbello, M. 2019. "Archaeological sensations in the archives of migration and the Ellis Island sensorium". Archaeology and Information Research, a special issue of *Information Research* 24 (2). www.informationr.net/ir/24-2/paper817.html

Danius, S. 2002. *The Senses of Modernism: Technology, Perception, and Aesthetics*. Ithaca and London: Cornell University.

Feld, S., and K. H. Basso, eds. 1996. *Senses of Place*. Santa Fe: School of American Research Press.

Jay, M. 1994. *Downcast Eyes: The Denigration of Vision in Twentieth-Century French Thought*. Berkeley, CA: University of California Press.

Kearney, R. 2008. "Bachelard and the epiphanic instant". *Philosophy Today (Supplement)* 42: 38–45.

Kennedy, John F. 1964. *A Nation of Immigrants*. New York: Popular Library.

Koskinen-Koivisto, E. and Seitsonen, O. 2019. "Landscapes of loss and destruction: Sámi elders' childhood memories of the Second World War". *Ethnologia Europaea* 49 (1): 24–40.

Kuusisto-Arponen, A-K. and U. Savolainen. 2016. "The interplay of memory and matter: narratives of former Finnish Karelian child evacuees". *Oral History* 44 (2): 59–68.

Laakkonen, S. 2011. "Asphalt kids and the matrix city: Reminiscences of children's urban environmental history". *Urban History* 38 (2): 301–323.

MacDougall, D. 1998. *Transcultural Cinema*. Princeton, NJ: Princeton University Press.

*Oral Histories, The Statue of Liberty – Ellis Island Foundation* (accessed 2 December 2019). www.libertyellisfoundation.org/oral-history-library

    Vincent Cioffari, oral history interview conducted by Janet Levine, December 3, 1994, recording.

    Marie Di Bella (Kovac), oral history interview conducted by Janet Levine, September 22, 1995, recording.

    Rozia Frankel, oral history interview conducted by Margo Nash, September 5, 1974, interview NPS-73, transcript.

    Stephen Houbrick, oral history interview conducted by Nancy Dallett, February 5, 1986, interview AKRF-136, transcript.

    Andrew Lichanec, oral history interview conducted by Debby Dane, February 5, 1986, interview AKRF-170, transcript.

    Mary Thome, oral history interview conducted by Nancy Dallett, November 6, 1989, interview DP-54, transcript.

    Anna Vislocky, oral history interview conducted by Nancy Dallett, June 2, 1986, interview AKRF-179, transcript.

    Mary Vokaty, oral history interview conducted by Andrew Phillips, March 25, 1989, interview DP-007, transcript.

Pink, S. 2012. *Doing Sensory Ethnography*. 2nd edn. Thousand Oaks, CA: Sage.

Povrzanović Frykman, M. 2016. "Sensitive objects of humanitarian aid corporeal memories and affective continuities". In *Sensitive Objects. Affect and Material Culture*, edited by J. Frykman and M. Povrzanović Frykman, 79–104. Lund: Nordic Academic Press.

Rose, G. 2016. *Visual Methodologies: An Introduction to Researching with Visual Materials*. 4th edn. Thousand Oaks, CA: Sage.

Van Gennep, A. 1909. *Les Rites de Passage*. Paris: Emile Nourry.

Van Vleet, K. E. 2008. *Performing Kinship: Narrative, Gender, and the Intimacies of Power in the Andes*. University of Texas Press.

Varricchio, M. 2011. "Golden door voices: Towards a critique of the Ellis Island Oral History Project". *Oral History Forum d'histoire orale* 31: 1–28.

Williams, R., and M. Orrom. 1954. *Preface to Film*. London: Film Drama.

**APPENDIX 1** Summary table of cases analyzed in the Croatia, Austria–Hungary, and Italy groups (n=84)

*CROATIA CASES (N=1)*

| NAME | SHIP_OF_TRAVEL | AUDIO | TRAN-SCRIPT | INTVW_DATE_1 | IMMIGRATION DATE | IMMIGRATION AGE | BIRTHDATE | FOOD QTY | TOUCH QTY | SIGHT QTY | SOUND QTY | BULLYING QTY |
|---|---|---|---|---|---|---|---|---|---|---|---|---|
| Di Bella, Marie | N/A | X | | 9/22/1995 | 1913 | 6 | 1/30/1907 | 0 | 1 | 4 | 2 | 0 |
| Kovac, Marie* | N/A | X | | 9/22/1995 | 1913 | 6 | 1/30/1907 | 0 | 1 | 4 | 2 | 0 |

NOTE: *Marie Kovac is also listed as Marie Di Bella in the Ellis Island Oral History Project. They are the same person.

*AUSTRIA-HUNGARY CASES (N=10)\**

| NAME | SHIP_OF_TRAVEL | AUDIO | TRAN-SCRIPT | INTVW_DATE_1 | IMMIGRATION DATE | IMMIGRATION AGE | BIRTHDATE | FOOD QTY | TOUCH QTY | SIGHT QTY | SOUND QTY | BULLYING QTY |
|---|---|---|---|---|---|---|---|---|---|---|---|---|
| Kucich, Katherine | THE VERONA | X | X | 2/7/1986 | 1909 | 5 | 4/9/1904 | 3 | 1 | 0 | 1 | 0 |
| Houbrick, Stephen | THE IVERNIA | X | X | 2/5/1986 | 1912 | 5 | 10/20/1907 | 2 | 0 | 3 | 1 | 0 |
| Lichanec, Andrew | THE KAISER WILHELM II | X | X | 2/5/1986 | 1913 | 6 | 5/25/1907 | 13 | 5 | 4 | 1 | 2 |
| Thome, Mary | NOT MENTIONED | X | X | 11/6/1989 | 1909 | 7 | 2/26/1902 | 8 | 4 | 2 | 3 | 1 |
| Frankel, Rozia | NOT RECALLED | X | X | 9/5/1974 | 1913 | 10 | UNKNOWN | 2 | 1 | 1 | 0 | 1 |
| Turner, Annie | NOT RECALLED | X | X | 4/14/1989 | 1902 | 11 | 1891 | 3 | 0 | 0 | 0 | 0 |
| Vokaty, Mary | NOT RECALLED | X | X | 3/25/1989 | 1903 | 11 | 1892 | 4 | 2 | 0 | 0 | 1 |

(*Continued*)

**Appendix 1** (*Cont.*)

*AUSTRIA-HUNGARY CASES (N=10)**

| | | | | | | | | | | |
|---|---|---|---|---|---|---|---|---|---|---|
| Voboril, Louise** | NOT RECALLED | X | 1/31/1974 | 1900 | 14 | UNKNOWN | 2 | 0 | 0 | 0 |
| Vislocky, Anna | NOT RECALLED | X | 6/2/1986 | 1912 | 16 | 12/29/1895 | 3 | 2 | 2 | 2 |
| Nash, Louis | THE ROTTERDAM | | 11/30/1973 | 1900 | 19 | 12/12/1881 | 3 | 0 | 0 | 0 |
| Voboril, Joseph** | NOT RECALLED | X | 1/31/1974 | 1926 | 30 | 1899 | 2 | 0 | 0 | 0 |
| Lehrer, Charles | THE GEORGE WASHINGTON | X | 9/9/1985 | 1913 | | 1892 | 2 | 0 | 3 | 0 |

NOTES: *Only cases with transcripts were analyzed in this essay in the Austria-Hungary group. Charles Lehrer case has not been included in the sensorium analysis since we focused on the interviews with transcripts in this group.

**Louise and Joseph Voboril were interviewed together and counted as one interview.

## ITALY CASES (N=73)

| Name | Ship | | | | | 7 MONTHS | | | | | | | |
|---|---|---|---|---|---|---|---|---|---|---|---|---|---|
| Langlois, Mary | NOT RECALLED | X | X | 9/2/1992 | 1912 | 7 | 11/23/1911 | 2 | 0 | 2 | 2 | 2 | 1 |
| Testa, Frances | NOT RECALLED | X | X | 4/30/1991 | 1913 | 2 | 10/26/1910 | 0 | 0 | 1 | 0 | 0 | 0 |
| Trupia, Dick | THE RE D'ITALIA | X | X | 8/27/1973 | 1913 | 2 | UNKNOWN | 2 | 0 | 0 | 0 | 0 | 0 |
| Crimi, Charles | THE ST. ANNE | X | X | 6/21/1990 | 1911 | 3 | 1907 | 1 | 0 | 0 | 1 | 1 | 1 |
| Mele, Lucy | THE CANOPIC | X | X | 9/2/1992 | 1913 | 3 | 7/7/1909 | 3 | 0 | 0 | 1 | 1 | 1 |
| Tonetti, Hector | N/A | X | | 8/21/1995 | 1909 | 3 | 7/9/1905 | 3 | 1 | 1 | 0 | 0 | 0 |
| Greiner, Walter | THE ROTTERDAM | X | X | 11/24/1992 | 1910 | 4 | 6/29/1905 | 1 | 0 | 1 | 1 | 0 | 0 |
| Marchione, Vita | NOT RECALLED | X | X | 12/6/1990 | 1909 | 4 | 7/4/1905 | 3 | 0 | 2 | 0 | 0 | 0 |
| Negri, Anna | THE KAISER FRANZ JOSEF | X | X | 3/29/1993 | 1913 | 4 | 2/28/1909 | 5 | 0 | 2 | 2 | 0 | 2 |
| Sardonia, Carmeletta, Sr. | NOT RECORDED | X | X | 4/28/1995 | 1909 | 4 | 4/6/1905 | 1 | 0 | 0 | 0 | 0 | 0 |
| Sesso, Pauline | NOT RECALLED | X | X | 4/27/1994 | 1905 | 4 | 6/2/1901 | 4 | 0 | 2 | 2 | 0 | 3 |
| Gabriele, Mary∞ | THE STAMPALIA | | X | 8/21/1996 | 1915 | 4 | 6/20/1910 | 3 | 0 | 9 | 0 | 0 | 0 |
| Lorini, Mary∞ | THE STAMPALIA | X | X | 8/21/1996 | 1915 | 4 | 6/20/1910 | 0 | 0 | 0 | 0 | 0 | 0 |

*(Continued)*

**Appendix 1** (*Cont.*)

*ITALY CASES (N=73)*

| Name | Ship | | Date | Year | Age | Date | | | | | | |
|---|---|---|---|---|---|---|---|---|---|---|---|---|
| Verni, Laura | THE SAN GUGLIELMO | X | 12/15/1995 | 1915 | 4 | 12/5/1911 | 2 | 0 | 5 | 0 | 0 | 4 |
| Mauriello, John | THE SAN GUGLIELMO | | 12/15/1995 | 1915 | 4 | 12/5/1911 | 0 | 0 | 0 | 0 | 0 | 0 |
| Meritai, Anthony | NOT RECALLED | X | 9/26/1991 | 1910 | 5 | 5/26/1905 | 5 | 0 | 1 | 0 | 0 | 0 |
| Willitrs, Elda | THE ANCONA | X | 11/5/1990 | 1916 | 5 | 4/28/1911 | 5 | 0 | 3 | 0 | 0 | 2 |
| Pizzo, Lina | THE KOENIG ALBERT | X | 5/15/1997 | 1910 | 5 | 3/5/1905 | 4 | 0 | 2 | 0 | 0 | 0 |
| Ebetino, Fred | N/A | X | 8/22/1994 | 1910 | 5 | 2/25/1904 | 4 | 0 | 1 | 1 | 0 | 0 |
| Sandroni, Mary | THE AMERICA | X | 9/3/1997 | 1912 | ~5 | 4/6/1907 | 5 | 1 | 1 | 0 | 0 | 0 |
| Allatin, Joseph | NOT RECALLED | X | 9/27/1990 | 1894 | 6 | 8/23/1888 | 1 | 0 | 1 | 0 | 0 | 0 |
| Cassarino, Vincenza | THE EUROPA | X | 3/30/1993 | 1910 | 6 | 11/16/1904 | 9 | 0 | 2 | 0 | 0 | 0 |
| Fuschetti, Nancy | NOT RECALLED | X | 10/10/1985 | 1913 | 6 | 3/6/1906 | 7 | 0 | 0 | 1 | 0 | 0 |
| Lehan, Margaret | THE PRINZESS IRENE | X | 11/14/1985 | 1911 | 6 | 10/6/1904 | 5 | 0 | 2 | 2 | 0 | 1 |
| Migliorese, Helen | THE CANOPIC | X | 9/2/1992 | 1913 | 6 | 3/3/1907 | 3 | 0 | 0 | 1 | 0 | 1 |
| Catalfimo, James | THE ADRIATIC | X | 1/25/1993 | 1913 | 7 | 9/30/1905 | 4 | 0 | 0 | 0 | 0 | 0 |
| Luca, Salvatore | THE DANTE ALIGHIERI | X | 5/30/1992 | 1913 | 7 | 2/9/1906 | 0 | 0 | 0 | 0 | 0 | 0 |
| Milazzo, Rose | THE ANCHORIA | X | 9/4/1973 | 1901 | 7 | 1894 | 2 | 0 | 1 | 0 | 0 | 0 |

| Name | Ship | | | | | | | | | | | | |
|---|---|---|---|---|---|---|---|---|---|---|---|---|---|
| Scarantino, Ross | NOT RECALLED | X | X | 5/26/1992 | 1919 | 7 | 10/30/1912 | 3 | 0 | 1 | 0 | 1 | |
| Sullivan, Cosma | NOT RECALLED | X | X | 1/17/1986 | 1905 | 7 | UNKNOWN | 6 | 0 | 3 | 2 | 3 | |
| Ubaldi, Jack | THE DANTE ALIGHIERI | X | X | 5/21/1993 | 1918 | 7 | 9/16/1910 | 6 | 1 | 9 | 1 | 5 | |
| Constantine, Teresa | DANTE ALIGHIERI | X | X | 7/7/1993 | 1917 | 8 | 3/9/1908 | 8 | 0 | 7 | 1 | 1 | |
| Germi, Josephine | NOT RECALLED | X | X | 1/24/1985 | 1906 | 8 | 1898 | 6 | 0 | 1 | 1 | 0 | |
| Magi, Gene | THE ST. ANNE | X | X | 8/25/1993 | 1914 | 8 | 9/12/1905 | 11 | 1 | 4 | 2 | 1 | |
| Minniti, Beatrice | NOT RECALLED | X | X | 9/20/1992 | 1909 | 8 | 11/6/1901 | 1 | 0 | 0 | 1 | 1 | |
| Sabatino, Helen | NAVIGAZIONE GENERALE ITALIANA (NAME OF SHIP NOT KNOWN) | X | X | 4/6/1994 | 1910 | 8 | 10/16/1901 | 8 | 1 | 3 | 2 | 1 | |
| Sabia, Nicholas | THE SAN GUGLIELMO | X | X | 5/14/1991 | 1916 | 8 | 1/3/1907 | 1 | 0 | 2 | 2 | 2 | |
| Torino, Maria | THE CASERTA | X | X | 4/17/1993 | 1916 | 8 | 8/4/1908 | 11 | 1 | 7 | 0 | 2 | |
| De Salvo, Anthony | N/A | X | | 6/6/1996 | 1919 | 8 | 3/1/1911 | 1 | 0 | 0 | 0 | 1 | |
| Brandes, Elena | NOT RECALLED | X | X | 5/22/1989 | 1911 | 9 | 1902 | 0 | 0 | 1 | 0 | 1 | |
| Breci, Rose | THE ST. ANNE | X | X | 10/21/1985 | 1911 | 9 | UNKNOWN | 2 | 0 | 2 | 1 | 1 | |

*(Continued)*

**Appendix 1** (*Cont.*)

*ITALY CASES (N=73)*

| Name | Ship | | | Date | Year | | Date | | | | | |
|---|---|---|---|---|---|---|---|---|---|---|---|---|
| Carilli, Sadie | NOT RECALLED | X | X | 10/11/1985 | 1904 | 9 | 7/15/1895 | 7 | 1 | 3 | 0 | 1 |
| D'Amato, Rose° | THE PATRIA | | X | 8/13/1996 | 1919 | 9 | 9/18/1910 | 7 | 0 | 4 | 1 | 0 |
| Di Giore, Rose° | THE PATRIA | | X | 8/13/1996 | 1919 | 9 | 9/18/1910 | 0 | 0 | 0 | 0 | 0 |
| Adario, Carmella | THE PESARO | X | X | 10/8/1984 | 1919 | 10 | 1/14/1909 | 3 | 0 | 2 | 0 | 1 |
| Macera, Anna | NOT RECALLED | X | X | 7/29/1994 | 1912 | 10 | 4/24/1902 | 4 | 0 | 0 | 0 | 0 |
| Salvi, Elisa | THE DUCA D'AOSTA | X | X | 8/28/1995 | 1915 | 10 | 8/1/1904 | 8 | 1 | 4 | 2 | 2 |
| Corsale, Angela | THE AMERICA | X | X | 4/24/1995 | 1912 | 11 | 12/16/1901 | 2 | 0 | 0 | 0 | 0 |
| Rizzuto, Charles | THE DANTE ALIGHIERI | X | X | 12/6/1990 | 1919 | 11 | 2/15/1908 | 2 | 0 | 1 | 1 | 0 |
| Vacca, Angelo | NOT RECALLED | X | X | 8/3/1992 | 1909 | 11 | 8/3/1896 | 5 | 1 | 4 | 0 | 0 |
| Losso, Santina¥ | THE ANCONA | | X | 5/7/1997 | 1913 | 11 | 11/2/1902 | 0 | 0 | 0 | 0 | 0 |
| Merrusi, Santina¥ | THE ANCONA | X | X | 5/7/1997 | 1913 | 11 | 11/2/1902 | 3 | 0 | 0 | 0 | 0 |
| Cioffari, Vincent | N/A | X | | 12/3/1994 | 1917 | 11 | 2/24/1905 | 1 | 1 | 4 | 1 | 0 |
| Di Marzio, Cesare | THE VENICE | X | X | 8/20/1985 | 1913 | 12 | 7/31/1901 | 3 | 0 | 1 | 0 | 0 |
| Iozzia, Antonina | THE DUCA D'AOSTA | X | X | 6/8/1994 | 1916 | 12 | 9/3/1903 | 5 | 0 | 2 | 0 | 2 |
| Pasquale, Anna | NOT RECALLED | X | X | 4/9/1994 | 1916 | 12 | 8/11/1904 | 8 | 0 | 4 | 1 | 3 |

| Name | Ship | | | Date | Year | Age | Date2 | | | | | |
|---|---|---|---|---|---|---|---|---|---|---|---|---|
| Rosato, Carmela | THE SAN JOANN | X | X | 10/15/1992 | 1907 | 12 | 8/28/1895 | 7 | 0 | 1 | 0 | 0 |
| Teglia, Oreste | THE CASERTA | X | X | 12/20/1985 | 1916 | 12 | 12/16/1903 | 5 | 0 | 6 | 5 | 2 |
| Spinola, Remo | N/A | X | | 5/31/1995 | 1913 | 12 | 9/13/1900 | 7 | 0 | 0 | 0 | 0 |
| Salerni, Guerino | THE EUROPA | X | X | 1/25/1985 | 1919 | 14 | 11/3/1905 | 7 | 0 | 3 | 0 | 1 |
| Cappellino, Vincent | THE CANADA | X | X | 7/26/1993 | 1912 | 15 | 5/4/1897 | 0 | 0 | 0 | 0 | 0 |
| Martucci, Carmine | NOT RECALLED | X | X | 5/8/1992 | 1919 | 15 | 12/25/1904 | 3 | 0 | 1 | 0 | 0 |
| Nigro, Lucy | THE AUGUSTA | X | X | 2/7/1991 | 1909 | 15 | 5/6/1894 | 4 | 0 | 3 | 0 | 0 |
| Riccobono, Giuseppe | THE TAORMINA | X | X | 12/19/1990 | 1906 | 15 | 7/13/1891 | 4 | 0 | 2 | 1 | 0 |
| Messina, Carmela | N/A | X | | 7/5/1995 | 1918 | 15 | 4/24/1902 | 3 | 0 | 2 | 1 | 0 |
| Barbella, Giovanina | THE COLUMBUS | X | X | 8/26/1992 | 1913 | 16 | 6/3/1896 | 2 | 0 | 1 | 0 | 0 |
| Fichera, Salvatore | THE TAORMINA | X | X | 6/3/1992 | 1908 | 16 | 12/21/1891 | 9 | 0 | 3 | 1 | 1 |
| Marino, Domenica | LA PERUGIA | X | X | 8/28/1973 | 1907 | 16 | UNKNOWN | 3 | 0 | 1 | 0 | 0 |
| Istria, Mary# | THE DANTE ALIGHIERI | | X | 7/19/1996 | 1917 | 16 | 5/8/1901 | 0 | 0 | 0 | 0 | 0 |
| Parachini, Mary# | THE DANTE ALIGHIERI | | X | 7/19/1996 | 1917 | 16 | 5/8/1901 | 4 | 0 | 3 | 0 | 1 |
| Minutella, Angela | THE MENDOZA | X | X | 12/8/1992 | 1910 | 17 | 8/31/1893 | 0 | 0 | 1 | 0 | 0 |
| Ricciardi, Elisa≈ | THE AMERICA | | X | 10/4/1996 | 1919 | 17 | 3/2/1902 | 4 | 0 | 1 | 2 | 0 |

*(Continued)*

**Appendix 1** (*Cont.*)

*ITALY CASES (N=73)*

| Name | Ship | | Date | Year | Age | Date | | | | |
|---|---|---|---|---|---|---|---|---|---|---|
| Vellucci, Elisa≈ | THE AMERICA | X | 10/4/1996 | 1919 | 17 | 3/2/1902 | 0 | 0 | 0 | 0 |
| Riva, Maria§ | THE VERONA | X | 7/29/1996 | 1914 | 17 | 3/5/1896 | 0 | 0 | 0 | 0 |
| Tesio, Maria§ | THE VERONA | X | 7/29/1996 | 1914 | 17 | 3/5/1896 | 3 | 0 | 1 | 3 |
| Protano, Carmine | THE LA VELOUCHA | X | 4/18/1993 | 1914 | 18 | 2/9/1896 | 3 | 0 | 0 | 0 |
| Zitani, Concetta | NOT RECALLED | X | 3/24/1992 | 1910 | 18 | 10/28/1891 | 0 | 0 | 0 | 0 |
| Balliano, Concettina | THE AMERICA | X | 4/23/1996 | 1909 | 20 | 11/30/1888 | 3 | 0 | 0 | 0 |
| Garrone, Concettina | THE AMERICA | X | 4/23/1996 | 1909 | 20 | 11/30/1888 | 0 | 0 | 0 | 0 |
| Scarantino, Arcangela | NOT RECALLED | X | 5/26/1992 | 1919 | 24 | JULY 1895 | 2 | 1 | 1 | 0 |

NOTES:

*The exact name of the ship is not known.

#Mary Istria was also listed as Mary Parachini in the Ellis Island Oral History Project.

∞Mary Gabriele was also listed as Mary Lorini in the Ellis Island Oral History Project.

§Maria Riva was also listed as Maria Tesio in the Ellis Island Oral History Project.

°Rose D'Amato was also listed as Rose Di Giore in the Ellis Island Oral History Project.

≈Elisa Ricciardi was also listed as Elisa Vellucci in the Ellis Island Oral History Project.

¥Santina Losso was also listed as Santina Merrusi in the Ellis Island Oral History Project.

# 12

## THE INVOLUNTARY ETHNOGRAPHER AND AN EAGERNESS TO KNOW

Sofie Strandén-Backa

One Saturday in September 2011, I was about to wash my carpets in the basement in the apartment building I used to live in. I put the carpets to soak in the morning. Later that day, my husband and I went down to the laundry room to deal with the carpets. The door was open. A young woman with long dark hair, dressed in silky black clothes, was also there, starting to wash her carpets. After some practical rearrangements, the three of us got started with our carpets – my husband and I with pine soap and a brush in the tubs, she on the floor with a brush on a stick. I admired her way of washing her carpets, and told her so, too. She, on the other hand, was wondering why I did not let the washing machine do the job. I pointed at a note on the wall and told her that it was not allowed to use the washing machine for this purpose. We talked a bit about this and that, as much as it was possible in the noise.

This practice of washing carpets is not something I do on a daily basis, but still, it is an everyday situation. Even though washing can be studied for its layers of meanings, so beautifully shown by Verdier (1981), Kaufmann (1998) and Klepp (2006), I had no intentions to continue this quest during this particular day. I never intended my carpet washing Saturday to be of any greater importance, and I certainly did not plan for it to be the starting point of a two-day long ethnographic event with several participants. Still, it became a "thick moment" – in analogy with Geertz's (1973) notion of *thick description* – that has returned to my mind many times, always with a puzzling feeling because of the absurd setting. What was it that really happened during these days? And, what did I miss?

Ethnographic fieldwork is ideally described as carefully planned and designed. The ethnographers have good pre-knowledge of what is going to take place and about the content of their study. The right persons have been contacted beforehand and given their informed consent of participation. The ethnographers enter the roles of the researchers as they get started, and take part in the events with a clear aim of research and a set of methodological and theoretical tools. This was, however, not the case in this study, which deals with my unexpected encounters with a Finnish Romany woman. Focusing on the non-linear in ethnography is a growing field of interest (see Smith and Delamont 2019). The overreaching aim of this chapter is to show the importance of an ethnographic process that is not linear and strict, nor foreseeable and controllable. That is precisely why a new understanding can be drawn from the surprises, ruptures and crises of it. As Halstead, I do not see a crisis as a problem, but as "a notion that facilitates the transformative spaces in which ethnographers do fieldwork and produce their ethnographies" (Halstead 2008, 2). A crisis is, at its best, something you learn from.

## The Finnish Romany

Writing about the Romany is difficult for a number of reasons. Not only are they viewed as a relatively closed group and, having their reasons, not wanting to let other people know about their ways. For centuries, this ethnic group has been persecuted by authorities throughout Europe, its members have been accused of a vast number of crimes, and their children have even been taken away from them in the name of decency and civilisation (Rekola 2015; Tervonen 2015). The Romany group is hard to grasp and one troublesome feature comes up already when naming it (see Rekola 2015). The neutral term – today – is Romany. Not long ago it was gypsy (Swedish: *zigenare*, Finnish: *mustalainen*). The group has also been called "*tattare*" in both Swedish and Finnish languages, a misleading term, and not well seen today. The term Romany is also problematic in many ways, since it covers a wide range of ethnic groups in Europe with perhaps more differences than similarities (see Tervonen and Enache 2015). The Finnish Romany people call themselves "*kaale*" in Finnish or "*kàlo*" in Romany, a term that is relatively unknown outside the community, and therefore I have chosen not to use it in this text. I use the term "Romany". I also use the term "gypsy" when I wish to show stereotypes and prejudices. As I see it, the stereotypes have been sticking to the word gypsy (see Ahmed 2004, 11, 63–64).

In Finland, the Romany have been categorized as a so called "old-minority" together with the Saami, the Tatars, the Jews, the Russians that moved to Finland prior to 1917, and the Finland-Swedes. All of these have their own respective and specific history and position, which differ greatly from one another (Tuori 2009, 29, 69). The Romany people has been discriminated and subjected to violence based on ideas of race (Tuori 2009, 72), while the Finland-Swedish people is differentiated due to language, and stereotypically viewed as "the Swedish-speaking better people" (Klinkmann 2017). I am Finland-Swedish, from the rural region of Ostrobothnia, a geo-linguistic position that is viewed as quite the opposite to the capital city of Helsinki (Strandén-Backa and Backa 2017). While the Finland-Swedes as a group are well-educated with their own Swedish-speaking university Åbo Akademi, the Romany got their first Romany language teachers in the 1980s (Friman-Korpela 2015, 237). The Finland-Swedes have been called the most studied group in Finland, but when it comes to the Romany, much remains to be done, particularly from an emic perspective.

Bearing in mind the pain that, according to feminist philosopher Adriana Cavarero (2000), occurs when other people do not see *who* you are, just *what* you are – in this case a Romany woman and a non-Romany woman (*valkolainen/ kaaje*) – I would like to unfold my own taken for granted ideas of an imagined ethnographic script and my feelings of hurt and frustration when I could not act according to it because the script was not accepted by the rest of the participants. It felt as if the rest were acting according to another script, one that I was not introduced to. As an analytical tool for this chapter, I will therefore use concepts that originate from Erving Goffman's famous *The Presentation of Self in Everyday life* (1959). The perspectives that he introduces are those from a theatrical performance in order to study how individuals present themselves and their activities to others, how individuals guide and control the impression that others form of them. It is important to keep in mind that an everyday event studied in this manner is reciprocal, in the sense that there are at least as many plays as there are participants. There are no stars or leading roles. This is certainly true when it comes to my own experiences of washing carpets.

## Washing carpets

I liked talking to this woman – let us call her Rosita – but, at the same time, I felt a bit uncomfortable, partly because of the language. I am not as fluent in Finnish as I would like to be despite my ten years of Finnish classes at school, and it is difficult to hear in a noisy place such as the laundry room. But there were other things, too, things I did not understand from Rosita's behaviour. My washing project kept me in the basement until I was done with the carpets, but Rosita had a constant connection to the world outside. In my view, she ran around most of the time – in and out of the basement, making several short phone calls, instead of focusing on the job at hand. Once a woman in big skirts knocked on the basement window, and Rosita immediately went out to her. Then I started to think that Rosita was Romany, and when she once returned from her visit to the outer world wearing her beautiful black velvet skirt, white blouse and ornament jacket, I finally became sure of her ethnic background. Some of the Finnish Romany women choose to wear their traditional dress, which distinguishes them visually from the majority of the population. It is not just any dress, but carefully sewn to fit. It is an expensive dress, as it is custom made with many parts sewn by hand, and also because of the amount of fabric. Approximately ten meters of velvet is needed for the skirt.

When Rosita entered the laundry room, she took her traditional clothes off before starting to work with her black and silky clothes on, and it was not until then I realised that her black clothes actually were her undergarments. To my surprise she was working only partially dressed, despite the fact that my husband was present, and his presence did not seem to bother her. When she was about to set off again, she said: "On with the skirts again." I looked up and asked her how much they weigh, and she told me that the dress weighs about ten kilogrammes. She told me that she had a chronic back pain because of her heavy dress, and continued to say that she did not want to use it if it were not for the fact that she was obliged to wear it. I asked her why she felt she had to wear it, and she told me that the dress is a mark for her being a grown-up woman.

## A job offer

Finally, my husband had to leave, and I stayed in the laundry room to finish up. All of a sudden something happened that took me by surprise. Rosita asked me if I was busy and had a lot of work to do, and since I did not give her an answer right away, she asked me if I *had* a job. Back then, I was in the middle of a research project, I taught at the university, and beside this I had some extra studies at the business school. She explained why she had asked me, and the reason was that she wanted me to help her to clean every now and then. I was stunned, and I did not know what to say. She told me that she would take part in the cleaning, and that she would pay me, but that the payment would not necessary need to go by the book. So there I was with my shining new PhD and was offered an under the table job by a gypsy woman. Everything felt upside down.

I was saved by another of Rosita's telephone calls, and got a couple of minutes' time to collect my thoughts. When she asked me again, I told her that I both worked and studied, but that I could ask my students. This was an excellent idea, according to her, and she encouraged me to keep in touch. She said that she wanted help with cleaning the windows and dusting on top of cupboards – her culture did not allow her to do this herself. And I got curious, of course, and wanted to know more. I thought that now I had an opportunity to learn more about Romany culture and traditions. Rosita seemed to be open and talkative. When she learnt that I was studying, she lit up, and told me that she was going to start studying. She wanted to become a social worker, but lacked the school grades. She pointed out that Romany people nowadays want to study and work. Rosita was very proud of her brother who just had been appointed leading welfare worker in a congregation. She told me he was helping poor people with food and clothes. She told me her Swedish-sounding surname, and asked if I knew what it meant. When I said that I did not know, she asked if it does not mean "honest". I explained that there was one letter too much.

I thanked her for asking me about the job and for the language immersion in the laundry room. I told her that if she wanted to practise Swedish with someone, now that she was going to study, she could practise with me. She looked happy, and seemed to realise that this was an opportunity for her. She asked me if I could teach her Swedish and write her a certificate. I promised her to try, but I explained that I, in exchange, wanted her to teach me about her culture. She asked me when I could come over to her apartment, and we scheduled our first lesson for the following day, which was Sunday. This suited her well, and she suggested that I would come for a visit at 4 pm. I explained to her that I have a food intolerance that requires a special diet, and that I say to people that I visit them for their company, not for the food. But she answered that it is different in her culture – all guests have to be treated with something to drink, and preferably, also something to eat. She asked me if I drink juice, and I said yes, and she made sure that I would come the following day.

## A Swedish teacher popping in

On Sunday afternoon, I felt both excited and nervous. I thought about what I would learn and whether or not I would get access to unknown territories. I wondered what I had put myself up to, what I would do and how I would be able to teach Rosita Swedish. I was a bit worried about breaking some sort of taboo and messing things up. According to Viljanen, the grounding pillars of Romany culture are honour, decency, and a literal and symbolic purity (Viljanen 2015, 395). I also thought about possible physical dangers. As a teenager, I was taught to watch out especially for Romany women, since they were said to be prone to violence, while male gypsies were not considered a threat. When I rang the doorbell of her apartment just before 4 pm, I felt pretty stupid, but the door was answered by a bright-eyed girl of school age and I asked for Rosita. She showed me to the sofa where Rosita was sitting next to the woman who had peeped in through the basement window the day before. I got a bit surprised when I entered. There were three grown up women and two girls and it did not seem as if it were going to be any Swedish lesson. I was invited to enter. In the kitchen, there was a slightly older woman and she held out her hand. I took it and told her my name. She introduced herself as Rosita's cousin. She asked if I was "that cleaning lady", but I told her that I was not. Rosita told the other women to make room for me between them in the sofa.

Earlier that day I had been picking apples at a friend's house, and with a vague notion about Romany rules of purity, I made sure to pick the apples directly from the tree and not putting the plastic bag on the floor. I had in mind that things that had been on the floor or on the ground were considered unclean. I held out my plastic bag with apples. I explained that I had picked them the same day, and I put them down on a table. Then I sat down on the sofa. It was cramped for room and I felt small between the big skirts. The two girls wanted to try the apples right away and Rosita also asked for one. I said that they might be a bit sour, but she told me that she liked them. She asked if I had brought any books, but I explained that I wanted to talk to her about her studies before we got started.

The other two women in the apartment *wanted* me to be the cleaning lady, and they complained that their legs hurt and that they needed help with the cleaning. The older woman encouraged the other one to show me her legs. She stood in front of me as I was sitting on the sofa, pulled up her skirts right in front of my nose, showed me her legs, lamented and tried to convince me that I really had to help them with their cleaning. Rosita explained to them that she had asked me already, and she told them that I had promised to ask my students. The two women went out on the balcony to have a cigarette – a tobacco treat was obviously expected of Rosita. Rosita thought that it probably would be better if we had our lesson some other time when she was alone, and I agreed. It seemed to me that she could not ask the older women to leave her apartment. And personally, I just wanted to get out of there. We decided to meet the next evening instead. I said goodbye and went home.

## The dress that made me think

There was nothing extraordinary with Rosita's and my first acquaintance. I was experiencing my ordinary feeling of anxiety when having to cope in the Finnish language, and my need to position myself against the stereotype of snobbish Swedish-speakers who just do not want to speak Finnish. I thought it was strange to wear black silky clothes while washing carpets. But when I saw Rosita entering the laundry room in her traditional dress, everything changed in a second. I understood that she was something very specific that I was not. The female Finnish Romany dress is a key symbol in many ways. The dress is part of the identity of Romany women in Finland. For them it is a symbol of pride and distinction of Romany culture and belonging, while for the non-Romany majority it is a factor of segregation, of otherness. To the majority of the population it is a strong marker, combined with stereotypes and behaviour that are not seen as valuable. Romany people are stereotypically not viewed as honest and trustworthy Finnish citizens. They are said to con, lie and steal, and to be unwilling to have a decent job and to rely on the Finnish welfare system. They are still viewed as criminally burdened, with a lot of alcohol, drugs, thefts, fights and even killing. Seeing this dress, all the culturally transmitted non-Romany knowledge about the group categorized as Romany overwhelmed me. Prejudice of various kinds is deeply rooted in common knowledge and popular imagination.

As I noticed the difference between Rosita and myself, I immediately categorised her as "the Other", and got more cautious. This piece of culturally transmitted knowledge is like a filter I had to deal with, something risking to distort my perception. In this particular case, I wanted to appear as extra nice, since I did not want Rosita to believe that I was one of "those people" with stereotypical opinions of her ethnic group. But, of course, I am affected by the cultural values circulating in the community where I have spent my whole life. At the same time, I also got less nervous about my non-fluent Finnish. It was as if we had something in common as none of us were part of the Finnish majority population, even though Rosita's mother tongue is Finnish, and I, based on my looks, quite likely, would pass as Finnish. To Rosita I was nevertheless a member of the majority population.

If we borrow the usage of back stage and front stage from Goffman (1959, 97–99), we can see that Rosita definitely considered the laundry room as back stage. She took her traditional skirt off there – most likely because she did not want it to get wet – and changed back into her dress when leaving the basement. I suppose that she must have felt at ease. Otherwise she would not have worked in clothes that she considered as underwear in public. She commented her own changing of clothes with "On with the skirts again" as she was entering the role of an adult Romany woman (Viljanen 2015, 398). Certain clothes, for example, can, according to Goffman, become institutionalized social facades in the sense that they give rise to abstract, stereotypical expectations. Goffman states: "The facade becomes a collective representation and a reality by its own force" (Goffman 1959, 33). Rosita's reflective comment made me pause in what I was doing, as I realized that it was not just any dress she put on. I did not know what to say, so I asked about the weight and was amazed by it. Physically the dress is a heavy burden, and Rosita also complained about chronic pain since starting using it. To me it seems that the dress also metaphorically can be seen as a burden since it is a marker that produces a stigma in the view of the non-Romany population (see Viljanen 2015, 390–392). And the sticky (see Ahmed 2004) stigma of "gypsyhood" is hard to bear: stealing, lying, cheating, and fighting. Rosita commented directly on some of these stereotypes and thus positioning herself and her peers against the flourishing stereotypes.

The laundry room was the only place I saw her without her dress. In her apartment she appeared fully dressed, even though a person's home usually is viewed as typically back stage in comparison to public domains (Goffman 1959, 106–108). Anything else would not have been possible, since she was in the company of elder Romany women. I have learnt later, that since the kitchen is considered pure, the traditional dress is required there (Viljanen 2015, 398). Rosita treated me like any other person, and, in some way, I believe she liked me, too. At least she felt safe to ask me whether I could be her cleaning company. During our talk in the laundry room, I made sure that I did not have the time for that, and I thought the whole thing was over with. But later, in her apartment, the two older women took me for the cleaning lady that they all so desperately seemed to be in need of. I was thrown into a play I did not want to take part in, when one of them enacted what Goffman calls an "idealisation" (1959, 39), that of the poor gypsy woman suffering from her aching legs due to her heavy dress. By doing this, she wanted to convince me that I really needed to help them with their cleaning. But, at the same time, it felt threatening and provocative. To be honest, I was afraid in Rosita's apartment, and I did not want to be there any longer than necessary in order not to be impolite to her. Many years later, I have been told by a woman, who is a layman expert on Romany culture after working for many years at a public sauna, that this kind of behaviour is a common test of whether it can make the *valkolainen,* the white person, afraid. It did, but I managed to keep cool, and did not reveal my real feelings, but continued to show my sympathies for their aching legs. At the same time this event is full of culturally interesting meanings, meanings that I, at the moment, did not manage to decode.

In Rosita's apartment I was directly interacting with three adult Romany women. And I was an intruder, even though I had an invitation. Obviously, Rosita had visitors that she did not expect, and she was forced into a situation that was impossible to handle since she was acting in two different plays simultaneously. Goffman (1959, 123) talks about the problems that appear when the participants fail in keeping two audiences apart, when an outsider happens to take part in a play that was not meant for him or her. The two other Romany women were intruders in the play that I and Rosita were involved in, that is teaching Swedish and learning more about Finnish Romany culture. And I was an intruder in another play, just because I was a white person who refused to be their cleaning lady. It is natural that a certain amount of confusion appeared, and I just felt that I was the wrong person, at the wrong place and at the wrong time. I was looking for a back stage pass into the fascinating world of the Finnish Romany population, but there seemed to be plenty of pitfalls and obstacles that I was not aware of.

## "The gypsy fight" in the parking lot

Back in my apartment, I heard loud and high-pitched screams as if several people were in life-threatening danger. The screams did not stop, so I went to the window and looked out. In the parking lot behind a couple of trees, I saw the legs of a woman kicking fiercely. I also saw a whole bunch of women in traditional skirts. I could see that other people from the block of flats were outside watching. The yelling continued, and I thought it best to go out and take a look. I even thought that someone could be harassing Rosita because of me.

The other residents were gathered at a safe distance. I wanted to go nearer and see what was going on, but I did not get any closer than a couple of cars away from the main stage. The two little girls from Rosita's apartment were hiding behind one of the cars, and they were crying with tears running down their cheeks. I asked them what was going on, and they told me that their mother and aunt were fighting. I saw an upset unknown woman with blood smeared all over her mouth and to me it was a truly scary sight. I turned to the girls and asked them if anyone had hurt them, but they shook their heads. A man approached the girls and told them to go inside, but they did not want to. I told them to come and sit with me in the swing, and so they did. They sat there for just a little while, and then ran back to their relatives when the situation had calmed down a bit. I could still hear the angry sisters screaming, but I could not catch the words. The only thing I could hear was the older woman from Rosita's apartment encouraging the two women to fight each other.

It felt like I had a ringside seat in a theatre during a very realistic and scary play. The stage was the parking lot between the garage and the dust bins, and the actors were convincing in their roles. It felt as if the participants in the fight were conscious of acting in front of an audience, like they were staging their "gypsyhood" in a strange strategic essentialist manner (Spivac 1993) in front of a grateful audience who, once again, got their prejudice manifested. The non-Romany audience, once again, got confirmed how "those gypsy people" behave. My eyes met the eyes of the younger woman from the apartment, and what I saw was something that I interpreted as a combination of pride and challenge – this is how we, the "gypsies", are. This woman chose another way than Rosita did when coping with stereotypes about the "gypsies"; it was like she acted them out through her challenging gaze. Earlier that day I had asked to know more about Romany culture, and now I got it shoved into my face. It felt like Rosita and the rest of the persons in the parking lot were enacting the type figures of "The Romany" and "The Gypsy" (see Strandén 2010).

Rosita was, of course, outside as well, trying to put an end to the fight. I approached her to ask what the whole thing was about, and she said that it had been just a little fight between sisters, and that everything was all right by now. I felt strange. I had just been given the role as a border-being, someone with passage to two different spheres, although a limited passage to one of them. An hour earlier, I had met three of the women and the two girls back stage on their home ground. I had been friendly and shown my interest towards them, despite my feelings of uneasiness. During this short period of time, I felt that I had won some kind of confidence – I thought I was given a back stage pass. I did not behave like the rest of the non-Romany audience. I reached the edge of the stage which changed my role into a walker-on, someone without a part of her own. But I was an actress without any screenplay. When I approached the stage, I felt unsure whether or not I would become physically or verbally assaulted as I was stumbling around in the play "The Gypsy Fight". I was really surprised when the two girls let me lead them away from the stage into the side stage when their male relative did not succeed. At the same time, I felt that I had gained some kind of respect due to my acting. I did not put my nose in, I did not try to break the fight off, but neither did I stand far away and watch the spectacle from a safe distance. I felt alarmed, but I wanted to act like a "good citizen", and I was happy with my role, which I felt was a success.

## An annoying eagerness to know

This could be the story about how I met my Romany friend Rosita, how I had many discussions with her over the years while teaching her Swedish and how I was invited to learn about her life and the ways of the Finnish Romany people. But this is not the story.

On Monday evening I rang the doorbell, as agreed, but despite me hearing someone being at home, the door remained locked. I never saw Rosita again, and the next day I saw the apples that I had given her scattered on the ground. At the time, I did not know what had happened. One thing I knew for sure was that I felt hurt, both by the clear rejection of my well-meaning gift and by the door that was shut despite her invitation.

Regarding the events accounted for above, one can dwell upon aspects of power, as both I and the Romany women had hierarchical and cultural ideas about each other. While the non-Romany community harbour deep prejudice against Romany people, the same is also true vice versa (see Okely 2008). According to Viljanen, the Romany struggle for purity and against impurity is not only about the literal and symbolic meaning, but also about a multidimensional cultural structure building on knowledge of the Romany identity. The Romany continually identify and measure each other based upon criteria of purity and honourability, and these criteria are also used to draw lines of their ethnicity within the group and, in particular, against non-Romany people. Persons belonging to other Romany groups and non-Romany usually neither notice nor understand these messages (Viljanen 2015, 399). During one instance, I clearly felt I was put to test and that was the uncomfortable situation when having someone's bare leg right in front of my face. What I did not know then, is that feet and legs are considered impure by the Romany (Viljanen 2015, 401). This act can be seen as a combination of a test and an insult. Since the feet and the lower part of the body are impure, everything that gets in contact with it becomes impure – hence carpets are impure textiles (Viljanen, 2015, 398). Since I was someone dealing with washing carpets, I was the right kind of person to ask to do cleaning chores for them, things they could not do themselves. In order to solve this part of my mystery case, the only thing that will help, is to learn more about the Finnish Romany culture.

When it comes to the part where Rosita did not open her door despite her invitation, I can only speculate. One reason could be that she was feeling threatened by her peers because of her socialising with me. I can be seen as a representative of the research community, one, that prior to the 1960s, showed an interest in the Romany in order to change them, to assimilate them more effectively. There has been widespread suspicion towards the majority population (Viljanen 2015, 385). This suspicion might also have been awakened by me handling the two crying girls during the fight in the parking lot. As a part of the assimilation plan, many of the Romany children were taken away from their families, and I suspect that there are all too many wounds to heal. Not knowingly, on a symbolic level, I did the same as the authorities and the Romany mission did for decades, that is putting the children in a safe place away from their family.

"Involuntary" is perhaps a word that is too much of a twist, but, in many senses, this is how I feel about the whole thing. This chapter is based on my experiences from an unplanned ethnographic event – I just wanted to wash my carpet. Then I realised that Rosita could offer a gateway into a community that has fascinated me ever since I, as a child, was watching the Romany women in their beautiful clothes and golden jewellery, the overwhelming flower decorations on the graves in the churchyard and the big Mercedes cars – their exotic Otherness. Yet, my brief knowledge of the complicated taboo system, their presumed negative attitudes towards white people, and the violent and criminal reputation made me feel cautious. But my curiosity was awakened and started an analytical process. The feeling of being involuntary is, thus, partly due to my training as a cultural analytical folklorist. I have been trained to stop and think in situations where my emotions start signalling, because there might be a situation at hand where the normative and what is taken for granted is contested (see Strandén-Backa 2013; Nilsson and Marander-Eklund 2018). However, I am not used to meeting neither silent nor open hostility towards myself. I am used to noticing details and carefully scrutinizing them in order to find out deeper levels of meaning, but in this case nothing made any sense to me because I lacked the necessary knowledge. The ethnographic moment that I have unfolded here has a somewhat dreamlike quality. As in a dream, I was thrown into situations I could not control, that seemed "queer", upside-down and even bizarre. The feeling that "anything can happen" never left me, and the logic was out of my reach. And indeed, it is a thick moment filled with symbols: a black silky dress, in the basement, a woman's leg in my face, a bloody fight in the parking lot, and apples on asphalt.

Writing this text, I have been struggling with questions concerning research ethics. I would like to appear as a neutral and objective researcher before my audience, but since I have chosen to reveal my prejudice and stereotypical beliefs, I let everyone know my low standards as a person. I definitely had my doubts about writing this text, and I still do. I have even been advised not to publish it because of the many problems arising when dealing with people that meet cultural negative expectations. In an interview with female Romany painter/writer Kiba Lumberg, she talks about problems arising when trying to have an open dialogue about the culture specific violence and subordination of women that, according to her, is frequent within the Romany community: "If a Romany deals with these issues, he or she receives threats of violence from the Romany population, and if someone from the majority population touches these matters, he or she is called a racist" (Bruun 2013). In many ways, it feels as if this is a case of ethnography seeking its ethnographer. Now it has found me, the involuntary ethnographer with all her doubts, giving me this problem: I cannot let go of this case – it haunts me like an unsolved criminal case haunts a retired detective. I do not want to get my hands dirty, but I need to close this case.

## References

Ahmed, S. 2004. *The Cultural Politics of Emotion*. New York: Routledge.
Bruun J. 2013. Tystnaden är den största skymfen, 34–39. *Astra* 3. www.astra.fi/wp-content/uploads/2013/10/astra_03_nät_kibaintervju.pdf
Cavarero, A. 2000. *Relating Narratives: Storytelling and Selfhood*. London and New York: Routledge.
Friman-Korpela, S. 2015. Den finskromanska politikens internationella förbindelser. In *De finska romernas historia från svenska tiden till 2000-talet*, edited by P. Pulma, 226–251. Helsingfors: Svenska litteratursällskapet.
Geertz, C. 1973. Thick description: Toward an interpretive theory of culture. In C. Geertz, *The Interpretation of Cultures: Selected Essays*. New York: Basic Books.
Goffman, E. 1959. *The Presentation of Self in Everyday Life*. New York: Anchor Books.
Halstead, N. 2008. The ethnographic present: Knowing through crisis. In *Knowing How to Know: Fieldwork and the Ethnographic Present*, edited by N. Halstead, E. Hirsh, and J. Okely, 1–20. New York: Berghahn Books.
Kaufmann, J-C. 1998. *Dirty Linen: Couples Seen Through their Laundry*. London: Middlesex University Press.
Klepp, I. G. 2006. *Skittentøyets kulturhistorie: Hvorfor kvinner vasker klær*. Oslo: Novus.
Klinkmann, S-E. 2017. "Svenska talande bättre folket": Mellan ironi, stereotyp och humor. In *Föreställda finlandssvenskheter: Intersektionella perspektiv på det svenska i Finland*, edited by S-E. Klinkmann, B. Henriksson, and A. Häger, 301–328. Helsingfors: Svenska litteratursällskapet.

Nilsson, F., and L. Marander-Eklund, eds. 2018. *Under ytan: Kulturanalyser av det bortglömda, dolda och triviala*. Åbo: Åbo Akademi.

Okely, J. 2008. Knowing how to know. In *Knowing How to Know: Fieldwork and the Ethnographic Present*, edited by N. Halstead, E. Hirsh, and J. Okely, 55–74. New York: Berghahn Books.

Rekola, T. 2015. Romernas tidiga skeden i Finland. Från 1500-talet till mitten av 1800-talet. In *De finska romernas historia från svenska tiden till 2000-talet*, edited by P. Pulma, 20–82. Helsingfors and Stockholm: Svenska litteratursällskapet and Atlantis.

Smith, R. J., and S. Delamont, eds. 2019. *The Lost Ethnographies: Methodological Insights from Projects That Never Were*. Bingley: Emerald Publishing.

Spivak, G. C. 1993. Can the subaltern speak? In *Colonial Discourse and Post-Colonial Theory: A Reader*, edited by L. Chrisman and P. Williams, 66–111. New York: Harvester Wheatsheaf.

Strandén, S. 2010. "I eld, i blod, i frost, i svält": Möten med veteraners, lottors och sjuksköterskors berättande om krig. PhD diss, Åbo Akademi.

Strandén-Backa, S. 2013. Dealing with emotions. In *Therapeutic Uses of Storytelling*, edited by C. Asplund Ingemark, 85–100. Lund: Nordic Academic Press.

Strandén-Backa, S., and A. Backa. 2017. Den kategoriserade forskaren: Om självreflexiv intersektionalitetsanalys och normativ finlandssvenskhet. In *Föreställda finlandssvenskheter: Intersektionella perspektiv på det svenska i Finland*, edited by S-E. Klinkmann, B. Henriksson, and A. Häger, 84–105. Helsingfors: Svenska litteratursällskapet.

Tervonen, M. 2015. Vagabonder och gränsöverskridare: Romer i den framväxande nationalstaten. In *De finska romernas historia från svenska tiden till 2000-talet*, edited by P. Pulma, 83–139. Helsingfors: Svenska litteratursällskapet.

Tervonen, M., and A. Enache. 2015. De nyanlända. In *De finska romernas historia från svenska tiden till 2000-talet*, edited by P. Pulma, 282–285. Helsingfors: Svenska litteratursällskapet.

Tuori, S. 2009. The politics of multicultural encounters: Feminist postcolonial perspectives. PhD diss, Åbo Akademi.

Verdier, Y. 1981. *Tvätterskan, sömmerskan, kokerskan: Livet i en fransk by genom tre kvinnoyrken*. Stockholm: Atlantis.

Viljanen, A. M. 2015. Den romska kulturens föränderliga former och permanenta strukturer. In *De finska romernas historia från svenska tiden till 2000-talet*, edited by P. Pulma, 380–427. Helsingfors: Svenska litteratursällskapet.

# 13
# ETHNOGRAPHY, ARTS PRODUCTION AND PERFORMANCE

Meaning making in and for the street

*Jessica Bradley*

## Introduction

This chapter considers how ethnographic approaches to creative practice, in this case devised street theatre, might enable new understandings of communication. In focusing on the theatre of the street it demonstrates how people draw on their communicative (Rymes 2014), or semiotic (Kusters et al. 2017) repertoires to produce creative work. It also sheds light on how short-term, intensive periods of research might be embedded within a longer-term commitment to working with research participants (see also Bradley 2017a). In choosing to foreground methodology, reflections on processes, and significant moments during the production process, it offers insights into ethnography as transdisciplinary dialogue. It therefore contributes an innovative methodological approach, interweaving ethnographic research with the wider contextual space of collaborative working with creative practitioners. This demonstrates the possibilities for engaging across sectors in gaining deeper understandings of the intersections of arts practice and language.

The data and reflections in this chapter derive from a doctoral research project with street arts performers in the UK and Slovenia, which considered language use in relation to the entanglements of bodies, objects and space. The main fieldwork took place in Ljubljana, Slovenia between March and July 2015 (Bradley 2018). The research was part of a wider multi-site ethnographic project which investigated multilingual communicative practices across superdiverse cities in the UK (TLANG, PI Angela Creese 2014–2018), funded by the UK's Arts and Humanities Research Council (AHRC) under its Translating Cultures theme. The TLANG project methodology was underpinned by linguistic and visual ethnography with researchers situated across four cities working with key participants across four different broad areas of activity: business, heritage, sport and law (e.g. Baynham et al. 2015). My own study, as part of this broader research, was to focus on *community* arts and my research centred on the creation of a street arts performance. This performance was devised and performed by a UK-based community arts organisation and a Slovenia-based street arts theatre as part of a wider collaborative project around street arts education in Europe (Adams 2015).

In this chapter I first pay attention to the stages of production, how these were developed during the observations I undertook and how they worked to frame the analysis. I then consider the theoretical concept of translanguaging, bringing it together with ethnography. This is followed by focusing on short-term immersion in research, in the context of longer-term engagement. I illustrate my arguments using excerpts of data and return to the questions posed at the beginning of the chapter.

## The stages of production

Over a period of five months, professional and aspiring performers worked together to create and perform a production, led by the artistic director of a UK-based arts organisation. This was based on a traditional story told by one of the performers during one of the initial project workshops (see also Bradley 2017a). This traditional story was a cautionary tale about a mythical goat with golden horns – *Zlatorog* – whose anger at the impulsive acts of humans destroys the paradise of the Julian Alps (see Copeland 1933). As the production process progressed, the story was transformed into a series of multiple, co-existing and intertwined texts, propelled onwards by the performers. Although the process of producing a theatre piece for the street was fluid and emergent, I organised the activities into four stages, as emerging from my observations over the course of my fieldwork and through dialogue with the artistic director. In this way I developed a model for understanding the different stages of production which aligns generally with the kinds of practices and negotiations involved in creating a production. Across these stages, which also formed the analytical core of my thesis, I incorporated different analytical tools to gradually encompass the performers' multimodal, multilingual and multisensory practices. The stages are summarised as follows:

- First, the *conceptualisation stage*, during which the performers shared stories of place (including the story of Zlatorog), the aim of which was to find the starting point for the production itself (March 2015).
- Second, the *making stage*, which was characterised by activities to create costumes and puppets and finding source material for props and objects to tell the story (May 2015).
- Third, the *devising stage*, for which the focus was co-designing the production itself, allocating parts and rehearsing the performance (June 2015).
- Fourth, the *performance*, which took place across villages, towns and cities in Slovenia as part of an international street arts festival (June–July 2015).

Dividing the activities by stage was in many ways artificial, imposing borders that were time- and space-bound but not necessarily able to describe the fluidity of the activities under investigation. The stages were porous. The activities which defined them were not necessarily restricted to a particular time period or location: for example, making took place across all four stages. But methodologically they provided scaffold for the analysis, imposing a structure on the creative process. In this chapter I focus on a small extract of interactional data taken from a conversation which took place at the beginning of the second stage of production: *making*. First, I set out the context for my research, translanguaging as the guiding concept and short-term ethnography as a methodological and epistemological strategy.

## Context: extending the translanguaging lens

Translanguaging was an initial focus for my research (see also García and Li 2014; Li 2018). As a theoretical concept that has gained significant traction, translanguaging is one of a number of ways of describing, analysing and theorising dynamic multilingual (and multimodal) practice. These include metrolingualism (e.g. Pennycook and Otsuji 2015), polylanguaging (e.g. Jørgensen et al. 2011) and plurilingualism (cf. García and Otheguy 2019). Li Wei highlights translanguaging's multimodal and multisensory nature (2018). Trans- approaches to all kinds of areas of social life are highly prevalent, and include, as Hawkins and Mori (2018, 1) state, concepts such as "transnational, transcultural, translocal, transpatial, transmodal, translanguaging, and translingual". Hawkins and Mori go on to suggest that trans- works to extend ways of understanding the flexibility and fluidity characterising society, opening up possibilities for understanding communication and social action.

Translanguaging is therefore one of multiple concepts which aim to offer a holistic lens for understanding fluid communicative practice. Much critiqued (e.g. Pennycook 2016; Jaspers 2017; Auer 2019), its application across a wide range of contexts has pushed it to outer limits, going beyond not just named languages but also language (e.g. Li 2018). Li (2018, 9) suggests that its broad take up could risk it seeming interchangeable with other sociolinguistic analytical constructs or indeed that it might compete with other terms, a critique which aligns to some extent to those made by Peter Auer (2019), whose concern is that translanguaging's differentiation from codeswitching is misconstrued (see also MacSwan 2017). Li underlines that translanguaging offers more than a description of communicative practice and is instead what he describes as a "practical theory of language" (2018). It is not within the scope of this chapter to critically engage with the theoretical and disciplinary discussions around the concept and what it can and cannot encompass. Rather, and crucially for the activities under investigation in my research and foregrounded in this chapter, translanguaging offers significant transdisciplinary affordances as Li explains:

> Ultimately, Translanguaging aims to present a new transdisciplinary research perspective that *goes beyond the artificial divides* between linguistics, psychology, sociology, etc, and as such it requires analytic methods that move the focus

away from treating languages as discrete and complete systems to how language users orchestrate their diverse and multiple meaning- and sense-making resources in their everyday social life. (Li 2018, 27, emphases added)

Lou Harvey (2020) takes the notion of trans- further in an analysis of reworking narrative research in language education for performance in collaboration with theatre practitioners, suggesting "entangled trans-ing" as concept to account for the transformative potentialities of translanguaging, attending to voice, narration and authorship. So, as many scholars are arguing (e.g. Hawkins and Mori 2018; Harvey 2020), trans- approaches offer potential for opening up new ways of thinking about the complexities of communication.

My own research examined how, in line with current theories of dynamic multilingualism, attention might be paid to the multimodal and the material, extending the analytical lens towards the multimodal practices of the creative practitioners through following the story of Zlatorog as a thread. Of course, for my research with street performers, many of the practices I observed were non-verbal and highly visual. Trans- approaches in research offer a way to holistically encompass these dynamic and creative communicative practices which go *"across, through or beyond"* (Jones 2016, 2) languages and language. I adapted a posthuman lens on translanguaging, incorporating the New Materialist concept of intra-action (Barad 2007) into a translanguaging perspective on communicative practices in street arts production and performance. This shifts the focus towards "the mutual constitution of entangled agencies" (Barad 2007, 26), presupposing that agencies are not independent: "they don't exist as individual elements" (ibid.). But, as demonstrated through imposing stages on the production process, there are also risks in eliminating categories and destabilising boundaries. What happens if we attend to wider semiosis in translanguaging (e.g. Pennycook 2017)? We may gain significantly in terms of our scope and what gets included in our analysis. However, we may also lose something important: there are gains and losses (cf. Kress 2005). As Ofelia García (2020) cautions, how can researchers committed to breaking down structures which increase inequalities foreground the embodied experiences of languaging by language-minoritized communities, whilst also destabilising bounded notions of named languages? Is there a risk that these actions might be in opposition? These questions are central to my research.

I will now reflect on ethnography as an underpinning approach to my research, pivotal to the questions raised above, problematizing it and highlighting some of the challenges I encountered during my fieldwork.

## Ethnography, translanguaging and transformation

In an article setting out some directions for ethnography within the context of Modern Languages, Naomi Wells, Charles Forsdick, and colleagues state that "the openness and curiosity on which Modern Languages are founded are, in many ways, ethnographic impulses" (2019). The authors go on to suggest that a "transformative" ethnographic approach to Modern Languages is urgently needed, contributing to a "public idea about language" in Mary Louise Pratt's terms, "which goes beyond an instrumental focus on language skills" (ibid.).

Although in this example Wells and colleagues are focusing on Modern Languages as a discipline, the argument that ethnography can create spaces for us not only to *reflect on* what we do but also *interrogate* it applies much more broadly. The authors describe ways in which ethnography is and might be incorporated within research, teaching and public engagement with research, even in shorter time periods. Incorporating ethnography in the ways described in the article makes the case for a trans- approach to activities within the field, disrupting some of the artificial boundaries set up between languages as defined by nation states (see also Bradley 2017b). The authors therefore argue that ethnography enables deeper understanding of the fluid communicative practices we deploy in our everyday lives, pushing to observe "beyond" the languages themselves. This underpins linguistic ethnographic approaches to research (e.g. Copland and Creese 2015) as opening up and extending aspects of linguistic analysis (cf. Rampton et al. 2014). So, if ethnography, as an approach to understanding communication in context in everyday lives, is compatible with translanguaging as a concept, what can focusing on street performance bring?

## Short-term immersion, longer-term engagement: approaching street arts production and performance from ethnography

In conceptualising the four stages of production for the process of creating the street arts performance, I sought to bound what were short, immersive periods of ethnographic fieldwork embedded within a longer-term commitment to working with the creative practitioners. I considered these time-bound periods of ethnographic research as "short-term ethnography" following Pink and Morgan (2013). Ethnography is a long-term undertaking, in some cases a lifetime's work. Moreover, doing ethnography is often painstaking and emotionally complex work, requiring many years of engagement. During the first year of my doctorate I was advised that in order to be able to call a piece of research an ethnography it must be long-term, intensive research, indeed perhaps longer than a doctoral research timescale would ever allow. Tensions therefore arise – how can a long-term ethnographic project fit not only into a doctoral research project but also into a life, in which multiple priorities compete? A critical approach to ethnography allows reflection on what insights ethnographic research might offer and what might also be missed. The concept of short-term ethnography accepts that ethnographic research is always constrained and always partial. Pink and Morgan explain that "short-term" ethnographic approaches are different from "quick and dirty" approaches to research. They situate it theoretically within what Pink (2009, 354) has called the "ethnographic place", a concept which seeks to "explain how a range of different types, qualities and temporalities of things and persons come together as part of the process of the making of ethnographic knowledge or ways of knowing".

As Pink and Morgan state, there are ways of working in even short-term, intensive and immersive contexts which in fact involve ethnographic engagement on a much wider scale and for the longer term. They describe four aspects of short-term ethnography as a starting point for further engagement. These are summarised as follows:

- the intensity of the research encounter, or "encounters with moments in other people's worlds" (Pink and Morgan 2013, 356) as learning and empathy;
- the different possibilities for focusing in detail in contexts in which the researcher cannot possibly learn how to "do" the practice under investigation;
- the ethnographic-theoretical dialog, as developing through continuous engagement (ibid., 358); and
- the use of audiovisual technology as "traces of ethnographic encounters" (ibid., 358).

Again, these features are perhaps artificial. But they allow for an exploration of the ontological possibility of short-term ethnography, not, as the authors argue, as a replacement for longer-term engagement but as something with distinct affordances.

Beyond the four stages in my research into street arts production, intense encounters with the worlds of the performers were embedded within the context of creating a series of collaborative projects with the organisation's artistic director (see McKay and Bradley 2016; Bradley et al. 2018), therefore extending far beyond the five-month fieldwork period. I did not (and could not) train to do street theatre myself while undertaking my research. However, I did participate in other ways: the time-bound nature of the production process meant that I was entangled in elements of the activities, for example in making props and costumes. There was an "all-hands-on-deck" approach. I sewed long strips of fabric onto puppet wigs and daubed detail with pink paint onto large puppet hands made from ping-pong bats. The rapid collection of data took place alongside engagement with theory, with the analytical framework developing across the process in dialogue with the ethnographic encounter and the data. Data collection across the process of the longer-term collaboration, but in particular during the four stages, included video and audio recordings, again, allowing me to return to the data in a way which will inform my work for years to come. Researching in this way – moving backwards and forwards from the data corpus, to theory and to the ongoing projects I worked on with Bev – foregrounded the tensions in ethnographic research in general. This enabled me to build constructive relationships, making deeper insights possible than the initial fieldwork would allow. In this sense, the ethnographic place was extended and complexified: an *entangled* ethnographic place. But that is not to say that this approach was without its challenges. I noted the following during my fieldwork which expresses some of how I felt about what I considered to be the partiality of my lens with regards to particular challenges faced by the performers:

I am participating and observing. But I am also missing so much. This raises questions for me about the partiality of any kind of observational research and the partiality of ethnography in terms of the "slice" of experience I am documenting and analysing. It poses interesting challenges for how I, as researcher, might write about these tensions, clearly inevitable in any kind of collaborative process. I am conscious of my "invited" presence. (Fieldnotes, May 2015)

In some ways I created different tensions through my presence. But with ethnography the partiality is also foregrounded – and can and should be accounted for, reflexively, as I wrote in my thesis:

And yet, the writings presented in the four analytical chapters are interpretations of these agencies, as considered through particular lenses, each one partial. As Geertz puts it, "in short, anthropological writings are themselves interpretations, and second and third order ones to boot" (1973, 317). (Bradley 2018, 288)

With all research, and particularly in the case of short-term ethnography, the partiality of the ethnographer's gaze and of any analysis must be considered. The data present new questions and new challenges. As Maggie MacLure states, data here are emergent – in ethnography they ask "what next" (2013, 228).

My research, and short-term ethnographic research of this kind, represents what Monica Heller (2008) describes as a slice of experience. It is a slice of a story, or multiple slices and perspectives on a story, that is told and retold many times and in different ways. It seeks to understand how the performers do the things they do, why they make the choices they make and what else is at play. But my research is also my own stories of these slices of experience. As with all ethnography, even longer-term, "life-project" ethnography, it is incomplete. It aims to shed light on communicative practices and processes but it also aims to disrupt and develop new ways of thinking about translanguaging and its affordances for understanding these complex processes of production and collaboration. So, I situate the approach I take to my research as ethnography. But I do so cautiously and critically, with the awareness that, as Tim Ingold (2017) states, ethnography can be constraining and speculative:

But in what I write I can at least argue for what I consider to be true, or as close to the truth as I can attain, in the light of my reading, the conversations I have had, and my own critical reflection. (Ingold 2017, 23)

A commitment to researching with people and, therefore, to engaging in common activities with people is also a commitment to providing evidence for the claims we make and accounting for our observations (Miller 2017). But, as Ingold argues, it is not necessarily a commitment to represent the views and opinions of the people with whom we have been working – and herein lies another tension. Instead I present these slices of experience through the analysis of the decisions and processes behind each series of transformations across the production process. The analysis reflects my reading, my conversations, my observations, and my own critical reflection, an "ethnographic-theoretical dialog" (Pink and Morgan 2013). It is, in this sense, my interpretation of research findings developed through "educational correspondence" (Ingold 2014, 393). In my research (which is always an account of other texts, a travelling story) I do not claim to speak for the people with whom I have been engaging in "educational correspondence". Instead, I speak for myself, through the training and intellectual development that has opened up for me through engaging in ethnographic research. The process is therefore both "experimental and interrogative" (Ingold 2017, 24). Although not a street performer, as a researcher I contributed to many of the stories I write about and I seek to make this visible through reflexive engagement with my work (cf. Grenfell and Pahl 2019).

Having positioned my research theoretically and methodologically, I will now reflect on a number of challenges and opportunities which arose through this project. I have categorised these as humiliation of the anthropologist (Miller 2017) and the opportunities in unsettledness (Shuman 2011).

## Deep hanging out: opportunities in humiliation and unsettledness

Investigating the processes involved in creating a street arts production required what Clifford Geertz (1998) describes as "deep hanging out" with artists, performers, and people who are learning to be these things and do these things. Over the course of this process, I collected multiple modes of data, including observational notes, video recordings, audio recordings, photographs, vignettes, blog posts and interviews. This enabled me to develop different understandings of the complexity of what was happening within these short-term projects. The range of data and the approach described earlier, enabled me to better situate how these smaller projects function within the wider context of the collaborative relationships, of the broader frameworks (e.g. streets arts festivals and training programmes). I was able to investigate how the objects, the material, can be seen to embody the interweaving of histories, of practices and how the processes represent the meshing of wants, desires, and strategies. And how communication in its broadest sense is central to the process (the production) and to the product (the performance itself). In this sense, the methodology I developed through my research mirrored the practices of the performers with whom I was working.

As my research continued, I began to realise that I needed to work to de-centre language (e.g. MacLure 2013). From the outset I had made a theoretically-grounded decision to commit to working with a group of people, therefore following their lead and their activities. I could have developed this research in other ways, for example by taking a place-based approach. In this case I would have situated myself within a particular geographically-defined space, perhaps a cultural institution or a community centre, and observed the comings and goings of different people within that space. Both these, or even a combination of the two, would be legitimate methodological approaches. But in choosing to work with mobile people, whose work crossed the borders of arts "institutions" and who create work in public and often disputed spaces, I accepted that I would not necessarily know what the context might look like, and indeed that it might not look as I expected. Daniel Miller describes this process – the act of not finding what we're looking for – as "the humiliation of the anthropologist" (2017, 28), suggesting that this is something we should welcome:

> A problem for contemporary anthropological practice is that a student may be expected to spend up to a year preparing to study a topic of current anthropological concern, but almost inevitably when they get to their field site this proves to be completely different from what they expected and most of that initial preparation turns out to have been inappropriate. (Miller 2017, 28)

I followed where others led, hoping to commit "generous attention" to the activities and practices (see Bradley 2017a). There is a risk in doing research in this way and a risk of humiliation. However, in researching creative arts and working with creative practitioners the contexts are uncertain, often led by specific projects reliant on external funding. People do not necessarily do what you decided they ought to do in your research plan. Pink and Morgan (2013, 352) suggest that the contexts in which researchers are embedded "shape" ethnography, making it "slippery to define". There is therefore the combination of liquid contexts and a liquid approach. The approach takes on the characteristics of the contexts, requiring an openness and acceptance of this risk.

So doing ethnography might mean accepting degrees of unsettledness, discomfort and being on the verge (Shuman 2011). But this also means being open to rich opportunities for collaboration, enabling the exploration of spaces and places that would not necessarily been envisaged or conceivable at the outset of the research process. This includes the emergence of data in unplanned spaces. To exemplify this, I will now focus on a small extract of data taken from a conversation in a taxi during the making stage of the production process.

## Conversations betwixt and between

Over the course of my fieldwork I undertook a number of interviews as part of the broader data collection. The role of the interview in ethnographic research is an interesting one (e.g. Hammersley and Atkinson 1983; Conteh 2017), with Martin Hammersley and Paul Atkinson suggesting that ethnographers do not need to "shy away from interviews" (1983, 131) as a way of offering insights into the "perspectives of the participants in the context" (Conteh 2017, 32). In the main these were "go along" (Kusenbach 2003), taking the form of "structured conversations" (Conteh and Toyoshima 2005, 23). In many cases I did not consider these "chats" as interviews until afterwards. To me they were conversations that would allow me to better contextualise the practices and processes I was investigating. But, later on these short snippets of conversations became more central to the analytical process, offering particular insights. The table below (Table 13.1) shows the different methods I used across the stages of production:

**TABLE 13.1** Data collection across the stages

| Stage of production and location | Research method and data collected |
|---|---|
| **Stage One: Conceptualisation** <br> Tabor, central Ljubljana, Slovenia | **Participant observation of workshops** <br> Fieldnotes, video recordings of workshops, video recordings of interviews, photographs, fieldnotes. |
| **Stage Two: Making** <br> Studio, Šiška district, Ljubljana, Slovenia | **Participant observation of workshops and participation in making activities** <br> Fieldnotes, video recordings of activities, video recordings of interviews, photographs, audio recordings of activities, audio recordings of interviews, audio recordings of conversations, fieldnotes, reflective vignettes. |
| **Stage Three: Devising** <br> Tabor, central Ljubljana, Slovenia | **Participant observation of workshops** <br> Fieldnotes, video recordings of activities, video recordings of interviews, photographs, audio recordings of activities, audio recordings of interviews, audio recordings of conversations, fieldnotes, reflective vignettes. |
| **Stage Four: Performance** <br> Ljubljana streets and Tabor, central Ljubljana, Slovenia | **Participant observation during festival: backstage and performances** <br> Video recordings of two performances, audio recordings of interviews, audio recordings of conversations, photographs, fieldnotes, reflective vignettes. |

The example here is taken from a conversation between the artistic director, Bev, and me in a taxi from Ljubljana airport to the city centre. The conversation concerns setting out ideas and plans for the following days of making and devising. The data were audio-recorded and later transcribed. At the time I had not necessarily considered this conversation as an interview or as data. I was experimenting with recording conversations during the periods of time I referred to as "liminal" (cf. Turner 1969). This is one example of many interactions in transit. These moments emerged as more significant than I had originally thought with data presenting themselves in "surprising ways" (MacLure 2013, 231). This often occurred in opposition to the categories I sought to impose on my data. I gradually learned how to let the data speak and be open to my own engagement with them, to attention and experimentation, as MacLure puts it: "we need to be attentive and open to surprise to recognise the invitation; and once invited in, our task is to experiment and see where that takes us" (ibid.).

The taxi journey presented an opportunity for me to ask about how the production would develop. I wanted to understand more about the synopsis and plans for the following few days. Bev explains how she has conceived the story as it will be told and animated by the performers. Although an elicited narrative, it arose in natural conversation and multiple "small stories" emerge in the conversation (see Table 13.2).

**TABLE 13.2** Data excerpt, conversation in taxi, May 2015

| 1 | J: | Okay |
|---|---|---|
| 2 | B: | So when I wrote that little synopsis (.) what was (.) really important for me is to break down quite a complex (.) narrative into a series of action points? |
| 3 | J: | Yeah |
| 4 | B: | So that (.) it's (.) you know it's very simple even there's a there's not a lot of (.) there's a few bits of (.) description (.) as in the character or setting (.) but it's (…) so and so comes and does this (…) and then does that (.) and then (.) this happens<br>[It's very] (…) |
| 5 | J: | [Okay] |
| 6 | B: | Kind of (.) clear (…) so that (.) you don't (.) because when you then perform it you can put loads [into it] |
| 7 | J: | [Yeah] |
| 8 | B: | Makes it very clear what that (.) action is |
| 9 | J: | [Okay] |
| 10 | B: | [Action] to action (xxx) |

I re-initiate the conversation (*okay*) (1). We had started to talk about the plans already and I had asked whether I could record. Bev had laughed and agreed. She then starts to explain her rationale for writing a short synopsis which set out the production ideas that she has sent to the Ljubljana-based street theatre and to me previously prior to travelling. She had taken the story that will be used for the production narrative, Zlatorog, and, seeking to simplify it, created what she calls "action points". The purpose here had been to simplify the story and break it down into actions by each character (4), divided into paragraphs. Bev had worked from a number of sources, including the notes she had made during the initial telling of the story which took place during the conceptualization stage. For this Bev had also drawn on an article about the story I had sent her by the author and academic (and climber) Fanny Copeland from the 1930s and from the video I had made of the performer telling the story.

Bev explains that creating short actions is a way of making the story "clear" (6). Clarity of story-telling is important for a street arts production: the audience must be able to follow the story and understand what is happening in a busy street context. The translation of the text into a synopsis also functions to enable the performers to know what they must do at each point and the action they must execute.

## Discussion and implications

This chapter was framed around three questions and how these are explored in my research. Here I consider each question in light of the theory, approach and slice of analysis shown above. I then describe the implications and future directions for my research.

## How might ethnographic approaches to creative practice enable new understandings of communication?

The first of these questions engaged with the transdisciplinarity of arts-based research and how ethnography enables new understandings of communication. Although the data derive from short-term engagements with practitioners, there is no quick way to engage with creative practice and it requires approaching research design in ways which allow for the open-endedness and emergence of working in this way. My doctoral research shed light on the way that creative practitioners allow for an openness to come through, while being very conscious that projects must be delivered on time (and on budget). This way of working has influenced the way that I do research, becoming entangled with my own ethnographic research and understanding of ethnography, but this extends away from established models in educational and social science research which often assume a more linear process of question, theory, data and analysis. If it is to be meaningful, an ethnographic approach to creative practice must engage with different and conflicting ideas through research designs which encourage co-production and transdisciplinarity, and which therefore enable dialogue and learning at all levels and across all stages.

## How might focusing on the theatre of the street develop rich understandings of people drawing on their communicative repertoires to produce creative work?

The second question considers the context itself – the street arts production process. One of the most productive but also challenging aspects of conducting ethnographic research with street artists is in the multiple directions that each experience could have led in. The story selected by the performers as the basis for their production led me to explore its provenance and its geographical links and one of my thesis chapters focuses on Slovenian folklore, delving into the history of the region and the language. And when the folk tale is told through street arts production, it becomes a partial reflection of an imagined history: as imagined by multiple actors. My data led me to go beyond the bounded fieldwork period, to look backwards and consider trajectories of texts and material. It also pushed me to extend translanguaging towards the multimodal and embodied, encompassing the practices of the performers.

When the story is performed, it is in resemiotised form enabling it to be told in the street. De Certeau describes space as "practiced place" (1984, 117), stating, "the street geometrically defined by urban planning is transformed into a space by walkers" (ibid). For the performance, the street has been pre-defined by Ljubljana's city planning department, the sites determined by the theatre company negotiated with the city council and the festival legitimised. If city streets are transformed into space by those within it, street arts performance plays a particular role. Street arts performances are interventions in "public" places, making what Simpson describes as "significant interventions into the everyday life of cities" (2011, 416). The spaces "created" by street performers are liminal, like the practice itself, and as the festival title implies. The prevailing image of the street performer, *performing outside*, as a busker, as a juggler, as someone blowing giant bubbles contrasts with that of the performer *performing inside*, as an actor in the theatre, as a dancer in the ballet. Following street performers enables a particular lens on everyday activity: in public and in the street.

### How can short-term research be embedded within a longer-term commitment to working with research participants and collaborators?

The third question is methodological and epistemological. The evolution of the research methodology to follow the arts organisation's work is discussed in more detail in a book chapter (Bradley 2017a) in which I conceptualise the "liquid" ethnographic approach underpinning my research as encompassing short-term, intensive ethnography, consolidated through active participation and engagement across a longer period of time. This active participation and engagement led to collaboration with Bev, artistic director, and we developed a series of collaborative projects (Migration and Home, AHRC, e.g. McKay and Bradley 2016 and Migration and Settlement, ESRC LSSI). Through working together, the nature of the research collaboration changed considerably.

In this chapter I have focused on how new understandings of communication are enabled through ethnographic approaches to creative practice. I considered translanguaging as a conceptual framework for understanding dynamic communicative practices in community arts and followed by considering the challenges and opportunities in short-term ethnography. I included a small excerpt of unexpected data, emerging from a conversation taking place in a taxi. In describing some of the processes involved in creating theatre for the street, the chapter demonstrates how ethnography as an approach to research enables insights into how people communicate over the course of creating work together. It makes the case for short-term and intensive bursts of ethnographic research within the context of a longer-term commitment to working with research participants, as offering the opportunity for data, and new questions, to emerge.

## Acknowledgements

Thank you to Bev Adams, Faceless Arts and the Ana Monro Theatre. Thanks are also due to Louise Atkinson, Lou Harvey and James Simpson for their helpful critique of earlier drafts and to Sari Pöyhönen for her hospitality during the Ethnography with a Twist conference in February 2019 during which I explored these ideas. The ideas within this chapter were also developed through a Centre for Luxembourg Studies graduate seminar organised by Sarah Muller at the University of Sheffield. Jean Conteh is the wise colleague who provided food for thought on "ethnography" while I was a doctoral researcher. And credit where credit is due – to Emmy who was my super-conference-companion and Izzy my super-fieldwork-companion.

## References

Adams, B. 2015. "Street Arts Winter Academy #4 – Creating the European Federation of Education and Training in Street Arts". Circostrada. www.circostrada.org/sites/default/files/ressources/files/cs-publication-4-en-2_final.pdf

Auer, P. 2019. "'Translanguaging' or 'doing languages'? Multilingual practices and the notion of 'codes'". In *Language(s): Multilingualism and Its Consequences*, edited by J. MacSwan. Bristol: Multilingual Matters.

Barad, K. 2007. *Meeting the Universe Halfway: Quantum Physics and the Entanglement of Matter and Meaning*. Durham: Duke University Press.

Baynham, M., J. Bradley, J. Callaghan, J. Hanusova, and J. Simpson. 2015. "WP4 translanguaging business: Unpredictability and precarity in superdiverse inner city Leeds". Working Papers in Translation and Translanguaging. https://tlang.org.uk/working-papers/

Bradley, J. 2017a. "Liquid methodologies: Researching the ephemeral in multilingual street performance". In *Researching Education in Multilingual Settings*, edited by J. Conteh, 153–171. London: Bloomsbury.

Bradley, J. 2017b. "Translanguaging engagement: Dynamic multilingualism and university language engagement programmes". *Bellaterra Journal of Teaching and Learning Language and Literature* 10 (4): 9–31.

Bradley, J. 2018. "Translation and translanguaging in production and performance in community arts". PhD diss., University of Leeds.

Bradley, J., E. Moore, J. Simpson, and L. Atkinson. 2018. "Translanguaging space and creative activity: Theorizing collaborative arts-based learning". *Language and Intercultural Communication* 18 (1): 54–73.

Conteh, J., ed., 2017. *Researching Education in Multilingual Settings: Ethnographic Principles in Qualitative Research*. London: Bloomsbury.

Conteh, J., and S. Toyoshima. 2005. "Researching teaching and learning: Roles, identities and interview processes". *English Teaching: Practice and Critique* 4 (2): 23–34.

Copeland, F. 1933. "Zlatorog (A Slovene Folk Tale)". *The Slavonic and East European Review* 11 (33): 651–654.

Copland, F., and A. Creese. 2015. *Linguistic Ethnography: Collecting, Analysing and Presenting Data*. London and Los Angeles: SAGE.

de Certeau, M. 1984. *The Practice of Everyday Life*. Berkeley, Los Angeles and London: University of California Press.

García, O. 2020. "Foreword: Colabor and re-performances". In *Translanguaging as Transformation: The Collaborative Construction of New Linguistic Realities*, edited by E. Moore, J. Bradley, and J. Simpson. Bristol: Multilingual Matters.

García, O., and W. Li. 2014. *Translanguaging. Language, Bilingualism and Education*. Basingstoke: Palgrave Macmillan.

García, O., and R. Otheguy. 2019. "Plurilingualism and translanguaging: Commonalities and divergences". *International Journal of Bilingual Education and Bilingualism*. doi:10.1080/13670050.2019.1598932

Geertz, C. 1973. *The Interpretation of Cultures*. New York: Basic Books Inc.

Geertz, C. 1998. "Deep hanging out". *The New York Review of Books* 45 (16): 69.

Grenfell, M., and K. Pahl. 2019. *Bourdieu, Language-based Ethnographies and Reflexivity: Putting Theory into Practice*. New York, Abingdon: Routledge.

Hammersley, M., and P. Atkinson. 1983. *Ethnography: Principles in Practice*. London: Tavistock.

Harvey, L. 2020. "Entangled trans-ing: Co-creating a performance of language and intercultural research". In *Translanguaging as Transformation: The Collaborative Construction of New*

*Linguistic Realities*, edited by E. Moore, J. Bradley, and J. Simpson. Bristol: Multilingual Matters.
Hawkins, M. R., and J. Mori. 2018. "Considering 'trans-' perspectives in language theories and practices". *Applied Linguistics* 39 (1): 1–8.
Heller, M. 2008. "Doing ethnography". In *The Blackwell Guide to Research Methods in Bilingualism and Multilingualism*, edited by L. Wei and M. Moyer, 249–262. Malden: Blackwell.
Ingold, T 2014. "That's enough about ethnography!" *HAU: Journal of Ethnographic Theory* 4 (1): 383–395.
Ingold, T. 2017. "Anthropology contra ethnography". *HAU Journal of Ethnographic Theory* 7 (1): 21–26.
Jaspers, J. 2017. "WP226 the transformative limits of translanguaging". Working Papers in Urban Language and Literacies. www.academia.edu/34532582/WP226_Jaspers_2017._The_transformative_limits_of_translanguaging
Jones, A. 2016. "Introduction". *Performance Research* 21 (5): 1–11.
Jørgensen, J. N., M. Karrebæk, L. Madsen, and J. S. Møller. 2011. "Polylanguaging in superdiversity". *Diversities* 13 (2): 23–37.
Kress, G. 2005. "Gains and losses: New forms of texts, knowledge, and learning". *Computers and Composition* 22: 5–22.
Kusenbach, M. 2003. "Street phenomenology: The go-along as ethnographic research tool". *Ethnography* 4 (3): 455–485.
Kusters, A., M. Spotti, R. Swanwick, and E. Tapio. 2017. "Beyond languages, beyond modalities: Transforming the study of semiotic repertoires". *International Journal of Multilingualism* 14 (3): 219–232.
Li, W. 2018. "Translanguaging as a practical theory of language". *Applied Linguistics* 39 (1): 9–30.
MacLure, M. 2013. "The wonder of data". *Cultural Studies – Critical Methodologies* 13 (4): 228–232.
MacSwan, J. 2017. "A multilingual perspective on translanguaging". *American Educational Research Journal* 54 (1): 167–201.
McKay, S., and J. Bradley. 2016. "How does arts practice engage with narratives of migration from refugees? Lessons from 'Utopia'". *Journal of Arts and Communities, Special Edition with Amnesty International on Arts, Activism and Human Rights* 8 (1–2):31–46.
Miller, D. 2017. "Anthropology is the discipline but the goal is ethnography". *HAU Journal of Ethnographic Theory* 7 (1): 27–31.
Pennycook, A. 2016. "Mobile times, mobile terms: The trans-super-poly-metro movement". In *Sociolinguistics: Theoretical Debates*, edited by N. Coupland, 201–217. Cambridge: Cambridge University Press.
Pennycook, A. 2017. "Translanguaging and semiotic assemblages". *International Journal of Multilingualism* 14 (3): 269–282.
Pennycook, A., and E. Otsuji. 2015. *Metrolingualism. Language in the City*. Oxon: Routledge.
Pink, S. 2009. *Doing Sensory Ethnography*. London: SAGE.
Pink, S., and J. Morgan. 2013. "Short-term ethnography: Intense routes to knowing". *Symbolic Interaction* 36 (3): 351–361.
Rampton, B., J. Maybin, and C. Roberts. 2014. "WP 125 methodological underpinnings of linguistic ethnography". Working Papers in Urban Language and Literacies. www.kcl.ac.uk/sspp/departments/education/research/ldc/publications/workingpapers/abstracts/WP125–Methodological-foundations-in-linguistic-ethnography.aspx
Rymes, B. 2014. *Communicating Beyond Language*. New York: Routledge.

Shuman, A. 2011. "On the verge: Phenomenology and empathic unsettlement". *The Journal of American Folklore* 124 (493): 147–174.

Thomson, P., and H. Gunter. 2011. "Inside, outside, upside down: The fluidity of academic researcher 'identity' in working with/in school". *International Journal of Research & Method in Education* 34 (1): 17–30.

Turner, V. 1969. *The Ritual Process: Structure and Anti-Structure*. Chicago, IL: Aldine.

Wells, N., C. Forsdick., J. Bradley, C. Burdett, J. Burns, M. Demossier, M. H. de Zárate, S. Huc-Hepher, S. Jordan, T. Pitman, and G. Wall. 2019. "Ethnography and modern languages". *Modern Languages Open* 1. http://doi.org/10.3828/mlo.v0i0.242

# ETHNOGRAPHIC TWISTS AND TURNS

An alternative epilogue

*Tom Boellstorff*

## Introduction

Even most anthropologists are unfamiliar with Bronislaw Malinowski's *Coral Gardens and Their Magic: A Study of the Methods of Tilling the Soil and of Agricultural Rites in the Trobriand Islands*. First published in 1935, it is far less read than works like *Argonauts of the Western Pacific* (Malinowski 1922). However, while its title implies the work is limited to agriculture, it is actually an expansive study – including, for instance, a vital theory of language as social action. Yet even those generally familiar with *Coral Gardens and Their Magic* may not know of Section 3 from Chapter 9, "An Odyssey of Blunders in Field-Work." Malinowski chose his metaphors carefully, and the reference to Greek myth (like the reference to "Argonauts") indicates the section's conceptual importance, despite being buried in the middle of a chapter toward the end of the text.

What is remarkable about this 15-page essay is that it is not a chronicle of everyday blunders (compare Malinowski 1967). Instead, the section recounts an odyssey of conceptual blunders. Noting that he first suffered "from a belief of infallible methods in field-work," Malinowski came to realize that method was not enough. His early attempts at ethnographic analysis "contained some elements of truth. What was wrong ... was the perspective in which these elements were placed" (1935, 325–326). By acknowledging his mistakes, Malinowski sought to "retrace the steps by which, in a somewhat roundabout and blundering way, I finally arrived at an adequate theoretical grip of the problem, which in turn enabled me to collect and organize the evidence in a satisfactory manner" (1935, 329–330).

Let us say that his ethnography needed a twist.

The chapters comprising this book are linked to the Ethnography with a Twist Conference, held in 2019 at the University of Jyväskylä in Finland, where I was honoured to be a keynote speaker. Throughout these chapters – from the Introduction onward – the notion of "ethnography with a twist" is taken seriously. It is deployed as a creative point of departure from which to frame challenges and solutions to ethnographic research. Like Malinowski in his "odyssey of blunders," the authors frame these challenges and solutions by connecting methodological and theoretical innovation. The odyssey as such is not new. But the paths forward cannot be extrapolated from the past; present challenges demand novel trajectories.

In this Epilogue I begin by reflecting on the various ways the concept of "ethnography with a twist" shapes the analyses in this volume. The editors have grouped the chapters under four themes: 1) new collaborative practices; 2) visuality and multi-modality; 3) power dynamics in shifting contexts; and 4) embodied and affective ethnography. Below, I provide four alternative themes: 1) emergence; 2) memory; 3) representation; and 4) authority. These do not replace those of the editors: they are indeed "alternative," "like alternating current in an electric wire" (Maurer 2005, 50). Placing the two sets of themes in dialogue with each other provides a "twist" in its own right, and through this complementary discussion I hope to gesture toward unfolding odysseys.

## Let's do the twist

While the contributors to this volume come from a global array of backgrounds and address a global array of fieldsites, the English-language phrase "ethnography with a twist" serves as a remarkably consistent organizing principle. As the editors state in the Introduction,

> By twists we mean both a) an intentional aim to conduct ethnographic research with novel approaches and methodological tools but also b) sensitivity to recognize and creativity to utilize different kinds of 'twist moments' that ethnographic research may create for the researcher.

"Twist" is fascinatingly polysemous in this volume, and deserves closer attention as a keyword for ethnographic innovation.

As both a noun and verb, "twist" is extremely common in contemporary English and appears in a range of slang forms. (A comprehensive analysis is beyond the scope of my argument; its etymology dates back to the 1350s and cognates exist in many northern European languages.) One of the most common meanings of "twist" as a verb is "to join or unite by twining or interlacing; to twine together; to entwine (one thing) with or to another; to intertwine, interweave" ("twist, v". 2019). The sense is of a circular or screw-like movement, as when taking two threads and combining them into one by turning one's hands in opposite directions. This sense of non-linear movement shapes most uses of "twist" as a noun— in particular, the idea of a "twist" as "an unexpected development of events, esp. in a work of fiction; a change from usual procedure" ("twist, n". 2019). This appears in the notion of a "plot twist," and in adjectival forms like terming someone "twisted," meaning unusual or bizarre.

The phrase "with a twist" originally referred to cocktails – specifically, using citrus rind as a garnish, which is twisted to release its aromatic oils. It combines the noun and verb senses of "twist": the physically "twisted" rind imparts a new taste to the drink – a "twist" to its flavour.

These delightfully multiple meanings of "twist" shape the four themes by which the editors braid together these chapters. New forms of collaboration provide a "twist" on established norms for fieldwork. Multimodal forms of data collection and presenting ethnographic findings "twist" the dominance of textuality. Power dynamics between researchers and those they study "twist" ethnographic claims and their implications. Embodiment and affect "twist" not only methods of data collection and analysis, but how ethnographic work is articulated to varied publics. I will now weave my own four-part braid. This alternative does not replace the first braid: you, dear reader, might consider them as elements to "twist" into a thicker, stronger rope for scaling the heights of new ethnographic opportunities to come. Or you might consider them an alternative "twist" with which to concoct new flavours for the heady brew of ethnography. Cheers!

## *Emergence*

"Emergence," the first stand of my alternative conceptual braid, shapes each contribution to this volume in some fashion. As noted above, a common use of "twist" is in the sense of a "plot twist". In this regard Marilyn Strathern has asked "What research strategy could possibly collect information on unpredictable outcomes?" (2004, 5), answering:

> Social anthropology has one trick up its sleeve: the deliberate attempt to generate more data than the investigator is aware of at the time of collection. Anthropologists deploy open-ended, non-linear methods of data collection which they call ethnography; I refer particularly to the nature of ethnography entailed in anthropology's version of fieldwork. Rather than devising research protocols that will purify the data in advance of analysis, the anthropologist embarks on a participatory exercise which yields materials for which analytical protocols are often devised after the fact. (Strathern 2004, 5–6)

As Strathern notes, ethnographic fieldwork has never involved "purifying" the site of study, as in laboratory research. In place of purity, ethnography has always been "with a twist". Strathern emphasizes that this "twist" takes a temporal form: the ethnographer seeks to generate more data than they are aware of at the time of collection, and conceptual frameworks for analysis are often devised after the fact.

Ethnography always has plot twists: its conclusions cannot be predicted in advance because they appear through embodied participation in fieldsites. In other words, ethnography is emergent, and this provides one way to do ethnography with a twist. Turunen et al. emphasize how their notion of "poly-space" emerged from forms of collaboration that also produced poly-space as ethnographic object. The "bizarre moments" they describe are bizarre precisely because distinct social worlds emerge in unexpected ways. Cheesemen et al. explore the emergent forms of knowledge walking practices provide, while Strandén-Backa invokes the notion of the "involuntary ethnographer," whose research emerges from everyday interaction. In this sense ethnography might be said to seek the ethnographer, an emergent character of investigation that finds an analogue in Bradley's account of studying performers. Here, forms of intentional – indeed, "staged" – meaning making anticipate the ethnographic encounter.

Emergence involves not just fieldsites and projects, but method. Hänninen asks how elicitation shapes ethnographic knowledge production with regard to interviews. Noting that the question of elicitation is a classic methodological question (indeed, it can be seen in Malinowski's distinction between what people say they do and what they do), Hänninen asks how uses of digital technology emerge through everyday practice, and how accounts of those uses can emerge through an interview method that treats elicitation as a joint activity. Siim's discussion of drawing with Estonian children shows the value of an emergent methodology for ethnographic knowledge production, one well-suited for persons that might otherwise be deemed less insightful cultural commentators.

## *Memory*

Ethnography is always history, a fundamental condition of its existence masked by misleading notions of anticipatory ethnography. Short of owning a time machine, there is no way to conduct ethnographic research on the future. The desire for a predictive ethnography results from a misunderstanding of ethnographic research as seeking general laws (like the law of gravity), a misunderstanding anthropologists have sought to correct for over 125 years (Boas 1887).

The fact that ethnography is always history has sometimes taken the form of temporal othering, presenting cultures as stuck in the past or timeless (Fabian 1983). However, this is not inevitably the case, and we can find a thread throughout this volume of work that rethinks the historicity of ethnographic research, including how memory "twists" understandings of culture as an individual and social phenomenon. Sandberg's notion of "retrospective ethnography" builds on the reality that all ethnography is retrospective to ask what happens when memory itself can be said to serve as a fieldsite. In other words, history in this perspective represents both a method and a substantive place of fieldwork. Such a framework appears as well in Dalbello and McGowan's discussion of interviews contained in the Ellis Island Oral History Collection. By exploring these oral histories with regard to embodied data, they treat memory as a sensory narrative that reveals experiential dimensions of migration.

This approach articulates with Tervahartiala's processual use of drawing as an autoethnographical method. Tervahartiala shows how autoethnography like autobiography, is both personal and historical, literally "drawing on" memory to articulate the broader cultural logics memory can illuminate. For Hänninen, participant-induced elicitation allows older adults to reenact and collaboratively reflect on their experiences with lifestyle blogging, linking memories of the life course to recollections of their own digital media use. Indeed, the production of "poly-space" explored by Turunen et al. is fundamentally a production of memory as well: it is in this conjuncture between space and memory that "heritage" can be said to appear. We find a resonance between such practices of memory among older Finnish adults, and those addressed in Siim's study of storycrafting with Estonian children. A participatory ethnographic method allows these children to narrativize their social contexts, remembering past experiences of migration and their current implications.

## *Representation*

No matter how much ethnography twists, it still pivots around the fundamental issue of representation. Many ethnographically-inflected social sciences have advanced forms of nonrepresentational theory that contribute to our understandings of subjectivity, culture, and power (e.g., Thrift 2008). However, frameworks termed "nonrepresentational" are predicated on an oversimplified characterization of representation. Nonrepresentational approaches often index processualism and contingency rather than representation, and scepticism toward such approaches is warranted (Cresswell 2012). This work is best read as contributing to the body of scholarship reframing what "representation" might involve and how most effectively to conduct it. In that regard Koskinen-Koivisto and Lehtovaara join those (like Thrift and others) who explore how embodiment – and particularly the senses and emotions – reshape representation. As Dalbello and McGowan's work with the Ellis Island Oral History Collection indicates, such explorations can draw on archival data as well. Such work reveals how embodiment is profoundly personal, as is one's sensory experience.

Indeed, questions of the senses, emotions, and affect have an important relationship to ethnographic knowledge production. These are often understood as subjective and individually specific, outside semiotic regimes that make representation possible. A vibrant body of work in sensory ethnography and the ethnography of emotion has sought to rethink affect as a methodological resource and ethnographic object. This includes the sensory and emotional experience of the ethnographer, and treating this as part of the analytic frame leads to new ethnographic possibilities. An important strand of innovation in this volume extends this set of insights. Consider how Tervahartiala's exploration of autoethnographical drawing points toward its possibilities as a method for producing data as well as presenting research results. After all, the suffix *-graph* can refer to drawing as well as writing (for instance, in the notion of "graphic novel").

Because ethnographies in various ways represent cultures, issues of representation inform the epistemology and ethics of ethnographic practice. As both Stark and Everri et al. note, digital technologies make video far easier (and potentially, more collaborative) than film, but raise new concerns as well. These include questions of rapport with the researcher, but also privacy and informed consent, particularly with marginalized communities.

While representation is arguably the goal of ethnography, it is an emic category as well, a process in which all humans engage through language and a range of other semiotic forms. The study of representational practices themselves constitutes a form of ethnography with a twist, as in Sandberg's study of commemoration as a form of representation, and Turunen et al.'s study of heritage.

## Authority

One powerful way to "twist" ethnography is to confront questions of authority. For instance, through their "International Society of the Imaginary Perambulator," Cheesemen et al. explore how forms of authority can be constituted through movement articulated through collaboration. Instead of place-based claims to ethnographic authority, that "I was there" (Clifford 1983, 128), this imaginary perambulation raises questions of what we might term pedestrian authority – "I walked there" – with all the "pedestrian" implications of the everyday and taken-for-granted. While the focus is on walking practices, the questions of aesthetics and knowledge production they raise have implications for movement more broadly. For instance, they speak to ableist logics of mobility that shape the recognized authority of persons who cannot walk because they move in wheelchairs, or whose walking is assisted by canes, crutches, or other devices that might make them appear as "misfits" within dominant conceptions of perambulation (Garland-Thomson, 2011).

Discussions of authority are often muddled by unclear or implicit theories of power and inequality that undergird them. For instance, there are important differences between "speaking for" and "speaking about" another culture, and not all distinctions in social status or power are oppressive. New twists on such questions of ethnographic authority are provided by Koskinen-Koivisto and Lehtovaara, both of whom explore how sensory ethnography might transform questions of authorial voice. They appear as well in Bradley's discussion of entanglements with the interpretive practices of street performers. Lounasmeri reframes questions of ethnographic power when addressing contemporary dynamics of "studying up". Anthropologists have addressed such dynamics for over a half century, asking what happens to ethnographic authority in contexts where researchers have, in some sense, less power than those they research (Nader 1969).

## A personal twist

In setting out these themes of emergence, memory, representation, and authority, I have provided an alternative pathway for "twisting" through the contributions to this volume, one that complements the overall narrative by adding another strand to the discussion. While I have done so without reference to my own work, given the consistent emphasis on self-reflection appearing in every chapter, a brief exploration of my own ethnographic practice can serve to reinforce and conclude the analysis.

Many contributions to this volume touch on the role of digital technology with regard to ethnographic practice, from Skype to blogging to video production, but the digital as such is not a primary focus. This is valuable, because too often digital technology is taken as innovative by definition. In fact, the digital does not necessarily "twist" ethnography more than any other domain. The category itself must be disaggregated and specified: while there are some features of the digital that are broadly shared, others are specific to gaming, to social networks, to surveillance, and so on, or to specific places (be those places virtual or physical). In my own ethnographic work in the virtual world Second Life, the greatest "twist" has been the discovery that so many aspects of digital culture are similar to physical-world cultures, even when the sociality in question is exclusively online (in other words, when the persons in question do not meet in the physical world; see Boellstorff 2015).

Similarity can thus be the greatest twist of all in ethnographic practice, not least because of the mistaken assumption that the goal of ethnography is to document difference. Indeed, this is a powerful point of commonality between my digital ethnography and my work on LGBT Indonesians (inter alia, Boellstorff 2005; 2007). In that work, the most surprising twist was to realize the ways in which these Indonesians saw themselves as similar to LGBT persons outside Indonesia, including in the "West". It was to realize that the conceptual rubrics by which one understands something to be similar or different are themselves being globalized and reconfigured in a range of local and national contexts. Whether with regard to Indonesia or Second Life, I have also been struck by the relationships between widely distributed cultural practices and assumptions, and more specified cultural logics. These can be inflected by some notion of locality, or by forms of social and embodied specificity like disability (Boellstorff 2019; 2020). The idea that embodiment is a transcendental category is ableist.

Weaving together these reflections on my own work with the contributions to this volume, I see an unfolding tapestry of possibility for ethnographic practice and collaboration. Ethnography has always been twisty, always open to the contingent and unexpected. Building on that history and the kind of work represented by these chapters provides us with a new beginning for our own odyssey. That odyssey will certainly involve new blunders, but through that very process of learning and growth lead to productive new twists for ethnography itself.

## References

Boas, F. 1887. "The study of geography". *Science* 9 (210): 137–141. www.jstor.org/stable/1762738 (accessed 28 January 2020).

Boellstorff, T. 2005. *The Gay Archipelago: Sexuality and Nation in Indonesia*. Princeton: Princeton University Press.

Boellstorff, T. 2007. *A Coincidence of Desires: Anthropology, Queer Studies, Indonesia*. Durham: Duke University Press.

Boellstorff, T. 2015. *Coming of Age in Second Life: An Anthropologist Explores the Virtually Human*. Second Edition with a new Preface. Princeton: Princeton University Press.

Boellstorff, T. 2019. "The opportunity to contribute: Disability and the digital entrepreneur". *Information, Communication, and Society* 22 (4): 474–490. doi:10.1080/1369118X.2018.1472796

Boellstorff, T. 2020. "The ability of place: Digital topographies of the virtual human on Ethnographia Island". *Current Anthropology* 66 (S21): S109–S122. doi.org/10.1086/704924

Clifford, J. 1983. "On ethnographic authority". *Representations* 2: 118–146. doi:10.2307/2928386

Cresswell, T. 2012. "Nonrepresentational theory and me: Notes of an interested sceptic". *Environment and Planning D: Society and Space* 30 (1): 96–105. doi:10.1068/d494

Fabian, J. 1983. *Time and the Other: How Anthropology Makes Its Object*. New York: Columbia University Press.

Garland-Thomson, R. 2011. "Misfits: A feminist materialist disability concept". *Hypatia: A Journal of Feminist Philosophy* 26 (3): 591–609. doi:10.1111/j.1527-2001.2011.01206.x

Malinowski, B. 1922. *Argonauts of the Western Pacific*. New York: E. P. Dutton & Co.

Malinowski, B. 1935. *Coral Gardens and Their Magic: A Study of the Methods of Tilling the Soil and of Agricultural Rites in the Trobriand Islands*. London: Allen and Unwin.

Malinowski, B. 1967. *A Diary in the Strict Sense of the Term*. Stanford: Stanford University Press.

Maurer, B. 2005. *Mutual Life, Limited: Islamic Banking, Alternative Currencies, Lateral Reason*. Princeton: Princeton University Press.

Nader, L. 1969. "Up the anthropologist: Perspectives gained from 'studying up'". In *Reinventing Anthropology*, edited by D. Hymes, 284–311. New York: Random House

Strathern, M. 2004. *Commons and Borderlands: Working Papers on Interdisciplinarity, Accountability, and the Flow of Knowledge*. Wantage: Sean Kingston Publishing.

Thrift, N. 2008. *Non-Representational Theory: Space, Politics, Affect*. London: Routledge.

"twist, n.1" 2019. *OED Online*. Oxford University Press. www.oed.com/view/Entry/208149?isAdvanced=false&result=1&rskey=y4bLzb& (accessed 28 January 2020).

"twist, v". 2019. *OED Online*. Oxford University Press. www.oed.com/view/Entry/208152?result=4&rskey=y4bLzb& (accessed 28 January 2020).

# INDEX

affect xxi, 14–17, 32, 50, 87, 170, 175, 215; and embodiment xxi–xxii, xxvii; and emotion xxii, xxvii, 3–4, 7–8, 217; *see also* senses; emotion
affective xx, xxii, 3–4, 7–8, 12, 14, 16, 25, 38; dimensions xxviii; encounter 17; ethnography 159, 214–215, 217; experience xxii–xxiv, 7, 14, 17, 37, 161, 171; geographies 8; knowledge xxii, 7, 32, 50; meanings xxiv, 3; sharing xxiv, 3, 4, 17; space 9; turn xxii, 14; affective-sensory 161, 166, 169–171, 175; multisensory-affective 166; sensorial-affective xxvii
agency xx; autoethnographic xxvi, 56, 63, 84–85, 101, 107, 162, 171; social 4
ambivalence 12, 17, 171
anonymity 69–72, 74, 76, 79; anonymization 69–74, 76, 79, 133, 137, 149
anthropology xx, 5, 23, 55, 68, 70, 101, 132, 147, 215; of humanitarianism 118, 120; of relations 120; social 149; *see also* visual anthropology
annoying eagerness to know 193
anthropological 5, 55, 64, 147, 203, 205
artistic research xxiii, 51, 101, 103
atmosphere 21, 23, 27–28, 31, 59, 123, 125–126
audiovisual material 28,
autoethnography 39, 100, 216
autoethnographic drawing xxvi, 100, 102, 109, 216

bias; culture-oriented sensory 29
bizarre; moments 3, 11, 216; situations 195, 215
blog elicitation interview (BEI) 57
blogging 55–62, 64–65, 217, 219; blogosphere 57–61
body 21, 25, 37, 42–43, 45–47, 50; gestures 41; and mind 7, 14, 32, 150; as impure 194; language 154; and knowledge 7, 14, 26
bodily remembering 163

child-centred methodology 85; *see also* storycrafting
childhood 10, 85, 163, 173–174; as mobile xxvi, 84–85, 86; *see also* transnational families
children xxiii, xxvi, 10, 48, 62, 69–71, 74–75, 78–79, 135, 138–140, 216–217; migrant 84–97, 163, 171; refugee 117, 124–125; Romany 186, 194; sounds of 28, 45, 46
class 7, 142, 173
collaboration xxi, xxv, 8, 22–23, 55–57, 63–65, 73–74, 90, 107; 214, 216–218; with creative practitioners 197–198, 200, 202–205, 209; long-term xxiii
collaborative; ethnography xxi–xxii, 4, 5–6; decision-making process 76; interpretation 76; and interpretive flexibility xxiv, 3; knowledge production xxvi, 8, 17, 199–120, 122, 128; memory 121, 123, 127; methods

## 222  Index

xxi; sense-making practices 16; meaning-making 17, 38; methods xxi; practices xxi, xxiv; research xxiii; research teams xxii; and reflexive exercise 23; workshop 21–33; writing xxi, 8, 29
collective ethnography xx; understanding xxv; academic collectives xxii
comic art 101
commemorative practice(s) 117–119; volunteers' 121, 123
communication xx, xxviii, 5, 139, 197, 199–200, 202, 204, 208–209; audiovisual 28; authentic 157; difficulties in 61; between children and adults 87; oral xxiv, 3, 101, 106; political 153; studies 147
community 123, 137, 148; archives 175; arts 198, 209; as producing emotion 147; as in methodological 103; poor 131–142; Romany 186, 190, 193–195; research community xxiii, 194; transnational communities 84
confidentiality 69–72, 77, 79, 154
consent 30; informed 69–77, 79, 132, 134, 136, 185, 218; as negotiation 75–76, 79; processes 74; recommendations on 70; signed 22, 71; 137; written 90, 138, 142
courage 17, 30, 156, 173
creative 103; arts 205; knowledge 4, 17; means and tools 34; methods 38, 87, 97, 103–104, 107; modes 34; practice xxviii, 38, 47, 198, 200, 208–209; point of departure 214; practitioners 198, 200–201, 205, 208; processes 104, 109, 199; vocabulary 32–33; ways of expressing and interpreting 50; work xxviii, 109, 198, 209; writing 31–32, 36
creativity xx, xxi, 25, 36, 214
crises xx
cultural kinesthesia 26

data management plan 77, 79
data ownership 69, 71–72, 77
dependence; economic 135–136; networks 132, 136; relationship of 135, 136
dialogue 198, 208, 214; inner/internal 47, 106; between researcher and participant 59, 61, 65, 74; drawing as xxvi, 88, 108; open 195; transdisciplinary xxviii, 197; visual 106; with embodied knowledge 7; with ethnographic encounter and data 202
digital; environment(s) 55; technologies 217
dimension(s); acoustemological 169; acoustic 172; arbitrary and intuitive 172; bodily 27; historical 125; of migration 161,
216; multiple 105; of the "real" 171; sensorial-affective xxvii, 161; sensory 24, 27–28, 32; sound 170; spatial 4, 32; temporal 4, 127; *see also* affective dimensions; multidimensional
displacement 108–109
documentation; amateur-scientific 49; of identity 132, 137, 139; media of 28; method 162; of personal details 141; of research 150
doodling; as method 102
drawer xxvi, 100–102, 105, 107–108
drawing(s) xxii–xxiii, xxvi; by/with children 86–90; as data 56, 87–90, 94, 101; as method/tool 24, 40, 68, 87, 89, 96, 101, 106, 109; in motion 38; session 86–90, 96; *see also* autoethnographic drawing; storycrafting

economic dependence 135–136
email 5, 8–10, 13, 57, 133
embodied; knowledge xxii, xxiv, 7, 22–23, 32, 41; researcher xii
emotion xxii, xxvii, xxviii, 25, 123, 134, 140, 147, 154, 161; and affect/senses 3–4, 14–15, 32, 218; children's 90, 94–96; and memory 123, 174; and representation 217; researcher's xxiv–xxv, 7–9, 14, 31, 36, 42, 48, 134, 146–147, 150, 194, 201; sharing of 3, 8
emotional; experience 217; labour 8; and mental conditions/states 75, 140; meanings xxiv, register 8; sharing 17
empathy 4, 17, 156, 202
emplacement 26
emplaced experiences 88
encounter 47; anthropologists' 147; challenging 148; elite 149; ethnographic 127, 202, 216; with holders of power 146, 150; between people and matter 22; social 24; peaceful (with children) 93; between people and research audience 29; unexpected 186; *see also* affective encounter
encountering the world 102
engagement 50, 206; civil 119; emotional engagement; long-term 198, 201–202; and participation 209; perceptual (of emplacement) 26; public (with research) 201; reflexive 204; short-term 208; knowledge engagement 37
entangled relationships 16
environment 25–26, 27, 31–32, 45–46, 48, 84; digital xx, 55; interaction with 39; living and working 30; local 147;

# Index

Kiswahili 132; material 27; online and offline 6, 57–58, 61, 65; physical 21–22, 29, 163; research xx; sensitive 69; social and cultural 16; social-media 58, stressful 141; urban 166
ethics xx, xxiv, xxv, xxviii, 101; of autoethnographic drawings 101–102; boards/committees 70, 78; of ethnographic practice/research xx, xxiii–xxiv, 5, 217; guidelines xxiii, xxv, 69–70; research ethics xxiii, xxvi, 70, 73–74, 78–79; 195; visual 70
ethical twist xxvi
ethnographer; involuntary xxviii, 185, 95
ethnography; digital xxviii, 79n1, 219; mobile 4, 6; multisensory 21, 23, 25, 29; multi-sited 6, 62, 119–120; sensory xxiv, 21–24, 26, 29, 31, 218; team-based 3, 4, 29, 39; (ethnographic) lenses 24, 43 ; with a twist xx, xxiii–xxv, xxviii, 22, 39, 213–214, 218; virtual 219
ethnographic knowledge production xxiv–xxv, 23, 36, 216–217; *see also* knowledges
evaluation 95, 123; self-evaluation 24; re-evaluation 4
experience; bodily 31, 33; emotional 14, 150, 217; multisensory 27, 166, personal 16, 38, 89–91, 95, 100, 141–142; polysensory 15; sensory xxiv, 14–16, 21–24, 26, 29, 31
experimental setting 32

fact 86, 96–97
feminism xxi, xxvii,146, 149–150, 187
fiction xxii, 31, 36, 86, 96–97, 214
field-workshop 122; collective 120
fieldwork xxi–xxii, xxiv, xxvi, 3–7, 15, 22, 24, 39, 55–56, 58, 61, 63, 64, 96, 119, 135, 138, 185–186, 197–198, 200–202, 205, 208, 213, 216; among older adults xxv, 60; alternative methods for xxvi; with children 90; with individual and group interviews 85; interdisciplinary 118; joint 8–13; norms for 216; with poor residents in the South 140; field research 120
first-person perspective 72, 79n1, 175

gender 74, 137, 151, 155; differences 148; equality 148; hierarchies 148; and power xxvii, 146–147; roles 96; and urban poverty 132
global South 131–133, 136, 138, 140–141, 143; global North 132, 138–139

"gypsy" 186, 188, 191–193; "The Gypsy" 193; "gypsyhood" 191–192

heritage xxiii, 3–5, 10, 14–15, 126, 197, 217–218; cultural 126–127 ; European 5; European cultural 6, 8; sites xxiv, 3–4, 12, 14, 16; studies 11; heritage-making 119, 125–126 ; The European Heritage Label 3–4
heritagization 126
history 128, 147–148, 152, 162, 186, 208; as family history 172; as life history 170–171; imagined 208; oral 161, 163–164, 166, 168, 174–175, 177
humanitarianism 118, 120

ICT xxv, 55, 58, 60, 62, 64
identity documentation 132, 137, 139; *see also* personal data
imagination 16, 31, 36, 44, 49; popular 190
informed consent xxv, xxvii, 185, 218; among the poor 132, 134, 136; as negotiation 75–76; in video research; 69–79
innovation 217; conceptual 4; ethnographic 214; methodological and theoretical 214
intersubjectivity xxiv, 22
intervention 22, 24, 32, 78, 169, 208; collaborative 128; emergency 69, 75; ethnographic 119; ontological 174
interview 5, 9, 13, 41, 45, 56–65, 140–142, 204–206, 216; elite xxvii, 146–156; ethnographic 55; expert 13; group 85, 93, 121; individual 85, 94; in low-income neighbourhoods xxvii, 132, 135–140; and memory 140; as on "open notebook" approach 132; photo interview 55–56; pre-elicited xxvii, 163; running 37; in Skype xxvii, 133–134; thematic 58, 61; visual (interview methods) 55; with children 86–87, 90, 95–96; *see also* oral history interview; participant-induced elicitation interview (PIE); Replay Interview (RIW)
intuitive 106, 107, 172; knowledge xxii, 16; research method 65; un-knowing 104

knowledge(s); autoethnographic xxvi; co-created xxii; ethnographic xxi, xxiv–xxv; situated 31; inside/emic xxii; integration 6; (co)production xx–xxiv, xxvi–xxviii; *see also* affective knowledge; embodied knowledge; intuitive knowledge

# Index

learning 39, 46, 48, 50, 202, 204, 208, 219; about Finnish Romany culture 192; sensory ethnography 22, 30, 33
life; histories 137, 141, 162–163, 165, 170–171, 175; stories 171
lifestyle blogging xxv, 55–62, 64–65

material 12, 24, 204, 208; visual and written 5; materiality 16, 21–22; *see also* audio-visual material
memory xxiv, xxvi–xxvii, 16, 38, 43, 47, 127, 132, 141, 163, 170, 214, 216–218; and heritage studies 11; locus of 123; multidirectional 11; narrations xxvii, 161, 163, 172, 173–175; performances of 171; popular politics of 161; post-memory 11; sensory 26, 31, 166, 169; and stress 140; vernacular 171; of walking 51; work 118–119, 121–128; *see also* sensory-memory walks; remembering
verbalizing memories 96
memorizing capacities 126
midwifers of memory 127
migration xxvii, 84–85, 136, 141, 161–166, 169–175, 177, 209, 216–217; as threatening "flow" 125; the Great Migration xxvii, 162, 166; intra-EU migration 84; wave 165; migrants xxiii, 84, 125, 131–132, 135–136, 142, 163, 169–172; and asylum seekers 139; emigration 162, 163, 169–172; immigration/immigrants 122, 140, 161–166, 169–175; migrants and refugees 117, 136; *see also* transnational communities; emigration; immigration/immigrants; refugees
minorities 12; language-minoritized 200; "old-minority" 186
mobility 4, 6, 27, 36, 84, 86, 89–90; as ableist 218; mobile people 122, 204
mobilisation 121; of civil engagement 119
multidisciplinary xxi, 9, 22, 29–30
multidimensional; as in cultural practice 194
multilingual(ism) xxviii, 197–200
multimodal(ity) xxii, xxv–xxvi, xxviii 198
multisensory 23, 25, 198, 199; multisensory-affective 166; *see also* multisensory ethnography, multisensory experiences; sensory-affective; sensory awareness; sensory perception
multitemporality 10

narrative(s) 31, 42, 85–88, 96, 117, 134, 142, 171–172, 174, 200, 207, 216, 218; commemorative 123; elicited xxvii, 207: conversational 86; cultural 43; heritage 4, 12, 16; migration 171–172; personal 139; research 86, 96; vernacular 161; self-narrative 40, 101
neighbourhood 12, 47–48, 132–136, 138–142, 171

oral history interview xxvii, 161–175
Other(s) 12, 19; Otherness 190, 194
ownership; of data 69, 71–73, 76–77, 79

participant-induced elicitation interview (PIE) xxiii, 55–65
participants' rights xxv, 69, 71, 76, 79
participant observation xx
participatory action research (PAR) xxii, 56–57, 63; research xxi, xxii, xxiii
participatory interview methods 55–56
past presencing 11, 118
perambulator 36, 39, 218
perambulograph 40, 41, 49, 51
permission 22, 76, 90, 133; verbal 76
perceived causation 132, 141–142
personal data 132, 137–138, 141–142
photograph(y) 48, 55–56, 59–60, 62–64, 87; and video 32, 68–69, 71, 75, 102–103, 137, 204, 206
photo-diary 55–56
photo-elicitation 55–56
photo interview 55–56
place 6, 10, 14, 23, 25–28, 31–32, 84–85, 89, 97, 121–124, 137, 172, 174, 193; of employment 138; ethnographic 202–210; out-of-place 24; physical xxiv, 3–4, 16; public 148, 208; safe 194; sense of 16, 38, 40, 42–43, 45–46; space and 68, 72, 77, 205, 208; video-recorded 72; virtual or physical 219; *see also* emplacement; emplaced experiences, displacement; replacement; space
place-based; approach 204; claims to authority 218
place-beyond-place 6
polysensory 15
poly-space xxiv, 3–4, 8–10, 12–14, 16–17
postcolonial xxi, 5
positionality xxiii
posthuman 200
post-structuralism 100, 104–105
poverty xxvi, 131–132, 140, 141–142; poor communities xxvi; poor populations/

residents 131–133, 135, 137–138, 140; urban 132;
power relations xxi, xxvi–xxvii, 74, 94, 118, 146, 149; *see also* gender and power
prejudice 186, 190, 192–193, 195
primitivist reflex 131
privacy 68–69, 75–77, 79, 137; and informed consent 71, 74, 218; online 59, 61
process; cognitive 4, 16–17; of learning 22, 33, 219
pseudonymisation 22, 69–70, 90

qualitative research 68–69, 87, 132–133, 155; using video for 68–69

race 186; racism 195
reader(s) 31, 36, 39, 57, 61, 63, 105–106, 108, 109
re-enactment 121
reflection(s) 10, 21, 23, 31, 39, 42, 45, 48, 125, 127, 134–135, 148, 150, 155, 169, 197, 201, 203–204, 208, 118–119; ethical 78; methodological 118
reflexivity xxii–xxiii, 17, 32, 41, 60, 71, 73, 79, 120; critical 146, 150, 162; interpretive xxiv, 3–8, 17
reflexive; attitude xxiii, xxv, xxvii; knowledge production xxv; team ethnography 3
refugees xxiii, xxvi, 10, 117–126, 128, 136, 139
remembering 21, 41, 46, 60–62, 64–65, 90, 95, 140, 142, 150, 163, 166, 170, 171–174, 217; bodily 163; process(es) of 123
Replay Interview (RIW) 74, 77
retrospective ethnography 118
risk 68, 71, 74, 76–78, 136, 151, 156, 190, 199–200, 205; analysis 78
Romany xxviii, 186–191, 193–195; Finnish xxviii, 186–187, 190, 192–194; women xxviii, 191–195

scripted emergence 208
self-reflection 4, 32, 63, 118, 120; self-reflexive process 63
senior people 60, 62
senses 22, 24–25, 27, 29, 31–33, 36, 38, 45–46, 106, 161, 166, 170–171, 174; and affects xxvii, 14–16, 217; hierarchy of 24; multiple 25
sensory; awareness 60; perception 21, 26, 32; *see also* sensory experience
sensory-memory walks 26
serendipity xxi, 6, 175
sharing; *see also* affective sharing
short-term ethnography 199, 201–203, 209

sketching 101–102, 107
Skype xxvii, 8–9, 219; interviews xxvii, 133–134
slums xxiii, 132
smartphone 58, 60–61, 62, 73, 133
social media 58–60, 62, 64, 119, 153
socio-economic relations 132–133, 136
space xxviii, 6, 12–13, 21–22, 25–29, 31–32, 37, 45, 105–106, 156, 169, 171, 198, 201, 204–205, 208, 217; acoustic 43–44; affective 9; body in 43, 46; contextual 197; dialogical 105; everyday 131–132; inter-personal xxiv, 3; and place 68, 72, 77, 205, 208; poly-space 3–4, 8–10, 12–14, 16–17, 216–217; public 76; shared 96; transformative 186; transnational 84–85; time-space 11, 106
surprise 3–4, 13, 38, 88, 94, 100, 124, 133, 137, 139–140, 186–189, 193, 206, 219; flash of 4, 12
stereotype(s) 186, 190–192
stigma 72, 191
storycrafting xxiii, xxvi, 83, 96–97; method 86, 89; session 89–90, 96–97
stories (fictional) 86–87, 89–92, 96–97; emotionally loaded 94–95; small 86–87, 206
storytelling 72, 87, 90, 95–96, 169, 171, 207; oral history 161
street art 197–198, 200–202, 204, 207–208; street theatre 197, 202, 207
stress 132, 134, 140–142
Subjective Evidence Based Ethnography (SEBE) 72, 74, 76–78
subjectivity xx, xxiii, xxiv, 7, 85, 147, 175, 217
summer of welcome 117–119, 126

technology 46; audiovisual 202; digital xxiv, 56, 58–63, 65, 216, 219; GPS 24
temporal xxiv, 215–216; temporality xxii, 118, 128, 174, 201; multitemporality 10
thick; description 6, 185; moment 185, 195
third-person elicitation 132, 140–142
touch 16, 22, 24, 25, 27, 47, 157, 166–167, 169, 177; touching 9, 23, 25, 30
translanguaging xxviii, 198–201, 203, 208–209
translocal everyday life 94
transnational 6, 199; communities 84; everyday life 86; families 23, 84, 91, 93, 95; migration 84, 163; space 84–85; way of life 89; *see also* mobile childhood
triangulation 61
twist moments xxi; *see also* ethnography with a twist

video xxv–xxvi; 28, 69, 73, 75, 79; video-ethnography xxv, 29, 69
viewer(s) 73, 105–106, 108–109,
visitors 5, 9, 12,122, 128, 191
visual anthropology 29; dialogue 106, 108; ethnography xxii, xxv–xxvi, 29; autoethnography 101; interview methods 55; journaling 101–102; methods 55, 68–70, 72, 101–102; research xxvi, 62, 65, 69–71, 73–74, 78, 104; turn 68

voice 200
volunteering xxvi, 119–120, 122–123; melancholy of 122–123; as heritage-making 119, 125; refugee xxvi, 128

walk-along-ethnography 26
writing xxi–xxii, xxiv; collaborative xxi–xxii, xxv, 8, 29; ethnographic xxii, 6, 31, 36; co-produced 22; empathetic 31